Secrets Of The UFO

Don Elkins and Carla L. Rueckert

Secrets Of The UFO

First Printing, May, 1977
Second Printing, November, 1977
Third Printing, October, 1978
Fourth Printing, March, 1983
Fifth Printing, September, 1983
Sixth Printing, April, 1985
Seventh Printing, January, 1987
Eighth Printing, July, 1988
Ninth Printing, October, 1990

ISBN: 978-0-945007-00-5

L/L Research
P.O. Box 5195
Louisville, KY 40255-0195

On the cover of this 2011 reissue of *Secrets of the UFO* is the original illustration that appeared on the first edition. The drawing was commissioned for Don Elkins by Gray Barker, who asked an artist to create his interpretation of the tall, hour-glass shaped structure described by a contactee in Chapter Eight, page 157.

Dedicated to Hal and Jo Price

"Truth is the daughter of time, not of authority."
Sir Francis Bacon

Acknowledgements

Grateful acknowledgment is made to the following publishers for permission to reprint excerpts from the following copyrighted works:

Helios Publications and Dr. Francis I. Regardie, for permission to use excerpted material from THE ART AND MEANING OF MAGIC, ©1971.

Thorsons Publishers Ltd. for permission to use excerpted material from THE MAGICIAN: HIS TRAINING AND WORK, ©1963.

Doubleday & Co., for permission to use excerpted material from THE COSMIC CONNECTION, by Carl Sagan and Jerome Agel, ©1973.

Doubleday & Co. for permission to use excerpted material from THE ROMEO ERROR by Lyall Watson, ©1974.

Harvest House Publishers, for permission to use information taken from UFO'S: WHAT ON EARTH IS HAPPENING, ©1975.

Indiana University Press for permission to use material excerpted from THE UFO CONTROVERSY IN AMERICA, by David M. Jacobs, ©1975.

Mark-Age MetaCenter for permission to use material excerpted from VISITORS FROM OTHER PLANETS, by Nada-Yolanda, ©1974.

Ministry of Universal Wisdom, for permission to use material excerpted from THE COUNCIL OF SEVEN LIGHTS, by George Van Tassel, ©1958.

Oahspe Publishing Association and Palmer Publications, Inc., Amherst, Wis. 54406, for permission to use material excerpted from OAHSPE, by John Ballou Newbrough, ©1882.

Prentice-Hall, Inc., for permission to use material excerpted from PSYCHIC DISCOVERIES BEHIND THE IRON CURTAIN, by Ostrander and Schroeder, ©1970 by Sheila Ostrander and Lynn Schroeder.

G.P. Putnam's Sons, for permission to use material excerpted from ALIENS IN THE SKIES, by John Fuller, ©1969.

Saucerian Publications, for permission to use material excerpted from FROM OUTER SPACE TO YOU, by Howard Menger, ©1959, 1967.

Ballantine Books, a division of Random House, Inc., for permission to use material excerpted from THE MAGIC OF URI GELLER, by James Randi, ©1975.

Ballantine Books, a Division of Random House, Inc., for permission to use material excerpted from UFO'S PAST, PRESENT AND FUTURE, by Robert Emenegger, ©1974.

Neville Spearman, Ltd., for permission to use material from THE SAUCERS SPEAK, by G. H. Williamson, ©1963.

Neville Spearman, for permission to use material excerpted from OTHER TONGUES, OTHER FLESH, by G. H. Williamson, ©1953.

The Viking Press, Inc., for permission to use material excerpted from SUPERMINDS, by John Taylor, ©1975.

Doubleday & Co., Inc., for permission to use material excerpted from URI: A JOURNAL OF THE MYSTERY OF URI GELLER, by Andrija Puharich, ©1974.

BBC Publications, for permission to use material excerpted from EINSTEIN: THE MAN AND HIS ACHIEVEMENT, edited by Whitrow, ©1967, 1973.

Leaves Of Grass Press, Inc., for permission to use material excerpted from SECRET OF THE ANDES, by Brother Philip, ©1961.

Prentice-Hall, Inc., for permission to use material excerpted from REVELATION: THE DIVINE FIRE, by Brad Steiger, ©1973.

Grateful acknowledgment is made to the following individuals for permission to reprint excerpts from the following copyrighted works:

Mr. Clyde Trepanier, for permission to use material excerpted from MAN, CONSCIOUSNESS AND UNDERSTANDING, VOLUME FOUR, published by Understanding of Detroit in 1962, ©1962.

Baird Wallace for permission to use material excerpted from THE SPACE STORY AND THE INNER LIGHT, published by the author, ©1972.

Mr. Walter Rogers, Jr. for permission to use material excerpted from his unpublished material sometimes called "The Brown Notebook," copyrighted as of this date.

Mr. Dewey B. Larson, for permission to use material excerpted from QUASARS AND PULSARS, published by North Pacific Publishers, ©1971.

Prof. J. H. Bruening, for permission to use his letter published in Gray Barker's Newsletter, Feb., 1976, ©1976.

Carla Rueckert, for permission to use material excerpted from VOICES OF THE GODS, unpublished manuscript, ©1974.

Dr. T. Lobsang Rampa for permission to use material excerpted from THE HERMIT published by Corgi ©1975.

Table of Contents

Proem

A ufologist is a detective who is exploring the single largest mystery of our time. As he wends his way through the elaborate maze of red herrings, misinformation, cover-ups, fanatics, skeptics, true believers and nonbelievers, he may well find that his most valuable ally in his search is a good sense of humor. Or, as Groucho Marx said, "Either he's dead or my watch has stopped!"

Don Elkins
Carla L. Rueckert

Louisville, 1976

Chapter One

A Very Strange Phenomenon

The information in this book is either nonsense or it is the most centrally important thing that you could possibly learn. It is allegedly the answer to the strange riddle of the UFO's. The information contained herein is not speculation or theory, but a condensation and edited arrangement of received communications from the UFOs. The obvious weakness of this contactee information is that evidential proof of its validity is not obtainable. Its strength lies in its sheer bulk and in the similarity of messages produced by sources widely scattered around the world. The last 25 years have produced millions of words of these communications allegedly originating within the UFOs.

Approximately 15 million people in the U.S. have reported seeing UFOs, more than 2000 contact cases have been reported, and about 700 landings have left trace evidence.[1] There is no longer any real doubt that UFOs exist. The question is: who are they? And why are they here? It is quite possible that understanding them is the most important endeavor which we can undertake.

There are thousands of people around the world who are quite certain that they know at least some of the answers to the riddles of these elusive manifestations.

How did these people acquire the needed information? Their answer—one which many find hard to believe—is that they have been in contact with the occupants of the UFOs. There has been a widespread and growing pattern of people who claim contact with UFOs since the early '50s. At this point, the claims are so widespread that they constitute a pseudo-secret subculture, a sort of underground group, all over earth. I say pseudo-secret because even though many of these contactees tell their stories, the information is of a type that our culture does not easily accept. The insiders in this underground all seem to be getting approximately the same information, and they can be found in many places both in the United States and all over the world.

They are not all wide-eyed cultists, three steps in front of the men in white coats, nor are they little old ladies fresh from the medium's parlor. Primarily, contactees are normal people of average intelligence and background. Each year produces more of them. Few of these people receive or desire publicity.

I've been studying paranormal phenomenon for 25 years, and for the past 14 years I've specialized in unraveling the contactee riddle. You will find in reading through this book that it requires some background in paranormal studies. The first three chapters of the book are intended to function as a synopsis of this background, and the bibliography is available to those who wish to pursue this field in greater depth. A great deal of apparently unrelated material begins to substantively add to the evidence available in the UFO contactee literature, once this mountain of contactee data is condensed. I am now in a position to make such a condensation, and this analysis of the contactee story turns into an explanation of the nature, purpose, origin, and ultimate objective of at least one large group of UFOs.

The entire situation regarding the contactees reminds me of something which the late Dr. James E. McDonald said to Congress in 1968. He was reporting to the House Committee on Aeronautics and Astronautics on his conclusions regarding UFOs. He described a situation in northern France years ago, where many peasants reported stones falling from the sky. Since the reporters were "dumb" and "unscientific," they were ignored at first. Finally a scientist took the reports seriously and investigated the thing fully. Thus was born the science of meteoritics. Dr. McDonald suggested to Congress that in dealing with UFO reports, we now face a "very similar situation in science. We have tended to ignore it because it didn't make any sense. It definitely defies any explanation, and hence the situation has evolved where we can't get going because we aren't already going."[2]

Consider the case of Travis Walton of Snowflake, Arizona, taken aboard a UFO on November 5, 1975, in plain sight of six witnesses. The witnesses were given lie detector tests. All tests showed the witnesses were telling the truth. Travis himself showed up five days later. He was twelve miles from the place he had been taken on board. He had a story to tell that involved his waking up inside the ship and finding several very odd-looking creatures examining him, as well as four perfectly normal-looking human types.

Now, these details are pretty solid. Dr. James Harder, director of Research for the Aerial Phenomena Research Organization, personally investigated the case and stated that he felt there was no hoax involved. The lie detector tests given to the witnesses support the data. All indications are that this contact is authentic.

In spite of this, the news coverage was so conditioned by the old ridicule lid of the 1950s that few Americans found out about it until months after the occurrence.

Various UFO research groups such as APRO and MUFON (for complete listings, see bibliography) put out many reports, such as that of the Travis Walton case, which the national press passes by. And so the underground becomes more and more certain that UFOs are real and are communicating with us, while the cultural community as a whole continues to not know much of the important data.

This gap in knowledge was at one time at least in great part attributable to the U. S. government's handling of investigations into the phenomena. In the late 1940s and early '50s, when the sightings and stories were gaining momentum, the Air Force, like almost everyone else, was mystified. In addition, they were responsible for the safety of American skies. They were embarrassed and concerned about these unidentified flying objects. These were the days of backyard bomb shelters; the national feeling was that Russia might well launch a nuclear attack. So it is quite understandable that the Air Force was extremely upset about their inability to explain the phenomena. The result was that the UFO phenomena was brushed off, officially, as being a ridiculous fantasy. In this atmosphere, the reliable witness was liable to refrain from reporting his UFO experience, because it might damage his reputation. Dr. J. Allen Hynek spoke about this problem in 1953:

> … nothing constructive is accomplished … for science in the long run—by mere ridicule and the implication that sightings are the products of "birdbrains" and "intellectual flyweights," … Ridicule is not part of the scientific method and people should not be taught that it is.[3]

After Project Blue Book came into its own, the Air Force became gradually more confident that the UFOs were not a threat to American security, but by this time the habit of ridicule of UFO sightings and sighters was well set. Gradually, the official nature of the ridicule lid has vanished, although still today there is a military injunction against servicemen reporting UFOs before they have been debriefed. But the habit of ridicule is still in effect, and has continued to successfully stop the free flow of information on the subject that is so necessary for the average citizen to have before he can really decide for himself about UFOs. As Jacobs notes in his book on the history of the UFO controversy, Hynek first polled 44 astronomers for their interest in the UFO phenomena, and found that only 17% of them were interested. He wrote them, then, about several particularly unusual and provocative sightings, and re-polled for interest: nearly all of the astronomers had become interested in UFOs. As Hynek said, "their general lethargy is due to lack of information."[4]

In countries where UFO sighting information has been as freely distributed as any other news, there is a much more energetic feeling among the general populace about the significance of UFOs.

There is a basic problem encountered by those trying to use the scientific method to investigate UFOs. When one begins to investigate a new phenomenon, he needs to start from some aspect of the phenomenon which is linked to present theory. The UFO phenomena does not easily "compute" on the calculators of our present system of physical measurements and predictive judgment. I think that it is this reason more than any other which discourages most scientists and keeps even interested men from undertaking active investigation. Ufology is a frustrating discipline to a scientist. Since it is already unfashionable to be a UFO investigator, this frustration completes the decision, and only the most daring of the scientific community will link their names with UFO studies. This set of circumstances is also true of the whole field of paranormal research, of course, of which UFOs is properly a part.

It has been my personal experience that many of the researchers in ufology will, while appearing most conservative for the record, confide in sympathetic company their more esoteric theories. Some of the more experienced of these people are truly daring the outer limits of knowledge in general. I think it's high time that these outer limits be made more generally known.

I've been at this pursuit of UFO understanding for over 25 years now. I've tried to maintain a totally open-minded approach to the study, considering no piece of evidence too small or too ridiculous to consider. The theory which has gradually emerged from this approach may seem a bit wild or absurd, but it is dealing with a wild and absurd bunch of data. The one thing that recommends the theory is that almost all reports which come in day by day seem to fit into it very well. One thing to remember: almost everything which we now accept as normal in our present technology would have been considered a wild and absurd impossibility a scant 100 years ago. We do not know how many millennia ahead of our present understanding the UFOs might be.

I have chosen not to abide within the approved scientific method of verification of accepted data within the boundaries of currently accepted scientific opinion because this method has proven a tool ineffectual in dealing with this phenomena. I make the assumption that the reason for this lack is that the system is set up to investigate the present level of reality within our technological and scientific nexus of thought. I make the further assumption that the nexus of thinking or technology which underlies the UFO manifestations may not have any close connection to our present Earthman's philosophy of reality. History is replete with examples of the events in which reality itself proved unconformable with the current scientific or philosophical thinking. I think it is happening again. We thought that the Earth was flat at one time. Less than 400 years ago, Giordano Bruno was burned at the stake for suggesting that the Earth revolved around the sun. Now, again, there really does seem to be a growing amount of evidence pointing to the existence of a totally different type of reality than is generally appreciated by our philosophy.

If you ask anyone you meet on the street whether he believes UFOs are real, over half will answer, yes, they probably are. Most people have a lively interest in the subject and when a case is covered in their newspaper, read it and ponder it. But because most UFO cases are not covered in newspapers, the general public does not receive a great percentage of the very prevalent UFO contact information. The lack of coverage is not the only reason that many UFO cases go unreported. There are other reasons:

1. The person who is contacted by the UFO is afraid to tell about his experience, because he fears ridicule.

2. The contactee has no knowledge of UFO investigating organizations, and receives only incredulity from the people to whom he does tell his story. He would like to share his experience but does not feel he will be believed.

3. The contactee may not remember his contact experience consciously, because of a memory block affected by the UFOnauts.

UFO researchers have found these three causes for "silent" contactees to prevail again and again, and it is theorized that a large percentage of contact cases are never discovered by investigators. The pioneer ufologist, Dr. J. Allen Hynek, has estimated that around the world there are about 100 UFO sightings every day, though most of these remain unreported.

But there are still an incredible number of cases that we do know about. There is at present such a tremendous number of well-documented cases of contact with UFO occupants that Dr. Hynek has stated that it's high time we stopped looking for eggs, and started making the omelet. The problem is, of course, that these eggs are so weird that we're afraid to crack them open to make the omelet. This book is intended as an attempt to make this omelet, even if its taste is offensively pungent to some theorists' palates.

But before I begin, I would like to look at just a few "eggs" with you. I want you to get an idea of just how strange these eggs really are. So I've taken a sample of some fifteen cases, all of them UFO sightings which include a close contact with the UFO occupants. These few cases are taken from the many which are reported by the investigating organizations such as APRO, MUFON, and FLYING SAUCER REVIEW. Look in the Bibliography at the back of the book for a list of these information sources complete with addresses. I will not bore you with the well-known cases of the 1950s. This is a small sampling of more recent cases, in order to establish how common these UFO contact reports are, and to give you the flavor of the concoction these "eggs" are going to make.

CASE NUMBER 1

Date: 1963
Place: Fern Creek, Ky.
Investigators: Col. Verne Yahne, Ky. Air National Guard; D.T. Elkins, Independent Investigator

Four young boys, aged 5 to 12, observed a disc-shaped craft as it landed behind a small woods near where they were playing. A humanoid clad in a space suit, about four feet tall, emerged from the woods. Two of the boys threw dirt clods at the entity to provoke it into some action. The entity then shot them with a small black rod, producing a tingling sensation and slight pain. When the boys were individually questioned, all four stories matched. The description of the humanoid which they gave matched information in NICAP files of more than 200 other sightings in the Ohio River Valley area in considerable and exact detail.

The boys' mother stated that she got a "message in her head" (telepathic) to call the University of Louisville shortly after she called the National Guard to report the sighting.

Small footprints and clear landing marks were found. A day later, two unidentified men visited the landing site and eradicated the landing evidence. Although they stated that they were from the University of Louisville, this was checked out and found to be untrue.

CASE NUMBER 2

Date: 1965, and continuing, to the present.
Place: Spain

Investigators: Antonio Ribera and Rafael Farriols, both ufologists in Spain.

A planet called UMMO began contacting various people in Spain in 1965. The people were well-respected and educated: a writer, an engineer, a lawyer, etc. The contacts would be by telephone, and the contactee was invited to ask questions of the Ummites. Later, a report answering the question would come in the mail.

These reports were signed with a thumbprint bearing a distinctive mark much like the alchemical symbol for Uranus, an "H" with a shorter vertical line through the bar. The contactees were told that the Ummo craft would be at a certain place on a certain date. The craft showed up on schedule and pictures were taken of it. On the bottom of the craft there is the cross-barred "H" symbol.

The reports have continued to come in through the intervening years, and speak on many technical subjects, such as physics and biology. The "Ummo" words which are used in these reports, when collected together and considered, form a self-consistent language structure. They say that they are from a planet which revolves around a star which they have tentatively identified as being our "Wolf 424," and that they were first attracted to our solar system by a radio signal which was sent from Earth in 1934. They gave the frequency of the signal (413.44 megacycles). Between the ages of 14 and 16 the vocal chords of the children become sclerosed and for this reason most of the adult inhabitants of Ummo are unable to talk and must use telepathy.

These Ummo reports are an exceptionally interesting instance of UFO contact, and they continue at the present time. FLYING SAUCER REVIEW occasionally updates this continuing story.

CASE NUMBER 3
Date: May 4-9, 1969
Place: Bebedouro, Brazil
Investigator: Hulvio B. Aleixo of CICOANI, a research group of Belo Horizante, Brazil.

Jose Antonio da Silva, a 24-year-old soldier of excellent personal character and reputation, was abducted by small, red-bearded humanoids who forcibly took him aboard their craft. During his confinement aboard their strange vessel, a fair, tall, human-looking being appeared to him, though the smaller aliens did not seem to be able to see him. This being warned da Silva of a danger which involved the whole of mankind which might be avoided if man on Earth changed his ways. Da Silva was told that intervention by unknown beings, and possible calamities, might be involved.

Twelve days after his abduction, da Silva was awakened by a sudden urge to go outside. He did so and saw three of the red-bearded aliens, who had apparently summoned him telepathically. He quickly re-entered his house and locked the door against them, for he felt that part of the danger to come might involve them.

CASE NUMBER 4

Date: Summer, 1973
Places: All over Pennsylvania
Investigator: Stan Gordon, MUFON State Director

Because this is a report of 118 separate contacts with unknown creatures, the date and place have to be generalized. These reports vary somewhat but have the primary details more or less in common. The salient feature of these cases is the creature or creatures who are sighted. They are hairy, ape-like beings with glowing eyes and apparent ears, large noses, fang-like teeth, and the long arms of an ape. Where Gordon was able to take footprint casts, the print was a large and three-toed track. The sightings were, in the majority, in wooded areas or near rural or small-town homes. During the sighting, animals would be still, but before and after a sighting, both animals and small children acted as though they were quite disturbed, cows huddling, dogs barking, children crying all night. These creatures have been sighted often in connection with UFO sightings, have been seen entering and leaving UFOs, and on occasion a telepathic communication from a source connected with the creatures has been reported. In three of these encounters, a creature has been shot. One was shot with a 30-06 (see Case Number 6). Another was shot with a 16 ga. shotgun at close range, and the third with a .38 pistol. The latter two creatures both disappeared in a flash of light, like a photo-flash bulb going off, on being shot.

CASE NUMBER 5

Date: 10-11-73
Place: Pascagoula, Mississippi
Investigators: Dr. J. Allen Hynek, Chairman of the Dept. of Astronomy, Northwestern University; Director, Center for UFO Studies; Dr. James A. Harder, Prof. of Civil Engineering, University of California; Director of Research, APRO.

Charles Hickson, age 45, and 18-year-old Calvin Parker were fishing when an oblong, blue-gray craft 35 to 40 feet long descended and hovered near them. The craft made a "zipping" noise. A door appeared in the craft and three humanoids or robots came out and approached the two men. Like their craft, these entities did not touch the ground but moved just above it, proceeding without moving their legs. The entities were short and had elephant-hide skin, slits for eyes, and pincer-like hands.

When Parker saw the entities approach, he passed out. Hickson was paralyzed, but was able to continue observing what happened. Two of the entities picked up Hickson by his arms and carried him inside the ship. When he was picked up, Hickson lost all feeling, including that of weight. He was taken to a bare, brightly-lit room. He could not see where the light came from. The entities placed him in a reclining position, still "floating" in air, and an eye-like instrument scanned back and forth across his body with thoroughness, as if it were examining or photographing him. This episode lasted somewhere between 15 and 40 minutes, Hickson is not at all sure about the time. After the examination was over, the entities left Hickson alone for a while, and then "floated" him back to where they had picked him up on the river bank.

About an hour later, the two shaken fishermen went to the sheriff's office to report their story. They were interrogated exhaustively and afterwards were left alone, in a "bugged" room. The recording of their conversation at that time reveals that both men were quite frightened by their experience, the emotional trauma having been so great to Parker that, after Hickson left the room, he began to pray. Ultimately he suffered a nervous breakdown as a result of this experience.

Hickson, though plagued with nightmares, and continuing feelings of terror about the experience, came through it better, and was able to work with investigators who wished to ascertain the truth about his experience. A 2½ hour lie detector test, given by a highly skeptical polygraph operator, revealed that Hickson was telling the truth. When Dr. Harder used the technique of time regression hypnosis on Hickson, he too felt that Hickson was telling the truth about the experience, for he said "a strong feeling of terror is practically impossible to fake under hypnosis."

CASE NUMBER 6
Date: 10-25-73
Place: Greensburg, Pennsylvania
Investigator: Berthold Eric Schwarz, M.D., Consultant, Brain Wave Laboratory, Essex Co. Hospital Center, Cedar Grove, New Jersey, Consultant to FLYING SAUCER REVIEW.

This case is perhaps the most interesting and many-faceted of the 188 Pennsylvania creature sightings included in Case Number 4. It began at nine o'clock at night, when a young farmer, called Stephen Pulaski in the report given in FLYING SAUCER REVIEW, and at least fifteen other witnesses saw a bright red ball hovering over a field near them. Stephen grabbed a 30.06 rifle, and he and two ten-year old neighbor boys went to investigate it. Stephen's auto headlights dimmed as he neared the object, and as the object descended towards the field, Stephen's German Shepherd, back at the house, became very disturbed. The object was now bright white, and appeared to be about 100 feet in diameter. It was buzzing much like a lawnmower would.

They stood watching the object on the ground, and then the neighbor boys saw something walking along by the fence. Stephen thought it looked like two bears, and he fired a tracer bullet over the "bears" heads. The creatures were very tall, one 7 feet, the other over 8 feet tall. These measurements were easier than usual to get because the entities were silhouetted against the fence and so could be accurately judged. They were hairy and long-armed, with greenish-yellow eyes. They made a noise like a baby whining. A smell like "burning rubber" was present. Stephen, realizing that these creatures were not bears and that they were coming nearer to him, fired over the entities' heads once more and, when they kept on coming, fired directly at the larger creature.

When the creature was hit, the glowing 150 ft. diameter object disappeared from the field, instantaneously, and the motor noise stopped. The two creatures turned around and walked back towards the woods. In the field where the object had been was a glowing area about 150 feet in diameter, which was gone by the next morning. While it was still there, a State Trooper who came to investigate the story went up to within 200 yards of it, then stopped, went back to call in the UFO researcher Stan Gordon. The Trooper felt that Stephen was so disturbed that it was better that he be watched—and Stephen wouldn't go near the glowing area.

It was 2 a.m. when Stan Gordon's Study Group team and Stephen and his father went back to the landing site. The animals were acting scared, and Stephen's dog was tracking something which no one could see at the edge of the woods. Suddenly Stephen began rubbing his head and face and looking as though he were about to faint. Several people approached him, but he threw them off, growling like an animal and flailing his arms. His own dog ran towards him and Stephen attacked the dog. Two of the investigators also experienced some feelings of lightheartedness and difficulty in breathing at this point.

Stephen continued running around, growling and swinging his arms, and then collapsed in a manured area, face-down. He lay there for a time, then began to come to himself, and said, "Get away from me. It's here. Get back." Sulfur-like odor was noticed. Stephen and the group got away from the area, but Stephen kept mumbling that he would protect the group. He said he saw a man in a black hat and cloak, who told Stephen, "If Man doesn't straighten up, the end is near." The man also told Stephen, "There is a man here now, who can save the world." Needless to say, the investigators present felt quite concerned about Stephen's health, and it was here that Dr. Schwarz was called in. Dr. Schwarz's subsequent psychiatric study of Stephen yielded results that he feels point clearly to the incident having occurred just as reported, for indeed it would be terrifying for a man such as Stephen, used to a very practical and realistic type of life, to shoot and hit an 8-foot antagonist which then was not harmed in any way. The numerous other witnesses to the various phases of the incident also bear out its having happened. Who was the man in black, and what do the predictions about Mankind really mean? That is a matter for interpretation. But that Stephen had the experience has been thoroughly documented.

CASE NUMBER 7

Date: 10-28-73
Place: Bahia Blanca, Argentina
Investigator: Liria D. Jauregui, APRO Investigator

Very early in the morning, truck driver Dionisio Llanca had a flat tire and pulled off the road in an isolated area. As he set up the jack to change the tire, he saw lights in the distance, but thought little of them until, as they approached, they suddenly changed to a brilliant blue. When Llanca tried to get up and look for the source of this odd light he found he was apparently paralyzed and could not move. He was able to see, however, as a dome-topped disc came to rest, hovering just above the ground near the truck. On the ground by the craft were three humanoid entities, two men and a woman. They had long blond hair and elongated eyes, and wore silver, one-piece suits with high boots, no helmets, no weapons.

After the entities had talked among themselves, one of them lifted Llanca by the neck of his sweater. Llanca was desperately frightened, but the man put a small black box against his left index finger and instantly he began to relax. In a few seconds, he was unconscious.

The next morning he awakened on the roadside and made his way back to civilization. He told his story and investigation was undertaken, but although competent doctors used hypnotherapy and truth serum with

Llanca, he could not remember a portion of his experiences aboard the craft. He was able to tell the investigators that these entities had been contacting people on Earth "since 1950," and that their purpose was to discover whether Earthmen could live in their world. He described the interior of the ship, and said that he went into the ship not by stairs or a ramp, but on a ray of light. But he reported that the beings did not want him to remember some of his experience aboard their craft, and he would not be able to. The message that came from him after intense probing for information was this, "I have a message from the beings in the craft but I can't tell you what it is. No matter what you or any other Earth scientists do, there will remain the memory lapse while I was on the ship."

The medical personnel working on this case agree with this statement, and feel that to probe any deeper in Llanca's subconscious for this experience might damage his health. But they feel that his experience was, though unbelievable, quite real.

CASE NUMBER 8
Date: 1-7-74
Place: Warneton, Belgium
Investigators: Mssrs. Bazin Sr. and Jr., Mr. Bigorne, Mr. Boidin, MUFON investigators.

An anonymous witness driving along the French-Belgian border experienced engine failure. His lights and radio also went out. At this point he saw a landed UFO about 160 yards away across a field. The 30-foot wide craft was shaped like a World War I British helmet and was glowing a patchy orange, with white light coming from beneath it. Two entities were walking slowly and stiffly toward the witness. Both were about 4 feet tall, with grayish skin, round eyes, a rudimentary nose, and a slit-like, lipless mouth. They wore helmets and metallic gray coverall-type uniforms. One had an object in his hand shaped like a short, thick ruler with a pointed tip. He was aiming it at the car.

When the beings came to within 12 feet of the car, one of them opened and closed his mouth and the witness felt a slight shock at the back of his head and heard a low-pitched, modulated sound. Then the entities turned about and reboarded their craft, which began pulsating an electric-blue glow. Its tripod legs withdrew, it rose and hovered momentarily, then rapidly ascended at a 60-degree angle. As the witness prepared to leave the site, another car drove up; its driver had also seen the UFO and the beings.

CASE NUMBER 9

Date: Easter Sunday, 1974
Place: Bardstown, Ky.
Investigators: Lawrence Allison and D. T. Elkins.

A boy in his late teens was driving alone at night and wondering why he was doing so—he had almost compulsively gone out to take the ride and had no purpose in mind—when a man appeared beside him in the car. He asked the startled boy if he remembered him, which he did not.

Then suddenly he was inside a large room, he and his car. The "passenger" welcomed him aboard, and proceeded to show the boy around the craft.

After the tour was completed, the guide, who looked like a normal Earth man and was casually dressed in a shirt and blue jeans, asked him to get back into his car. The boy did so and found himself suddenly back on the road.

Investigations to find more details of this encounter are continuing.

CASE NUMBER 10

Date: 4-10-74
Place: Whitehouse, Ohio
Investigators: Earl Neff and Larry Moyers, MUFON field investigators.

"Sam" (an alias) had spent an evening with a friend who claimed to be a contactee of the UFOs. During this meeting, he had asked the contactee for proof of the UFO's reality. On the way home from work the next night, shortly after midnight, his car's engine and light died. As he got out of the car he noticed another car stop behind him. A very prosperous-looking, gray-haired man got out of the car and came over to him. This normal looking human then offered Sam "proof," by dematerializing a rock with a small hand-held implement. Then he told Sam to "save his marriage," and promised that he would be contacted again.

CASE NUMBER 11

Date: 5-26-74
Place: Mitchell Caverns, California.
Investigator: Idabel Epperson, MUFON field investigator.

This witness had seen UFOs several times in the past. One evening he was awakened in his camper by a humming sound and pulsating lights. He tried to call his family, but was immobilized. He saw four pinwheels of odd-shaped colored lights, red, orange, yellow, and blue-green. He awoke the next morning with bloodshot eyes and an aching body. It was two hours later than his usual rising time.

He had impressions of having been inside a UFO, but a memory lapse blocked out details. At a later date, under hypnosis, he recalled being inside the craft and described a row of gyroscopes along an inner wall. "The pinwheels of colored lights energized these to form an artificial gravity field." He had seen eight men, normal-looking, seven of them dressed in maroon "foil-like" uniforms, the eighth clad in a soft, pale-blue outfit. He saw a view screen which was showing a close-up view of Saturn, a control panel, and three recliner-type chairs. The entities examined his eyes with a magnifying glass. The witness says that he expects to receive further contacts from these entities.

CASE NUMBER 12
Date: 9-3-74
Place: Duxbury, Mass.
Investigator: John Giambrone, MUFON field investigator.

One day, early in the morning, this very reluctant woman witnessed a red pulsating UFO at treetop level, and two light beams which shone across the bog caused her car to die, while the radio gave out static. Not long after this incident, the woman got a telepathic message to drive her car down a certain road, which she did. Again the radio and engine quit, but this time four small humanoids appeared, moving rapidly towards her, each astride a small vehicle that looked like a roto-tiller but moving rapidly above rather than on the ground. One of the entities approached her car and telepathically asked her to open the door, but when she did not comply, all four doors flew open anyway. The entity examined her and touched her on the nape of the neck with a small implement which left five small puncture marks. She was told that they have thousands of ships which have been visiting Earth for many years. They have a mother ship nearby, she was told, and their home planet is called "Omnius" or "Omnigus." They have examined many people, not all of them voluntarily. She was asked not to touch them because of possible contamination and was warned that she would have severe headaches for several weeks after this contact. These entities were four to five feet tall, had helmets on which concealed their faces but through which small, shiny eyes could be seen. They were dressed in uniforms, the belts of which featured an emblem with vertical wavy lines.

This witness was terrified by this encounter and has refused to allow any investigation by any group. The details given here were supplied to

MUFON in strict anonymity by her husband. This woman denies to any questioner that the event ever occurred.

CASE NUMBER 13

Date: 10-25-74
Place: Medicine Bow National Park, Wyoming
Investigators: Dr. Leo Sprinkle, Prof. of Psychology, University of Wyoming, Investigator for APRO and MUFON; Rick Kenyon and Robert Nantkes, MUFON field investigators, and Frank Bourke, *National Star* investigator.

Carl Higdon was hunting elk in the northern area of the park. He fired at one, but saw his bullet leave the rifle in slow motion and drop to the snow about 50 feet away. Feeling a tingle, he turned and saw a humanoid entity over six feet tall standing nearby. The entity wore a black jumpsuit with a wide belt, upon which was a six-pointed star and a yellow emblem. The entity had bristle-like, straight hair standing straight out from his head, small eyes, no eyebrows or chin, bow-legged, long-armed, and with rod-like manipulators instead of hands. He might have had hands but Higdon never saw them.

The entity approached Higdon and asked if he was hungry, and flipped him a little bunch of pills, which Higdon swallowed. (Perhaps the entity felt that Higdon would not be hunting unless he needed food.)

The entity pointed at Higdon, and suddenly Higdon found himself within a transparent, cubical "craft" in company with two UFOnauts and five elk. They told him they were on their way to their home planet some 163,000 light years away, and shortly they were there. They had put a helmet with wires sticking out of it on Higdon's head. He saw a tall, Seattle space-needle-type building and a type of sunlight which was very intense and made his eyes water. The entities told him that our sun does the same thing to their eyes.

The next thing Higdon remembers is being back in the park, about 2½hours having elapsed since the first sight of the entity. He was cold, disoriented, and nearly hysterical. His truck was not where he had left it; he found it about three miles away, stuck in a mud hole. From here he sent out a distress call over his CB radio, and the Sheriff picked him up at midnight. By now, Higdon was in a state of panic and near nervous exhaustion, shouting, "They took my elk!" They took him to the hospital and checked him over; oddly, his blood tests showed a very rich supply of vitamins—those food pellets must have been nutritive—and old TB scars on his lungs had disappeared!

Later investigation found that Higdon's wife and two others had seen a red-green-white flashing light moving back and forth across this area. When Dr. Sprinkle used time-regression hypnosis on Higdon, he found out more about his experience. Higdon was able to recall that other "Earth people" had been present, and he said that the aliens had come to Earth to hunt and fish for food.

CASE NUMBER 14
Date: 8-13-75
Place: Alamogordo, New Mexico
Investigator: NATIONAL ENQUIRER, APRO

Staff Sgt. Charles L. Moody, a 32-year-old Air Force man, was parked near Holloman Air Force Base in the desert, watching for a predicted meteor shower, at about 1:20 a.m., when suddenly like a flash, an object appeared, dropping from the sky about 300 feet away. It stopped about 25 feet above the desert floor and "wobbled" for a while, then glided toward Moody. As it came closer, Moody could see that it was a disc-shaped craft which glowed a dull, metallic gray. It was 40 to 50 feet across and 18 to 25 feet high, with three globes showing on its underside.

The terrified Moody leapt back into his car and tried to escape, but his month-old battery was completely dead. Then the craft halted again, about 50 feet away, and Moody began to hear a high-pitched voice, and to see shadowy figures through a window which had appeared in the craft. Quoting the ENQUIRER report: "Suddenly an odd glow enveloped my car, and I felt numb all over." Immediately after the experience, this numb feeling was the last thing Moody remembered before coming to, sitting in the car, and watching the craft leave, shooting straight up. But in time, the memory of the hour and 20 minutes he'd "lost" came back to him.

Two beings had come from the craft, gliding rather than walking. They started to open the car door and Moody panicked, striking out at one of the aliens. Then, "the lights went out." When he regained consciousness, he was on a table, and an alien was studying him. Moody was unable to move. The alien, which was hairless, large-skulled, with no eyebrows and round, large eyes, small nose, mouth, and ears, and thin lips, "spoke," but with no lip movement. He asked if Moody was well, and told him he would release him from the paralysis if he promised not to strike out. Moody agreed, so the frail, five-foot tall being in the skin-tight white suit, with whitish-gray skin, touched Moody with a metal rod about seven inches long and half an inch thick. Instantly, Moody could move freely.

Moody asked if he could see the craft's propulsion system, and the alien agreed, so they left the circular room in which the examining table was in, and went through an arched doorway and then into another room, which, Moody reported, seemed almost as large by itself as the whole craft had looked from the outside. It was as though the interior of the ship were larger than the outside. In this room, there were three other beings, one apparently a woman, floating about a quarter-inch above the floor. The leader told Moody to stand on a certain part of flooring, and as he did so it dropped, like an elevator, to a room below. Protruding up from the floor of this room were the top sides of the three globes he'd seen on the underside of the craft. The globes contained large crystals, on each side of which were rods which sloped in toward the crystal.

The aliens gave him other information too, says Moody. They said that this ship was a small observation craft from a much larger main craft which stayed 5,000 to 6,000 miles out in space. They also told Moody that they would be making themselves "known to mankind" within three years, though they plan only limited contact at first. These aliens belong to a league of races, which our human race may one day be invited to join—if they decide to accept us. But whatever happens, the aliens will never hurt us.

After this conversation, Moody was told to report to a medical facility, and he lost consciousness again, to wake up in his car. He watched the craft leave, then easily started his car and went home. Both his wife and his superior officer are convinced that the very conservative Sgt. Moody is telling the truth.

CASE NUMBER 15

Date: 11-5-75
Place: Apache-Sitgreaves National Forest, Arizona
Investigators: Coral and Jim Lorenzen, Directors of APRO, Dr. James Harder, Dir. of Res., APRO.

Travis Walton and six other men had been working in the forest all day, thinning wood with chain saws. They were riding back to town at about six o'clock when they saw a yellowish glow ahead of them and to the right. The truck was on a right-hand curve, and it bumped along until suddenly it came to a clearing, where they had a very clear view of the object causing the glow. It was about 15 feet in diameter and 8 feet high, and was hovering about 15 feet above the ground, about 90 feet from their truck. They were able to estimate the size of the craft because it was hovering over a pile of slash and was about its size. The craft was glowing with a color "like a Coleman Lantern being lit."

When Travis saw the object he asked the driver to stop; then without waiting for the truck to completely halt, he jumped out and walked quickly over to the pile of slash. The object gave off a beeping noise and began to oscillate around its vertical axis. There were other rumbling noises. Then a bright, narrow ray of greenish-blue light shot out from the craft and struck Walton. A bright, soundless flash surrounded Walton's body and lifted him a foot into the air and backwards, with his head knocked back and his arms outflung. One of the other men saw Walton fall to the ground after this, but all were busy running from the scene.

They stopped about a quarter of a mile away, just as a light lifted up through the trees in the direction from which they had just come and streaked away. They decided to go back and find Walton. They were back at the landing site in 15 minutes, but could find no trace of the craft or of Walton. They finally gave up searching and went to the Sheriff's office to report the incident and the missing Walton. The Sheriff noted later that these men were extremely upset, one even weeping. Later polygraph tests bore out that they were telling the truth about their experience.

In the next days, a thorough search, involving about 50 men, was made for Walton. After 2 days, the search was called off, and a missing persons report filed.

On November 11th, Travis Walton called his sister from a telephone booth in a nearby town. His voice was extremely weak. Her husband and her brother went to find Walton, and discovered him slumped on the floor of the booth from which he had called. He was twelve miles from the spot at which he had last been seen. He had a strange story to relate, and little by little the details were told. When he regained consciousness after being hit by the ray, he was lying on a table in a low-ceilinged room. There was apparatus resting on his lower chest. He had pains in his head and to a lesser extent all over his body. Around him stood three entities, about 5 feet tall, with large eyes, small noses, mouths, and ears, and no hair. They wore brown coveralls. Travis was panicked by the sight of these "human fetuses" and knocked the apparatus off his chest, striking out at the entities. The creatures calmly left the room, turning right out the doorway. Travis followed them, turning left. He went down the hall and into another room, which featured a transparent wall through which he could see what he thought were stars. He sat in a chair which had push buttons on its arm, and pushed one of the buttons. But the stars then started to move, so he left the buttons alone. A man in a blue outfit and transparent helmet came into the room and beckoned that Walton follow him. He did not answer his questions, but merely led him out of the craft, through an airlock, and down a ramp. He was now in a large enclosure in which several disc-shaped objects were parked. The air was fresher than before, the light brighter. His guide took him into another craft where he met three more humans, two men and a woman, who wore blue clothing but no helmets. They all closely resembled one another. At this point a mask, resembling an oxygen mask, was put over Walton's face, and he lost consciousness.

When he regained his senses, he was lying on his back on a road. He felt the heat of a disc-shaped object which was rising into the sky above him, the doors on its bottom just closing. Walton recognized the road, walked unsteadily to the nearest phone, and called his sister. Six days had elapsed.

Tests performed immediately after Walton's return show some dehydration but no malnutrition and no possibility of drug use. The lost time is blocked by a strong memory block, and APRO's careful report stated that it might be months before further information about the lost time can be extracted from Walton's subconscious.

This concludes our small sampling of contact cases. These few interesting cases make up only a tiny percentage of the well-documented contact cases, which now number over 2,000. This total increases almost daily. Over 2,000 reliable witnesses have reported contact not only with UFO's but with their occupants. Trained investigators have found these stories to be given in good faith by credible people. *Something* is happening.

Chapter Two
The Telepathic Contact

> Do a movie on Uri. Melanie is the one to do it. Work at it; it will come out at the right time. You are not to entrust anyone with the secret of our existence—no one.[1]

This message was received at 2:00 p.m., April 14, 1972. It appeared as if by magic on Dr. Andrija Puharich's cassette tape recorder, and was alleged to have been transmitted from a UFO. At 1:03 a.m. on August 27, 1972, the following was received in the same manner by Dr. Puharich:

> One of our failures is that we cannot contact you directly. We can only talk to you through Uri's power on the tape recorder. It is a shame for such a brilliant mind we cannot contact you directly. Maybe in time we shall be able to contact you directly …
>
> This afternoon we heard the movie script … it is a brilliant movie but not the story we want. We want you to prepare the earth for our mass landing, a mass landing on earth. We landed in South America 3,000 years ago, and we must land again. We want you to tell our story, what you call the UFO experience. Use all the collected data and literature.
>
> A.P.: How do we know which is the relevant or true data?
>
> Research the data published. You will know what is correct. Write the movie script carefully, slowly, properly, and cleverly.[2]

Six years earlier, in 1968, I had received essentially the same message, not on a tape recorder but by the direct mental process referred to by the source. I had been experimenting since 1962 with dozens of subjects, pursuing an investigation into the possibility of mental or telepathic contact with UFO sources. By August, 1972, when Dr. Puharich was being asked to prepare Earth for a mass landing by producing a movie on the subject, I was already in the middle of producing a motion picture. My reason for doing so: a UFO source had requested the same task of me.

The important part of this is that each of us had received the same information, totally independently, and allegedly from a UFO source. In fact, most of the information from the UFO source recorded in the book, URI, by Puharich, correlated with the telepathically received data I had accumulated as a result of my own experiments.

My own interest in the possibility of telepathic contact with UFO sources stemmed from my original study of the UFO literature of the 1950s. Most of the people who claimed contact with UFOs were considered charlatans or crackpots by the scientific community in general. It seemed to me, however, that this was the historically classic attitude of men of science toward genuinely new ideas.

This is true to this day, and was emphatically true then. The numerous contactees of the '50s, as well as many of the more recent contactees, seemed to have a common denominator: most of them claimed direct, mind-to-mind contact with the aliens, rather than verbal communication.

It was not hard to see why the scientific community would be sorely tempted to classify all UFO contacts in a lump under cultist claims because of the metaphysical or religious orientation of most of the messages. On the surface, such contacts seemed like highly imaginative science fiction stories, or like the creations of fanatic cultist groups seeking frantically for their new Messiah.

What the scientific community chose to overlook was the independence of many of the claims from other claims of contact, and the extreme degree of consistency in the content of the messages. This independence was a fact in several of my own contact experiments: the participants did not know when they started what their goal was or what they should expect to happen to them. The messages which they eventually produced were extremely consistent in content with other alleged UFO messages.

I have found increasing numbers of functioning contact groups around the country, in Canada and England, and elsewhere in the world. And in addition to the growing number of voluntary contacts, one can come across many sincerely told stories of involuntary contact.

An example of this which has been well documented is Herb Schirmer's story. Schirmer, a highway patrolman in the midwest, reported sighting a flying saucer during a routine patrol in 1967. The Condon Committee heard of this and put him through time-regression hypnosis. Under hypnosis, Schirmer recounted contact with the UFOnauts themselves, rather than a simple sighting of a flying saucer. Repeated testing of Schirmer's memory only proved that he sincerely believed that his story of contact with extraterrestrials was true. The Condon Committee people could not shake his faith in what he remembered of the UFOnauts.

Herb Schirmer's story is told rather fully by an investigating reporter who seemed well versed in this area. He offered a list of general observations regarding the UFO contactees. Among his points was this one, concerning the way the contactee allegedly receives his messages from the UFOnauts:

> While he is being interviewed or questioned, the contactee often seems to be listening to another "voice" or presence in the room. Often there are pauses in his conversation which last as long as forty-five seconds to a minute. After this pause, the answer to a query is given with great lucidity. In interview sessions wherein the contactee has been hypnotically regressed to the time of contact, he begins his entranced re-creation of the experience in "normal" hypnotic voice trance patterns. When he reaches the time when the "message" was relayed to him (usually after the mental and physical examination) his voice and manner changes, even under hypnotic trance and he *recites*, rather than *recalls*, the dogma which saucer people have relayed to him.[3]

I recognized this description of the contactees' manner when speaking as messengers for alleged UFOnauts as being similar to the style of speaking used by all of the "telepathic receivers" that I had investigated. Another extremely apt description of this telepathic contact is found in John Fuller's book, INTERRUPTED JOURNEY. Included in this volume is a great deal of directly transcribed and quoted material from the file of Betty and Barney Hill. They had gone to a psychiatrist with anxiety problems. The doctor had performed time regression hypnosis on both of them, and uncovered an alleged contact with the UFO people. When Barney was asked to recall the language used by the UFOnaut, Barney stated that the being did not speak to him by word, but told him what to do by the alien's thoughts making his thoughts understand. When the psychiatrist asked Barney if this was some kind of mental telepathy, Barney said that he did not know the definition of the word "telepathy." Yet he described its process quite well.

It seemed to me to be rather an exaggeration of scientific caution to declare, as so many did, that all of the people who claimed this telepathic communication were suffering from identical forms of mental aberration. The more appropriate response seemed to me to be to attempt to check this common denominator out.

For this reason, I set up a control group of people whose sanity and habitual veracity I could vouch for, and proceeded to expose them to conditions which allegedly would produce UFO contact. The instructions, of course, had come from an alleged UFO source which I had come across several times in my research.

Since 1962, I have worked with over 100 of these human guinea pigs who were successful in mentally receiving what I believe to be messages from UFOs.

The data collected through these telepathic receivers created a problem in evaluation. I had originally hoped to be able to extract material of a scientifically evidential nature from these experiments, but soon after the start of the experiment, I realized that rigorous analytical control was not possible. Telepathy itself is still proving extremely difficult to investigate scientifically, when the receiver and the sender both can be monitored exhaustively. And, needless to say, if we could put our hands on the UFO senders to test them, we would have our experiment's end.

Yet it was possible to produce an unending supply of data. So I simply chose to generate a great deal of data, figuring that it was a mistake to expect material of this nature to fit any preconceived notion that I might have had.

After carrying on this experiment for over 13 years, I now feel that I can make the following statement: *The information claimed to be received by numerous UFO contactees can be duplicated in a controlled situation.*

For example, in numerous instances, I have been able to produce the telepathic contact in people who have no previous knowledge of UFO literature. In each case the message which they receive has correlated in its content to a very high degree with other UFO contactees' messages. The results of this experiment indicate to me that we should take a very close look at this UFO contactee information. It is my belief that within this information is the key to creating a much more direct contact with the elusive UFO phenomenon.

When I work with Uri Geller, the results we achieve with telepathic experiments are remarkably good.

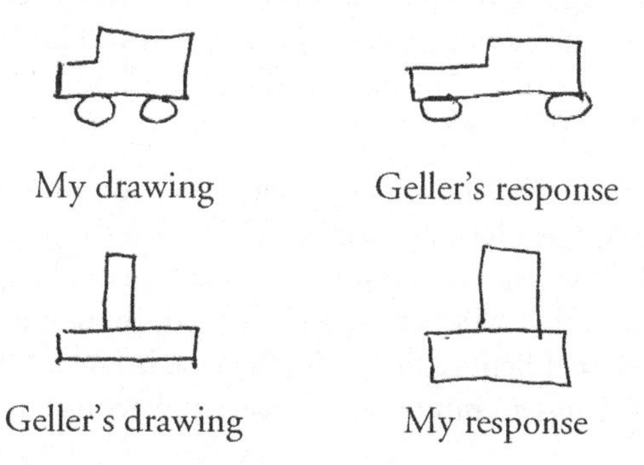

Many professional magicians have stated that Geller is actually a very clever trickster with no special mental ability. It seems that few of them have applied the scientific method of repeated experiment to determine his ability.

I found that, for my own edification, the most conclusive tests were those performed in a random fashion during the normal daily routine, completely unannounced. That is, Uri did not know that I was testing his telepathic ability as we carried on a normal conversation during the day. The result: for me, there is no doubt that Uri Geller is a first-class telepathic sender and receiver.

Telepathy is not a difficult technique to learn. I am convinced that it is a basic form of communication that our civilization has forgotten due to lack of use. It is analogous to the ability to do one-arm pushups. Anyone can do them, with enough practice and conditioning.

Most of us can show evidence of a telepathic "muscle," since we've usually had experiences of starting to talk about a subject simultaneously with a close acquaintance.

Telepathic communication is very similar to radio communication. If you think of everyone having a radio transmitter and receiver in their brain, you have a close analogy. Our problem is to learn to tune this mental radio for clear transmission and reception. It is my theory that the UFO contactees are receiving, on often poorly tuned receivers, the powerful and accurately tuned signal of the UFO's transmitter.

Learning to receive is very simple. It requires practice in making the mind a total blank. This is easier for some of us than others! One way to do this is to make a daily practice of sitting in a comfortable position and letting the conscious mind "run down" or become less active. Finally, short periods of consciousness with no thoughts can be achieved. This is the beginning to tuning the receiver, and is the condition necessary for the UFO contact experiment to succeed. Now this is still far from perfect tuning, but it can be sufficient if, as in the case of the UFOs, the transmitter is very strong.

It seems that language is no barrier to telepathic communication. For instance, a German sender may think, "messer," meaning knife, and the American receiver will get the impression of a knife. The general contact of that communication will have been achieved, though perhaps nuances in meaning are lost. I believe this to be the case in most UFO contact communications, and accounts for the seemingly common nature of the language.

Once the subjects in my experiment were trained, it was necessary to attract the UFO transmitter. The most efficient way of doing this seemed to be a simple hand-off. The trained receiver was exposed to a contactee for a brief period, not long enough to dilute the evidential quality of the data which the new receiver might be expected to produce.

Since a study of this nature takes years to produce, and since most of the evidential quality is extracted slowly and cumulatively by the experimenter, it is difficult to prove to the casual observer the nature of the alleged contact. To most researchers, this evidence is simply not conclusive.

Since I have observed over 100 people go through this process and have read millions of words of contactee literature, both published and unpublished, I believe that I am now in a position to select the highly correlative material from the masses of communications. Moreover, the material in the body of this book is selected by me to best represent the material received from the large number of contactees whose material I have studied.

I have no way of vouching for 100% accuracy; however, I have tried to reduce my personal bias to a minimum by investigating as much material as I could find.

The answers you find here are the result of a careful selection from literally millions of words of alleged UFO communication spanning over 20 years and involving contactees both "silent" and published, as well as my own experimentally fabricated contactees.

I will make the following observations concerning the general nature of the alleged telepathic communications from UFOs:

1. People who have had face-to-face encounters with UFOnauts report telepathic communication more often than any other form.

2. Those who claim communication at a distance with a UFO source report that telepathic contact was used in an overwhelming majority of cases.

3. The same general message permeates over 90% of the millions of words received by thousands of people around the world.

4. I have been able to experimentally fabricate contactees who, with no prior background in UFO literature, produced the general UFO "doctrine" in detail.

5. Most of my fabricated contactees who have seen a UFO have done so shortly after becoming contactees.

6. There are over 100 contactees which have been fabricated in my group. Their backgrounds represent a general sampling of our society with educational levels ranging from grade-school to post-doctoral.
7. Over 90% of these fabricated contactees experienced identical physical symptoms during the time of the contact.
8. A single message would sometimes be delivered through a dozen contactees, a part through each one. Though the contactees were of different backgrounds and educational levels, the message would be uniform, of coherent continuity, and largely free from normal errors and hesitations of speech.
9. Two of my fabricated contactees were given only one day of training before returning to their home some 600 miles away. Their progress was monitored by mail, and the result was still the same.
10. I have found that some people can achieve the contact phenomenon simply by being hypnotized. No preparation or training is necessary for this type of contact. The content of messages received is the same as the great majority of all other contacts.
11. It is not necessary for the fabricated contactees to believe in UFOs or the reality of the contact phenomena to produce the communications. One of my best hypnotic contactees has never believed, and still refuses to countenance, any part of the phenomenon, although her communications have in all cases been excellent and have matched in exact detail the bulk of other contactee material.
12. Several of the contactees, particularly those with extensive training in the physical sciences, maintained a highly objective and somewhat skeptical attitude throughout the experiment and still produced excellent communications, precisely analogous to the bulk of material received.

The process of receiving contact is so simple that it is difficult to adequately describe it. Some people seem to have a terrific natural ability to receive this contact, and some almost none. To receive the contact it is only necessary that a person learn to clear his mind, by any process that seems to work, and then await the contact. I realize that this sounds much too simplistic to yield results. Yet this is the method, if you can call such a simple concept a method, which has produced in my own experimental work many contactees who have produced many thousands of words of standard contactee "doctrine."

Chapter Three

Reality, Etc.

In our culture there seems to be very little communication between science and religion, and yet the practitioners of both disciplines claim that their studies are fundamental to an understanding of basic truth. What emerges from the UFO communications is the attitude that there is a single valid approach to the complete understanding of the universe, and that this approach blends what we presently consider to be two separate disciplines and philosophies.

My personal bias, at least during the initial stages of my investigation, was wholly on the side of the scientific disciplines. As the investigation continued, however, I kept finding what seemed to be a religious or spiritual factor in the contact phenomena. My determined bias towards open-minded and impartial observation led me finally to acknowledge this factor as a genuine part of ufology. At present, I no longer regard this factor as separate from a scientific understanding of the phenomena. The seemingly religious content of the communications is seen as such because of our own cultural conditioning: we interpret these messages as religious. It is my belief that the foundation of a much more nearly absolute and true philosophy of natural phenomena is being made available through the UFO contacts. At present, our languages are inadequate to communicate anything but the first step in the evolution of our thinking. It will be necessary for us to make this first step, in order to begin to understand how to make the second.

Paranormal Phenomena

Several years ago, I had the opportunity to converse with some ghosts that materialized into our physical world and then vanished after our conversation. To many psychical researchers, this phenomenon, known as materialization due to ectoplasmic emission from a medium, is an established and accepted occurrence.

It is my belief that anyone following the rules and conditions laid down for this type of contact can achieve it, assuming that he is in the presence of a suitable materialization medium (an individual capable of producing ectoplasmic emissions.)

The most evidential of the ghosts which I saw and talked to was a tall, ghostly individual who grew solid before my eyes, carried on a conversation with me, and then to prove his ability to manifest in the physical world, slapped me and my companion, Carla, solidly on the arms. Then he slowly walked through us, while we watched closely. Thus in the space of a few seconds, he displayed both the properties of a perfectly solid substance and those of total absence of solidity.

Psychic researchers have for many years reported and photographed these ghostly materializations, but because of their inability to produce the phenomena at the demand of skeptical observers, little general interest has been developed in this research.

As we unravel more of the UFO mystery, we will discover the reason why the skeptical or "prove it to me" approach is quite often the defeating factor in paranormal investigations. I also noticed this same factor in evidence as I recently observed several hundred seemingly miraculous bare-handed surgical operations in the Philippines. I saw native "psychic surgeons" seemingly plunging their hands directly into the patients' unanesthetized bodies, pulling out all sorts of bloody parts while the patients remained perfectly conscious, watching the process and feeling no pain. The patients displayed no wounds or scars after the operation was completed. Here again the evidential quality of the operation witnessed was very dependent upon the attitude of the witness. It has been aptly stated that, with paranormal phenomena, "believing is seeing."

There are many observers who attend demonstrations of paranormal phenomena and who conclude that what they have seen was all trickery. I've had a lot of experience in witnessing these demonstrations, have seen several hundred authentic ghosts materialize, have watched much psychic surgery and had minor operations performed on myself, and in every case I have noted a common factor. If skeptical observers were present, the phenomena either didn't occur at all, or their quality was so poor that trickery would naturally be suspected.

Now the skeptical observer doesn't like this facet of the phenomena at all and uses it as evidence of the fakery. His problem is that he doesn't understand why he, as a skeptic, can't be given evidential and inalienable proof of the reality of the phenomena. He absolutely cannot accept the necessity under the circumstance of his skepticism of taking the word of some "believer," whom he usually considers deluded. The reason that this lack of proof must accompany skepticism will become evident as we further explore the UFO communications.

My own stance is a balanced one, I hope, that of the believer who is skeptical of tricksters among the real practitioners. There are many fraudulent mediums and many quack psychic surgeons. I have seen both practicing their trades and am aware of their methods. Yet their existence does nothing to compromise the reality of the paranormal phenomena generated by the real mediums and psychic surgeons.

A pertinent question when considering psychic demonstrations is: how does the paranormal event happen? The answer may well lie in the area of occult theory which is concerned with the existence of various "planes."

The theosophists say that there are fourteen mental planes associated with this planet. After death, they say, an individual finds himself at one of these 14 levels of existence, the level being dependent on the spiritual nature or development of the person at the time of his death. The cliché that covers this theory is a heavenly "birds of a feather flock together." When a ghost materializes into our reality, it is from one of these 14 levels that he usually comes for his earthly visit. In general, it is theorized that a planet is a sort of spiritual distillery, with reincarnation taking place into the physical world until the individual is sufficiently developed in the spiritual sense that he can reach the higher states of existence, and is no longer in need of this planet's developmental lessons.

Most of this theory was developed as a result of reported contact and communication with the inhabitants of these supposedly separate realities.

The most satisfactory term I have come across for these different levels of reality is the word, "density." I have come to believe that these densities interpenetrate with our physical space and mutually coexist, though with very little awareness of each other. A simple analogy, to which I've referred before, is to consider the actors in two different TV plays, both receivable on the same set, but each play being exclusive of the other. This seems to be what we experience in our daily lives: one channel or density of existence, being totally unaware of the myriad entities occupying other densities of our physical space. The point of all this is that our density or reality is not ultimate or singular; it is in fact our reality only at the present.

Many of the UFO reports display ample evidence that the object sighted has its origin in one of these other realities or densities, just as do the materialized ghosts. I would like to emphasize that this does not in any way imply their unreality; rather, it displaces the UFOs' reality from ours. I'm saying the equivalent of: Channel 4 on the TV is equivalent to but displaced from channel 3 on the same TV.

If you were told to build a scale model of any atom using something the size of a pea for the nucleus, it would be necessary to have an area the size of a football stadium to contain even the innermost orbital electrons. If the pea were placed at the center of the 50-yard line, a small cotton ball on the uppermost seat in the stands could represent an electron of the atom. There is very little actual matter in physical matter. When you look at the stars in the night sky, you probably see something quite similar to what you would see if you could stand on the nucleus of any atom of "solid" material and look outward toward our environment. To demonstrate an electron to you, a physicist will probably show you a curved trace of one on a photographic plate. What he probably does not tell you is that this is second-hand evidence. The electron itself has never been seen, only its effect on a dense medium can be recorded. It is possible, of course, to make accurate mathematical calculations, about what we call an electron. For such work we must know some data on magnetic field strength, electron charge and velocity. But since a magnetic field is caused by moving charges, which in turn are empirically observed phenomena, we find that the entire mathematical camouflage obscures the fact that all we really know is that charged particles have effects on each other. We still don't know what charged particles are, or why they create an action at a distance effect.

Senior scientists would be the first to agree that there is no such thing as an absolute scientific explanation of anything. Science is, rather, a method or tool of prediction, relating one or more observations to each other. In physics, this is usually done through the language of mathematics. Our scientific learning is a learning by observation and analysis of this observation. In the sense of penetrating the fundamental essences of things, we really do not understand anything at all.

A magnetic field is nothing but a mathematical method of expressing the relative motion between electrical fields. Electrical fields are complex mathematical interpretations of a totally empirical observation stated as Coulomb's Law. In other words our forest of scientific knowledge and explanations is made up of trees about which we understand nothing except their effect, their existence.

Baba Ram Dass, formerly Dr. Richard Alpert of the Dept. of Psychology at Harvard University, met Sai Baba in India and was given a small medallion by that guru. Sai Baba held out his hand, a glow appeared in his palm, and the glow slowly solidified into the medallion. Dr. Alpert was amazed and commented to one of Sai Baba's associates on this miracle of creation. "Oh, don't be silly, he didn't create that," replied the devotee. He has a whole warehouse full of those things. He just transported it here mentally." Sai Baba's own attitude towards this sort of thing is that all is illusion, or maya.

This would seem to be a very accurate analysis of our physical world, which is most often apparent to mystics and atomic physicists. For an example of the mystical approach to our illusion, here is OAHSPE explaining about all the heavenly bodies which we cannot see, because they are outside of our illusion:

> When a planet hath attained to so great age she no longer giveth forth light or heat to radiate upon herself, she cannot be seen in the heavens. Of which kinds of planets there are millions in the etherean firmament. Some of these move slower than any of the planets man can see. Some of these at times eclipse the sun, and are taken for sun-spots, although, perhaps, not a million miles from the earth.[1]

To a person unfamiliar with the inner workings of modern science it may seem that modern man has his environment nicely under control and totally figured out. Nothing could be farther from the truth. The leaders of science who are researching the frontiers of modern theory argue among themselves, with their followers dissenting in droves behind them. As soon as a theory begins to receive wide acceptance as being a valid representation of physical laws, someone finds a discrepancy, and the theory has to be either modified or abandoned entirely. Perhaps the most well known example of this is Newton's "F=MA." This attained the status of a physical law before being found to be in error. It is not that this equation has not proven extremely useful: we have used it to design everything from a moon rocket to the television picture tube. But its accuracy fails when applied to atomic particle accelerators like the cyclotron. To make accurate predictions of particle trajectories it is necessary to make the relativistic correction formulated by Einstein. It is interesting to note that the reason for this correction is based on the fact that the speed of light is totally independent of the speed of its source.

If Newton had penetrated more deeply into the laws of motion he might have made this relativistic correction himself, and then stated that the velocity correction would always be of no consequence, since the velocity of light was so much greater than any speed attainable by man. This was very true in Newton's day, but is definitely not the case now. We still tend to think of the velocity of light as a fantastic and unattainable speed, but with the advent of space flight, a new order of velocities has arrived. We have to change our thinking from our normal terrestrial concepts of velocities. Instead of thinking of the speed of light in terms of miles per second, think of it in terms of Earth diameters per second. The almost unimaginable 186,000 miles per second becomes an entirely thinkable 23 Earth diameters per second. Or we could think of the speed of light in terms of our solar system's diameter and say that light would speed at about two diameters per day.

Einstein's assertion that everything is relative is so apt that it has become a cliché of our culture. Let us continue being relativistic In considering the size of natural phenomena by considering the size of our galaxy. If you look up at the sky on a clear night, nearly all of the visible stars are in our own galaxy. Each of these stars is a sun like our own. A calculation of the ratio of the number of suns in our galaxy to the number of people on planet Earth discovers that there are 62 suns for each living person on Earth today: Earth's population is close to 4 billion; and there are 250 billion stars in the Milky Way! it takes light over four years to get from Earth to even the nearest of these stars. To reach the most distant star in our own galaxy would take light 100,000 years.

These calculations are made using the assumption that light has a speed. This may be an erroneous assumption in the light of modern theory, but its apparent speed is a useful measuring tool, so we use it anyway.

So we have a creation in which we find ourselves which is so big that at a speed of 23 Earth diameters a second we must travel 100,000 years to cross our immediate backyard. That is a big backyard, and it would seem ample for even the most ambitious of celestial architects, but in truth this entire system of 250 billion stars is just one grain of sand on a very big beach. There are uncounted trillions of galaxies like ours, each with its own 250 billion stars, spread throughout what seems to be infinite space.

When you think of the mind boggling expanse of our creation, and the infantile state of our knowledge in relation to it, you begin to see the necessity for considering the strong probability that our present scientific approach to investigating these expanses is as primitive as the dugout canoe is in relation to the whole state of the art of Earthbound transport.

The most perplexing problem of science has always been finding a satisfactory explanation of what is called action at a distance. In other words, everyone knows that if you drop something it will fall, but no one knows precisely why. Many people know that electric charges push or pull on each other even if separated in a vacuum, but again no one knows why. Although the phenomena are quite different, the equations which describe the force of interaction are quite similar:

For gravitation: $F=Gmm'/r^2$

For electrostatic interaction: $F=Kqq'/r^2$

The attractive force between our planet and our sun is described by the gravitational equation. The attractive force between orbiting electrons and the atomic nucleus is described by the electrostatic interaction equation. Now each of these equations was determined experimentally. They are not apparently related in any way, and yet they both describe a situation in which attractive force falls off with the square of the distance of separation.

A mathematical representation of an action at a distance effect is called a field, such as a gravitational or electric field. It was Albert Einstein's foremost hope to find a single relation which would express the effect of both electric and gravitational phenomena; in fact, a theory which would unify the whole of physics, a unified field theory. Einstein believed that this was a creation of total order and that all physical phenomena were evolved from a single source:

> Over the years Einstein and other mathematical physicists published many unified field theories, none of them successful. A famous one, put forth by Kaluza, recast the mathematics of relativity in a space of five dimensions instead of the customary four. Kaluza hoped ... that unification of gravitation and electromagnetism would follow by a suitable interpretation of the fifth dimension. Einstein took up Kaluza's work, but once more no new physical understanding appeared. The most celebrated unified field theory, called the generalized theory of gravitation, was published by Einstein in 1945, and independently by Schrodinger at about the same time. By then Schrodinger was disillusioned by quantum mechanics, which he himself had helped to create. For some years both these eminent men believed that the new theory would solve the problems which they thought still beset fundamental physics.
>
> The mathematics of the theory is very complicated, and it is necessary to use approximate methods. With these it was shown that the theory failed to satisfy the basic requirement that its field equations must determine the motion of electric charges present. This was enough to convince Schrodinger that the theory was useless. Einstein was not prepared to accept the approximate results: he maintained that the theory could be judged only if certain exact solutions of the generalized field equations were found. These exact solutions, he believed, would represent matter by pure field. This was the position he took up until his death.[2]

This unified field theory, describing matter as pure field, has been accomplished now. It seems that the entire situation was analogous to the solution of a ponderously complex Chinese puzzle. If you can find the right key turns among so many wrong ones, the puzzle easily falls apart. Dewey B. Larson found the solution to this problem, and the puzzle not only fell apart, but revealed an elegantly adequate unified field theory rich in practical results. And, like a good Chinese puzzle, the solution was not complex, just unexpected. Instead of assuming five dimensions, Larson assumed six, and properly labeled them as the three dimensions of space and the three dimensions of time. He assumed that there is a three-dimensional co-ordinate time analogous to our observed three-dimensional space.

The result of this approach is that one can now calculate from the basic postulate of Larson's theory any physical value within our physical universe, from sub-atomic to stellar. This long sought after unified field theory is different because we are not accustomed to thinking of time as being dimensionally analogous to space. We have thought of time as one-dimensional, as a stream moving in one direction. Yet once you get the hang of it, co-ordinate time is mathematically a more comfortable concept with which to deal. Professor Frank Meyer, of the Dept. of Physics at the University of Wisconsin, presently distributes a quarterly newsletter[3] to scientists interested in Larson's new theory which explores perplexing questions in physical theory using Larson's approach. I was interested in testing Larson's theory and made extensive calculations using his postulate. I became convinced that his theory is indeed a workable unified field theory. If you are personally interested in checking this theory for yourself, I recommend obtaining his work and checking it as I did.[4]

I had been pondering several interesting statements communicated through contactees by the alleged UFO source prior to discovering Larson's work in the early '60s. Although the people who had received these communications knew nothing of the problems of modern physics, they were getting information which apparently was quite central to physical theory: first, they suggested that the problem with our science was that it did not recognize enough dimensions. Second, they stated that light does not move; light *is*. Larson's theory posits six dimensions instead of the customary four, and finds the pure field, which Einstein believed would represent matter, to move outward from all points in space at unit velocity, or the velocity of light. Photons are created due to a vibratory displacement in space-time, the fabric of the field. Furthermore, the contactees were saying that consciousness creates vibration, this vibration being light. The vibratory displacements of space-time in Larson's theory are the first physical manifestation, which is the photon or light. According to the UFO contacts, the UFOs lower their vibrations in order to enter our skies. The entire physical universe postulated by Larson is dependent on the rate of vibration and quantized rotations of the pure field of space-time.

The contactees were suggesting that time is not what we think it is. Larson suggests the same thing. The UFOs were said to move in time as we move in space. This would be entirely normal in Larson's time-space portion of the universe.

Lastly, and perhaps most importantly, the contactees were receiving the message that the creation is simple, all one thing. Larson's theory is a mathematical statement of this unity.

The New Science Advocates is a group of scientists and philosophers currently promoting Larson's theory. In a recent news release, they had this to say about Larson's Reciprocal System of theory:

> No previous theory comes anywhere near being a general theory in the true sense of the term. None of them is applicable to more than a relatively small part of physical science, and none is derived entirely from premises of a general nature. Everyone finds it necessary to make many assumptions specifically applicable to its restricted field of coverage. A theory of atomic structure makes assumptions about matter and about its basic forms; a theory of electrical phenomena makes assumptions about electricity and electric charges; a theory of quasars makes assumptions about quasars and about the radiation through which these objects make themselves known; and so on. Furthermore, all of these theories make use of a host of additional assumptions of a more general character that are embodied in the basic laws and principles of physics. But now we have a theory that makes no assumptions at all, other than those contained in the fundamental postulates as to the properties of space and time which define the theory. *All* conclusions, including those with respect to the basic physical laws and principles, are derived solely by deduction from those postulates, without invoking the aid of any supplementary or subsidiary assumptions, and without introducing anything from experience.
>
> In our opinion, this totally unprecedented accomplishment is sufficient in itself to justify the most serious and painstaking study of the new theoretical structure …[5]

An interesting extension of Larson's work is a conjecture which I have entertained that a more informed society might index events spatially rather than temporally. When IS talks with Puharich about time, it would seem that they do this, for they say that a certain event was planned hundreds of light-years ago.

The Metal-Bending Children

When Uri Geller performs on TV, mentally bending metal and fixing clocks, there are often many kids who try to duplicate Uri's "tricks." Sometimes the kids succeed. The number of children that can cause bends and breaks in metals and other materials just by wanting the break or bend to occur is increasing daily. John Taylor, professor of mathematics at Kings College, reports in his excellent book, SUPERMINDS, on the extensive tests run in England on several of these gifted children.

What physicists have never before considered worth investigating is now increasing at a very rapid rate. Action at a distance, apparently as a result of some type of mental activity, seems repeatedly the observed effect. If the Gellerizing children continue to increase in numbers and ability, the 1980's will see such fantasies of TV as MY FAVORITE MARTIAN, I DREAM OF JEANNIE, and BEWITCHED becoming a part of reality.

So far, most of the ability shown by these children is in the area of bending and breaking materials. But there is some indication that they, like Geller and Matthew Manning, will develop other abilities as well.

With controlled, repeatable experiments like those conducted by Taylor and by the Stanford Research Institute in the United States, we begin to have good, solid data available for study. Gradually we are moving into a position from which we can begin to create a science of "magic," for that which has been called magic through the ages is now being performed at an ever-increasing rate, primarily by children. In the future, we may even find this "magic" added to the curriculum of the sciences at universities. In point of fact, the present disciplines of chemistry, physics, etc., are still basically "magic" to us, since we are still in the position of having no ultimate explanation of causality.

Age Regression Hypnosis

During the past twenty years I have done several hundred age regressions, working with subjects from various walks of life. With very few exceptions, I have discovered that the reasonably good hypnotic subject can be helped to remember experiences which occurred before his or her birthdate into this present life. The large majority of these people remember lives which occurred prior to this life but identifiable as being in the recent historical past. I have had people who are in this life quite ignorant of a certain foreign language, who under hypnosis, while re-experiencing moments of a previous life, are able to speak that foreign tongue.

While there is no way to prove the theory of reincarnation, it is interesting to note that many researchers besides myself have reported many thousands of instances of these hypnotic regressions to previous lives. As one examines the mass of data which these regressions provide, one cannot help but note that the theory of reincarnation is a more substantively satisfactory explanation than some alternate theories, which attempt to be conservative and scientifically "safe."

Such latter explanations of the data of a good age regression case take each confirmed fact gained in the hypnotic session and say, "The subject could conceivably have known this another way. The subject could be using telepathy. The subject could be clairvoyant." The explanations offered in this way strike me rather as an instance of going around Robin Hood's barn, when there is a broad and well-trodden path right through the forest. I say well-trodden, because three-quarters of the world's population ascribe to religions which include reincarnation within their structure of religious beliefs.

Mediumship

The medium, a person who is able to act as a link with discarnate entities, is probably the most controversial of the common psychic types. I consider a good working knowledge of mediumship and its pitfalls essential to the study of alleged telepathic UFO contactees. As I have stated, there seem to be many planes or densities of existence, therefore it is not always possible to be sure of the source of a telepathic contact. A person visiting a medium for the purpose of communication with discarnate Uncle Herman may actually contact a residual portion of Uncle Herman's consciousness, another entity claiming to be Uncle Herman, or in many cases the subconscious of the medium. I am certain that many mediums and UFO contactees never intend fraud, and do not themselves realize the fraudulent nature of what they "telepathically" receive. The dedicated researcher will attempt to achieve an attitude of unbiased discrimination, listening to everything with suspended disbelief, yet reserving final judgment until his data is ponderous in quantity and correlations are extensive.

Magic
(Real Magic, Not Prestidigitation)

W. E. Butler defines magic as "the art of effecting changes in consciousness at will."[6] Generally, events are thought of as magical if they defy all rational or "scientific" attempts to explain them. As a consequence, as our scientific philosophy has expanded our inclination to view natural events as magical has shrunk. We no longer consider thunderstorms to be of magical significance, because we know the physical mechanics which create the thunderstorm.

That is, we think we do. What we have really done with thunderstorms is to find our way back to the more basic puzzle of electrostatics.

Born into this world, we wake up in our crib and very slowly become aware of our surroundings. As long as these surrounding, these conditions of existence, remain the same, we are satisfied to call our environment "normal" reserving the label of "paranormal" for that which is contrary to the great body of our experience. That is, as long as we drop a stone and it continues to fall rather than float in air, we will accept that as the natural event and see a floating-in-air object that looks as though it *should* fall as supernatural.

It is a difficult thing to do, but try to imagine for a minute a state of total lack of experience with this world. Try to look at it as if for the first time. Without labeling them, look at the people, the animals, the birds and insects; at foliage and sky. Feel the wonder creeping in. Now, in your mind, back off from the surface of the planet Earth and see it as a totality, a ball in space with a thin cloak of swirling air around it. You and the billions of others who live on Earth stand on its surface, the soles of your feet pointing inward, towards the center of the ball; your heads pointing outward, towards space. As you hold this in your mind, perhaps magic seems not so limited on our "normal" world. I believe that in truth, we have only a tiny sliver of understanding of reality, if indeed we have any at all. When a child stares at a spoon and it curls up, or breaks, we somehow find this more amazing than the magic of our daily experience. Perhaps these "magical" new events are clues to the real nature of man.

The Mechanisms of Real Magic

Motion in our physical world is usually the result of a potential energy such as gravitational, chemical, or electrical. The magician also works with potential energies, within consciousness, in order to create motion or displacement in mind. The magician works with potentials in consciousness similar to the physical activity of storing electrical charges in a battery. Just as a battery has a positive and a negative pole, so does consciousness. Many call this positive-negative polarity good and evil. There is ample evidence that it is possible to create a large potential through the manipulation of consciousness, whether it is done by intentional magical manipulation or by political rhetoric or religious exhortation.

I would suggest that consciousness is more fundamental than physical matter. I find it hard to see even the possibility of physical matter creating consciousness. The magician, then, is working with the more fundamental of energy fields, to attain a more fundamental objective.

The objective of the magician is to obtain predictive and manipulative control of consciousness. The white magician clearly defines for himself the limits of this manipulation of consciousness: his objective is the development of his own consciousness. The black magician is less careful about what consciousness he wishes to be able to manipulate, and thus becomes interested in the "evil" aspects of control over others' consciousness.

The white magician wants to develop his consciousness, for he knows that it is the only thing he will be able to carry with him through the physical death. His attitude towards this physical life is that its one purpose is to provide him with the catalytic effects of physical experience for use in the development of his thinking. He sees himself as a micro-consciousness dwelling within macro-consciousness, and attempts to consciously unite himself with all that there is, so that the microcosm is one with the macrocosm. To put it another way, he is attempting to achieve realization of union with his creator. The key to this attempt is control of consciousness. The more closely the magician approaches this goal of realized oneness with the creation, the more able he is to do seemingly magical things. He is tuning his mind to that of the Creator, and thereby displaying some of the abilities of creation.

The black magician has the reciprocal orientation in that he is attempting to achieve separation in mind rather than unification. He glorifies his own individuality and gains power by separating himself from all of creation and then declaring himself its master. Both white and black magical attitudes and practices are able to build high potentials in the field of consciousness, quite analogous to the creating of potential difference in electrical fields with positive and negative charges. Once a sufficient charge of consciousness has been stored, it may be used to create motion or change in consciousness, which in turn effects the physical world for what we call good or evil.

Because the essence of man is his consciousness, the true nature of man is perforce magical. All men have infinite potential to create whatever changes they may desire. But at present, man on Earth seems lacking in the knowledge of his true nature and the abilities of his mind. Most men fluctuate as a matter of daily habit between slightly good and slightly evil, building up a slight potential in one direction and discharging it, then swinging back a bit the other way. This puts him down in a "potential well" of thought. Since he is not polarizing steadily in either direction, he can do no magic. Those sufficiently polarized—like Jesus the Christ—perform this "magic" with no difficulty. Everyone does have the innate ability to do such magic. The beginning of the Gospel according to John in the Holy Bible contains this statement:

> The true light that enlightens every man was coming into the world … to all who received him, who believed in his name, he gave power to become children of God, who were born not of blood, nor of the will of the flesh, nor of the will of man, but of God.[7]

I am not in any way suggesting that the unity with God, or Creator, or the Christ, is only valid when approached through the doctrines of any particular religion, but the concept is clearly stated here.

When Jesus told his Disciples: "These things and more shall you do," he intended that those who heard those words polarize their consciousness until they regained the natural abilities which we presently call miraculous.

Many of the UFO sources indicate that they feel that man on Earth has trouble recognizing in many instances the difference between positive and negative thought, and for that reason is vacillating between the two.

There are lots of people who have heard about or read a little of the UFO contactee literature, who dismiss it as being a series of ridiculous fantasies, like the French peasants reporting stones falling from the sky.

If a handful of people reported contact instead of thousands, and if the communications they reported varied widely in content instead of matching, then there would be a much poorer case for UFO contact. I have worked with teenagers who had no previous background at all in UFO research or literature who, after a very short training period were able to receive, in a telepathic manner, hours of communications of the exact type reported by UFO contactees. Comparison of this information with information obtained by other widely separated contactee sources over the past 20 years always results in the same conclusion: that the basic message content, no matter where or who the receiver was, is the same. Earlier I spoke of the UFO contactee picture as a kind of puzzle, and a fairly big one at that. Some of the pieces of this puzzle seem silly or even crazy when one first picks them up, but carefully pieced together, these contactee stories begin to form a recognizable pattern of UFO motive. I think this pattern is not easily recognized or understood for the same reason that Gellerized spoons are hard to accept, there is very little previous experience on which to base an analysis. But that the pattern exists is hard to deny. As ufologist Brad Steiger puts it:

> For the past three years I have been conducting a serious study of certain contactees, whom I call "flying saucer missionaries," and I have noted that a certain percentage of the information dispensed in their cosmic sermonettes has contained a good deal of accurate information and that certain predictions have been realized. In my opinion, many UFO researchers—and nearly all news media and orthodox scientists—have been too hasty in their assessments that the contactees' messages are just so much nonsense and science-fiction-inspired pseudo-religious prattle. Although several of the contactees seem to parrot in a tedious manner a great amount of the same basic "message," there may be important clues hidden for us in their fanciful distortions if only we were to work a bit harder to separate the cosmic wheat from the celestial chaff.[8]

And long-time researcher, Professor J. H. Bruening of the University of Mississippi, has this to say about UFO phenomena, after studying it closely for 30 years:

> UFO phenomena is a *contrived* paranormal event created for the benefit of the viewer with a specific stimulus content. This phenomena is a show-and-tell device precisely geared to the culture to which it is presented.
>
> Note that all historical UFO sightings are always just slightly advanced for the viewers of the time. Medieval sightings were of a fully rigged sailing ship sailing along in the sky! The 1897 sightings looked like a Victorian science fiction book illustration and the crews were all reported as being dressed properly for 1890. Current sightings are "space ships" with astronauts as pilots dressed in space suits. Obviously neither a sailing ship fully rigged nor a Jules Verne ship could possibly travel through interplanetary space in those forms from another planet to the earth and back. They all were here in physical form to be sure and were reported as such, but they did not get here in that form by flying here.
>
> This display is intentional and is a part of a controlled program of cultural diffusion of special forms of information into current earth civilizations. The information is, however, in coded form! It is not obvious at all but is mixed in with considerable "noise." Not to be melodramatic but Toynbee has amply demonstrated that cultural

advancement periodically is based on the productivity of a small number of creative people who are able to pick the signal out of the noise and come up with new conceptual patterns as described by Sorokin and Kroeber. It would appear that the last quarter of this century is such a time, and perhaps ... (the) ... *Invisible College* may be that group who can decode the signal and thereby extract the key information. I hope they can do this before the Russians do it. The coded data in fact contains considerable information in the fields of technology, culture, philosophy, religion and sociology. To paraphrase McLuhan the phenomena is the message. The whole pattern must be considered as a total thing and not examined in a Spencerian fashion. If a piecemeal approach is used the total pattern will be lost with a resulting loss of information.

The rest of the model (of the UFO phenomena's meaning) is built around the proposals put forward as early as 1947 by the discussants in the Mark Probert group in California. I keep coming back to these ideas because they simply do in fact explain details of the UFO phenomena. (See THE COMING OF THE GUARDIANS, SEANCE REPORTS AND TRANSCRIPTS 1945-1960, ROUND ROBIN 1950-1960, Vista, Ca., The Borderland Science Research Association.)

This model is also found scattered around in a large part of published UFO data, especially in contactee reports, most of which seem to be true. The ones I have investigated do have a ring of truth about them. Now, the Extraterrestrial Intelligence (ETI) model which is an extrapolation of our civilization fails to account for either paranormal phenomena or for the reported engineering designs, while the continuous violation of the known laws of physics and aerodynamics eliminates the simple mechanical model of UFOs. The obvious limitations imposed on the use of a space vehicle of a mechanical sort by the sheer distance between solar systems again excludes the jet or ion-driven space ship as a possible model.

The model that does appear to fit the data is, incredibly enough, the one which is constructed around the concept of a multidimensional universe which contains technically advanced civilizations some of which have reached the capability of multidimensional travel. This travel is a space-time phenomenon where a change of frequency is equivalent to an instant change in location; i.e., they dematerialize "there" and materialize "here." Once here the ship or vehicle operates as a physical object in our dimension. It can violate the laws of physics by partially dematerializing. Its physical appearance is determined by

> its mission, not by any engineering demands, and the crew may appear either as themselves or as manifesting a contrived appearance, again depending on the mission.
>
> It would appear that what is considered as a change in frequency is that matter comprising other dimensions varies from our matter in that the distance from the electron shells to the nucleus is much lesser there than here. In a sense their matter is more "dense" than our matter is, so they expand their matter in order to materialize here and must hold it in this abnormal state in order to remain here. To return to their place they relax their energy field and immediately return. This difference in matter allows our mutual dimensions to normally coexist without interference except in some rare cases where a sort of splash-over takes place during which people and objects may appear or disappear suddenly.
>
> The general cultural impact of the UFO phenomena through its persistent and deliberate performances has been to create a knowledge revolution of a dramatic sort in the general population. This gives the creative minority a really favorable social climate in which to work. In a sense the phenomena have created a demand for new ideas—now someone has to come up with them.
>
> I have worked these ideas out in considerable detail and the more the concept is expanded the more it fits. You know the real problem in theory construction is timidity. We are all too often reluctant to move boldly into new domains and thus are unable to come to grips with intellectually explosive phenomena.[9]

What I am saying, then, is that the UFO phenomena are forming a pattern, the heart of which is a structure of being and thinking, or a philosophy, which can begin now to be put together. The contactee messages especially gives important clues toward the construction of this philosophy. These cosmic sermonettes, as Steiger terms them, do yield a harvest: there is "cosmic wheat" among the "celestial chaff."

Chapter Four

The Nature Of Man

Few of the many thousands of communications allegedly from UFOs which are available to the researching scientist are acceptable on face value to him. The reason for this is that the scientists have not formulated a general theory which can contain the contactee information. The scientist is not being particularly stringent or hard-nosed in this exclusion of data; this data simply does not "compute." Some scientists reject the data as being unworthy of their attention. Other, more interested researchers look rather longingly at the more dramatic aspects of the UFO-related evidence and declare themselves ready to forge ahead until the new understanding is reached. In his excellent consideration of the metal-bending and other unusual talents of Uri Geller and the children who are currently demonstrating the Geller-type abilities, Professor Taylor says:

> Part of the job of looking at the world through the eyes of a trained scientist is to look for ways of improving our current scientific models of the world.[1]

Hopefully, this is the thrust of this investigation as well. This chapter will begin the presentation of a theory of reality formulated as a result of long study of UFO and paranormal phenomena. The theory is still speculative, rather than conclusively proven. However, I believe the time has come for it to be presented for consideration by researchers and by the general public, because familiarity with the theory offers an entry into the myriad of UFO phenomena and contacts which seems to make sense.

The Real Nature of Man

Imagine yourself encased in a heavy rubber suit and the cumbersome divers' apparatus, with the big bell face mask on your shoulders. You are carefully and with some difficulty walking about on the ocean floor. The suit, and the relative difficulty of movement within it, is a fair representation of the physical body in which we are encased and with which we usually identify ourselves. The body that animates this awkward physical body may be called, as St. Paul did, the "spiritual body," or, as some occultists do, the "astral body." It has not been proven to exist in a certain known manner, no one yet has ascertained the precise composition of the astral body; yet there is enormous weight of common belief in it, stretching back to the Egyptian belief in the "Ka." Ghosts and apparitions throughout history have appeared as witnesses to the reality of this body. In their well-researched book, Muldoon and Carrington treat rather carefully the whole array of astral projection data that also lends credence to the assertion that there is an astral body.[2] And Kirlian photography is catching a luminescence around the physical body that, according to some clairvoyants, comes not from the physical but from the astral body. "We look, they say, something like an eclipse of the sun by the moon, the luminous astral body."[3] This astral body which all of us have, then, is the "double" of our physical body and in fact acts as the electrodynamic, or bioplasmic, mold from which is created that configuration of chemicals that manifests as our physical body. This finer body leaves the heavy material body at the time of death and is related to the spirit or soul. This again is not scientifically proven, but there is a great deal of descriptive evidence to indicate the truth of the statement. Much research has been done and is now in progress on the nature of death and dying by Dr. Elisabeth Kubler-Ross and others, and at this point in their research, they are asserting the presence of a good deal of collected data indicating a continuation of the individual consciousness through and after the death of the physical body.

Dr. Lyall Watson creates an elegant exposition in defense of the non-reality of what we call "death," but then concludes that in investigating the paranormal, the researcher is perhaps "kept in check by a cautious cosmic nanny."[4] It is his suspicion, and I share it with him, that in the investigation of the paranormal we are treading on the edges of a type of knowledge we are not intended to have, at least until we learn to use some new tools for understanding. And the study of UFOs very much falls within this category.

The spirit body is the more basic of the two bodies. We spend more time exclusively in the spirit body than in the physical, for besides dwelling within it before birth and after physical death, we remove our consciousness to the world of spirit regularly in sleep. It is a cliché of several religions that the spirit world is one in which we have greater abilities, freedom from the problems and pain of the flesh, and in general a better deal.

Much research has been done to investigate this spirit world, and the findings are that there are not one, but many spirit planes of existence.[5] Our physical plane, then, is not one of two worlds, but is very much in the minority, one of many worlds. The physical world which we are now experiencing is the anomaly. This point is getting at the crux of our problems with understanding UFOs. It is necessary to understand that we are forms of consciousness of a much more flexible and immaterial nature than is appreciated in our present state of awareness.

> As we progress on to higher planes of life, we shall incarnate in bodies far more ethereal than those now used by us, just as in the past we used bodies almost incredibly grosser and coarser than those we call our own today.[6]

Many people have either voluntarily or involuntarily experienced out-of-the-body travel for short periods. Perhaps the most common experience occurs in the pre-sleep, drifting period, when the person feels a floating sensation and discovers himself near the ceiling looking back down at his prostrate physical body. This ability to travel out of the physical body is learnable, and there are various methods taught to those who are interested, by such groups as the Theosophists and Paul Twitchell's Eckankar. As Twitchell has noted, this type of information is also in that area where knowledge is difficult to come by or to express:

"He who has fully accomplished soul travel finds it nearly impossible to communicate his experience to others once he has returned to the physical form, especially when his traveling has taken him above the astral world into the higher planes."[7]

So, hard though it may be to prove, my scheme of things into which the UFO phenomena seem to fit has as a basic tenet the concept that the physical body does not alone signify life, but consciousness signifies life, and that consciousness exists in a continuum of reality which includes what we now know as life, and death. When the physical body is no longer animate, still that consciousness exists in a continuing reality, having passed merely to another, lighter density of existence.

A natural addition to this line of thinking is the belief in reincarnation, that we have each existed through many incarnations, in various densities of existence, going from one to another largely through the gates of physical birth and death. There is an untold number of these densities throughout the universe. All are equally real. And each, presumably, has its own characteristics so that from many dimensions, other portions of reality are not perceivable. This is what has happened on our physical plane on Earth. We presently are experiencing an apparent isolation. Here we are, in the rather gross physical plane, moving about in the heavy physical body, restricted by the limitations of five physical senses, with little obvious reason to develop the psychic or non-physical senses which are part of our finer body. Why are we so limited in this density; why is it so difficult to expand our awareness? What is the reason for life in this density? In fact, what is the reason for life in all the densities?

Most of us Earthmen have some goals, usually concerning financial security or some accomplishment producing physical reward during our lifetime on Earth. Intertwined with these goals are other, more intangible goals, which show forth in our physical lives as feelings for the arts, for beauty, for philosophy, or for the ideal companion. The invisible side of existence constantly tugs at our awareness, through emotion and thought. This sort of pursuit of truth or beauty is one good example of the reality of more than just the visible, physical plane. At various levels of density, our objectives as an entity are quite different. Once we are completely removed from the physical density of experience, we realize the infinite nature of existence, the eternal span of our own conscious lifetime, and we begin to get a clearer sight of our primary objective. We become aware that there is something worth striving for that is lasting. This is the impulse, brought back into the physical density, which is responsible for the creativity in all areas of life: we see in our spiritual selves that which we wish to bring back into our daily lives. The religious impulse, in its pure and unchurched form, is the opposite impulse: to seek while in the physical plane to visit and experience the higher reality of eternity. Life is therefore redefined in terms of the physical death, which in religious terms becomes a gate to higher life. Both in aesthetic pursuits and in pursuit of spiritual understanding there is the key concept: life is not limited or tarnished as it seems, but life and the living are infinite and eternal. You cannot take your earthly gains with you when you die here. All your goals will die with your physical body, but one thing you may take, and that is your consciousness: your mind, your spirit, the eternal you. And in this dense physical atmosphere, you are presently at work shaping not just your earthly self, but your eternal self.

Whether we realize it or not, we are all in this process of self-change together. We are growing. Not in the physical body only or primarily, but most of all in the higher body. This is the real evolution. This is the reason for our present Earth experience. We have chosen to come into this Earthly density to experience the emotional catalyst of physical life. The experience we gain here has its results in the evolution of our minds, our consciousnesses.

You notice I am assuming an intended direction, an ultimately predictable path, to this evolution. I predicate that this evolution is in the direction towards the thought of our Creator. As we grow in mind, we more closely approach the fundamental thought of our Creator. I believe that this is our primary objective. No matter what path we think we are on, this one is either advanced within our experience, or it patiently waits for us to finish with our dawdling and get about the main business.

The aura is the observable edge of our higher body, seen just outside the surface of our physical body. People with well-developed psychic senses have seen them throughout history; hence the halos around revered models rendered by many an artist through the centuries. Now it would seem that Semyon Davidovich Kirlian of Krasnodar in the USSR has developed a process whereby this aura is rendered not only visible but recordable by photography. Through his process, a whole world of color and life becomes visible to the physical eye. All living things, plants and people, have these auras. The color and intensity of the aura is an indication of the nature of the higher body as well as the state of the physical body. The aura seems to change in response to mood or the health of the subject, but its nature is not limited by those qualities of intellect and education by which we set so much store within the physical illusion. A janitor, for instance, may possess a more intense aura than the well-respected physicist whose office he cleans.

As OAHSPE puts it:

> A man may be wise as to books and philosophy and mathematics and poetry and great learning, and yet be low in grade as to spirit. A man may know little of all such knowledge, and may be poor withal, but by hardship and experience, developed in sympathy and good works done unto others, and be high in grade as to spirit.[8]

Each of us, no matter what our circumstances, is experiencing life on Earth for the same purpose: further refinement of the spiritual, auric body. The condition of our auric glow is a quick index of our spiritual development.

There are 250 billion stars in our galaxy alone, and there are uncounted trillions of galaxies besides ours. The creation seems to be infinite, in terms of the present physical science as well as in philosophical terms. What is it that limits us from experiencing this infinite creation? Anyone who has ever tasted the heady taste of what lies in store for the developed consciousness knows that somehow, he must continue to seek that awareness of infinity again.

Many of the UFOs are attempting to play a part in this evolution of ours. A large percentage of them are in a different density than our physical world most of the time, becoming "real" to us and to the physical world for only short periods. The UFOnauts have good reason to act as they do, most of the reason being linked to this concept of the evolution of mind. They wish to assist us in the evolution of our minds.

There is much evidence that there is a wide variance between sources for UFO activity in our skies. Some UFOs are in contact with, and working with other UFOs. Some seem to be operating alone, as unaware of other

UFOs as we are of the finer densities. Various UFOs come from various densities both within our "real" universe and outside of our reality. Their mental state of evolution varies widely, some entities not so far ahead of us, some incredibly beyond our ken. But they are all interested in Earth now. This present time seems to be centrally important. In our contacts with the UFOs, we find out why they feel this is so.

The Flat Earth Syndrome

It wasn't so long ago that man considered himself to be living on a flat Earth, with edges that dropped off into the abyss. The night sky was a velvet black bowl, studded with small points of light, which turned about us. At present, we have made some progress in our understanding of Earth and stars. We see that the Earth is round, we see that it moves in space; we see that the points of light are either planets like us or self-luminous entities like our Sun. We have found that instead of the sky's darkness being a close and protective bowl-surface, space is unimaginably vast, so that even within the celestial backyard of our nearest star neighbor, it would take us 80,000 years to traverse the distance thereto. This is figuring a velocity of 7 miles per second, the reported escape velocity of our fastest launched space vehicle to date, Pioneer 10.[9] So far has our understanding brought us: space travel is a reality, but the thought of doing it, in person, is still absurd, especially if you begin to consider travel out of our planetary system. This is where our science is now: within the boundaries of our technology and daily routine we have a serviceable and solid philosophy of reality. But at the frontiers of physical space and time, we have a vast uncertainty. We are not equal to it yet. Its challenges lie there, waiting patiently for us to seek them out.

It is in this context that I feel the UFOs have arrived here. Perhaps we are on the brink of an unfoldment of understanding even greater than that which rounded the flat Earth and gave depth to the sky. And the UFOs are acting this time as the insistent clue to the new reality. That they do not "compute" according to our present understanding is a welcome characteristic, for it is this quality of data which historically has heralded a new level of advancement of man's knowledge. The careful study of UFO and UFO-related phenomena has brought me to a conclusion about the nature of reality that is the kind of departure from accepted doctrine that the flat-to-round earth claim was in its day. The theory has its seeds not just in the ufology data but in disciplines far afield: atomic physics, parapsychology, theosophy, and theology. I have paid attention to science and also to pseudo-science. I cannot and do not claim that the theory is scientific, properly speaking; nor do I claim myself as an infallible observer, or receiver of ideas. I attempt to state my theory in such a way that it can be quickly comprehended. The pleasure and challenge of further investigation is then yours as well as mine. Most of this theory is the work of others. I have only combined the ingredients, adding a few refinements. Parts of this theory may seem absurd at first, but then so did the idea of a round Earth, no doubt.

There is one aspect of UFO study which does not yet equal the round-Earth story: Columbus and his demonstrated proof has not yet arrived for us! There is ample data to substantiate the theory developed in this text. But a goodly portion of this data is not evidential: it lacks provable validity. This means that many a sane and sensible man will back off right here. James Randi, the prestidigitator, puts this point of view well:

> I have often been asked, "Do you deny the existence of ESP and other paranormal occurrences?" The answer is that I doubt their existence simply because I have never had evidence presented to me that would prove their existence. I cannot choose to believe something because I want to. Give me some hard proof, and I will change my mind: until then, I am burdened with Reality.[10]

And so are we all burdened with reality: a reality which is sending us numerous and obvious clues of an even greater reality. True science, I submit, is not only the explainer of the familiar, but the explorer of all that there is to explore. The UFO phenomena seem so often like the functioning in physical reality of the wildest imagination of our race. Carl Jung ascribed this phenomena to just that source.[11] Yet these UFO events are occurring, and it is a valid response to strive to understand them, using all the available material. This is what I have done; the material treated here is in my opinion the best material available for the formulation of a workable solution to the UFO mystery. The test of any theory is its value as a predictive and explicative tool. For several years now, the UFO events have been fitting comfortably into this theory. It is as though I have gotten enough pieces put into my puzzle so that the remaining ones are quite easily fitted into the developing picture of the whole.

The body of the theory has been distilled from 25 years of collection of alleged contacts with UFOs. No single piece of evidence was judged when received; but only added to the mass of other data. Out of this mass has precipitated a surprising amount of correlation of data with regard to a high percentage of UFO related phenomena.

Chapter Five

A Solution To The Mystery Of The UFO

In the 1950s, there were many contactees who wrote books, gave lectures, and in general profited from their alleged private liaisons with extra-terrestrials. The most well-known of these contactees included George Adamski, Orfeo Angelucci, Major Wayne Aho, Truman Betherum, Dan Fry, Howard Menger, George Hunt Williamson, and George Van Tassel. Serious UFO researchers of this period tended to feel considerable animosity towards these contactees because they confused and polarized public opinion. Most scientifically motivated researchers did not and do not feel that these contactees were anything but either charlatans or self-deluded crackpots.

I avoid this judgment, and include the data from some of these sources. Historically, it is the exclusion of data such as this that has at times inhibited science. I may point out here that there is a great distance between the accepting of data and the eventual weighting of it. I've carefully read the material published by the contactees, and have become personally acquainted with several of them.

The twenty years which have passed since the first contactee flurry have produced a plethora of new contactees around the world. However, because of the lack of respectability accorded to the first avowed contactees, the newer ones have tended to keep the contacts to themselves, except for reports to one or the other of the UFO investigative organizations. It has become downright unfashionable to be a contactee. I personally know numerous silent contactees, and am familiar with the cases of others who have related their strange experiences with UFOnauts only in strictest confidence.

The important thing about all of these contactees is that there is a remarkable correlation of the information which they receive, which becomes apparent to anyone who has taken the trouble to research the available literature.

One of the more prestigious silent contactees was cited in the television documentary, UFOs, PAST, PRESENT, AND FUTURE. Since he was a full commander in the U.S. Navy, it is not difficult to see why he was reluctant to have his telepathic contact publicized. Here is a partial account of the contact. It was made at 2:00 p.m. on July 9, 1959, at CIA offices at 5th and K Streets NW, Washington, D.C.

D. Cmdr. ____ pointed out that during the latter part of June he and another Naval Officer had flown up to Maine and visited Mrs. S ____ for the purpose of witnessing a contact and to interview the lady. Mrs. S ____, after the interview and contact, asked Cmdr. ____ why he didn't make a contact himself. The officer ____ then tried, but was unsuccessful.

E. After his return to Wash. Cmdr. ____ was discussing the case with Mr. ____ and Lt. Cmdr. ____ at CIA. At the insistence of these two gentlemen he attempted another contact and was app. successful in receiving messages from a person called AFFA, an inhabitant of the planet Uranus. Cmdr. ____ would pen his question on a large sheet of paper (ques. put to him by other 2) relax, and some unknown force would guide his hand in writing the answers. During the time that the message is being transmitted, is subjected to a very great physical strain. Of the many questions put to AFFA—some samples:

Q. Do you favor any government, religious group, or race?

A. No, we do not. Signed AFFA.

Q. Will there be a third World War?

A. No. Signed AFFA.

Q. Are Catholics the chosen people?

A. No. Signed AFFA.

Q. Can we see a spaceship or flying saucer?

A. When do you want to see it? Signed, AFFA.

Q. Can we see it now?

A. Go to the window. Signed AFFA.

(Mr. ____ , Cmdr. ____ and Lt. Cmdr. ____ all go to the window.)

Q. Are we looking in the right direction?

A. (answered vocally) Yes, signed AFFA.

At this time, approximately 1400, 6 July 1959, these three men saw what they have indicated was a flying saucer. They described the object as round, with the perimeter brighter than the center. Lt. Cmdr. ____ checked with Washington Center (radar) and was informed that for some unknown reason radar return from the direction in which the ship was supposedly seen had been blocked out at the time of the sighting.

> ... H. On July 10, 1959, Maj. Friend in the company of Cmdr. ____ visited the office of ONI to study the case file of Mrs. Swan. The record indicates that Mrs. Swan has been in touch with the following persons from the planet or (system):
>
> AFFA—Uranus
> Crill—Jupiter
> ALOMAR—Mercury
> PONNAR—Mercury (wanted to leave human race alone to stew in its own juice.)
> ANKAR—Centaurus
>
> The Navy indicates that through these contacts Mrs. S ____ has been able to answer technical questions beyond the level of her education or background. The case contains records of some of the exchanges that Mrs. S ____ has had, and while there is some loose mention of how spaceships work and of what they are made, there was little of value. ... indicated that the Canadians had exploited this scientific angle.
>
> I. The S ____ record indicated that there was an organization OEEV which means the Universal Association of Planets, and that the organization has a project EU or Euenze (?) (earth) which is being conducted. What this project was to accomplish was not mentioned.[1]

In George Hunt Williamson's book, THE SAUCERS SPEAK! we find some interesting correlation with the silent Commander's contact. Williamson was reporting on his 1952 contact by radiotelegraphy and telepathy. He included contacts with AFFA of Uranus, ANKAR-22 of Jupiter, and PONNAR of the planet Hatonn in Andromeda. This is an example of the correlations I'm talking about. One of these would prove nothing. Dozens of such coincidences begin to add up to a reasoned description of a theory which makes some sense out of the massive UFO chaos. One note: in dealing with these contacts, you have to remember that AFFA, PONNAR, and ANKAR-22 are most likely not denizens of our particular density of reality, and therefore would not be visible to astronauts landing on their planets.

The really significant bulk of correlations becomes evident during the reading and deciphering of the messages and meanings of the alleged communications. I have selected a small, representative portion of the millions of words of contactee communications that I have read through the years, in order that the essence of what I have come to believe is the message from the UFOs may be made easily available to the reader. I make heavy use of the Hatonn source in these two chapters to come because the material has been gathered by the experimental group which I set up and consequently, I have the confidence of knowing precisely how the information was obtained.

> I am in a craft, high above you. I am aware of your thoughts, even though I am quite some distance above. I am, at this time, in a craft which is capable of interplanetary flight. This craft has been seen by some of your people. It will shortly be seen by more of them. It may shortly be seen by yourselves if you look for it. The time is closely approaching now when we must be seen much, much more by the people of this planet. The time is now closely approaching when we must create a high degree of inquisitiveness among your people. They are quite inquisitive at the present, but they are not yet seeking. This is what we intend to do: we intend to provide a stimulus for them, to increase their seeking. The larger percentage of your people, although interested in our craft, are not sufficiently interested to seek an answer to what they see. This we intend to alleviate by stimulating a more intense interest.[2]

And Yolanda channels an echo of this reason for the continuing UFO sightings:

> Remember the purpose of these sightings. They are only to open the minds and hearts of the skeptical ones ...[3]

And another contactee, an Arizonan, relays this from his source:

> The man whose body and mind I am using to speak to you is being used by his own full cooperation. Had he not reached out, I would not have been beamed to him in answer. Yet all who reach out are not answered, for all do not reach out in honesty of purpose. Some wish to acquire some personal gratification of the moment; therefore, they do not reach a point of open acceptance necessary to receive me. I am beamed to many on your world. This man is not unique.[4]

It seems that they want the people of Earth to seek on their own some answers to the mystery of the UFOs.

> I am speaking to you from a craft known to you as an *otevana*. It is a very, very large craft compared to your standards. It is several miles in length. We have been aboard this craft here above your planet for some numbers of years. It is like a world in itself, and is used for intergalactic travel. Aboard this craft we have all of the facilities that you have in your world, plus many others.[5]

They seem to be describing an often-sighted, cigar-shaped "mother ship," which is normally not in our dimension of reality and is therefore not usually visible to us. An interesting correlation here is from the book, OAHSPE, written by Dr. John Ballou Newbrough, first published in 1882. The book is said to be the product of automatic (telepathic) writing. OAHSPE tells of etheric beings traveling to Earth in spaceships to aid in the evolution of mankind. One type of ship mentioned by them is the "otevan."[6]

Here is more about OAHSPE's ships, and their purpose:

> As I taught corporeans to build ships to traverse corporeal seas, so have I taught ethereans to build vessels to course My etherean seas.
>
> As I bound the corporean that he could not raise up in the air above corpor, save by a vessel, so created I My heavens for the spirits of men, that by manufactured vessels they might course My firmament.[7]
>
> ☙
>
> Go build me an avalanza capable of carrying three thousand million angels, with as many rooms, capable of descent and ascent, and east and west and north and south motion, and prepare it with a magnet that it may face to the north whilst traveling.[8]
>
> ☙
>
> And in this same time the descending stars of other Gods and Goddesses, the etherean ships from far-off worlds, were drawing nearer and nearer; and, on every side, the firmament was as if alive with worlds on fire.[9]

Another telepathic contact states:

> ... we are thousands upon this ship no. 1235, twenty-three hundred and fifty three persons, to be exact. We are not persons exactly as you see persons but we are of the different dimensions, different planets. We congregate on this etheric ship, which is the size of a city; as you understand it would be, to accommodate the comings and goings.
>
> The purpose of this ship in orbit is to stimulate and to work with all those who are being trained to be key light centers in the Western hemisphere of the Earth ...[10]

This is a more specific description, given by a channel in a Miami light center group called the Mark-Age MetaCenter. And how long has this type of help been coming our way?

We have attempted throughout what you would consider ancient times on your planet to bring to mankind, to those who would desire the knowledge, the knowledge that is necessary for experiencing all of the infinite experiences created by our Creator. Some of those who dwelt upon this planet in the past have accepted these teachings and have benefited from them. Benefited far beyond anything that could be imagined by those who are not experiencing the benefits. We have attempted for many of your years to bring to all of those who desire the teachings, the very simple teachings that allow you to know all. However, these teachings have not been understood very well.[11]

"Q. How long have they been coming into our atmosphere?

"A. For thousands and thousands of years."12

"Q. What is life like on your planet, as compared to our life?

"A. Life on our planet at one time was much like that upon planet Earth. However, at this time our entire population of sentient beings has developed into a completely unitary and combined ability of each brother of the planet known as Hatonn. The combination is so strong that we are able to do many, many things. Feeling and being as one, we are seeking as one, and as our seeking has led us forward, we have found our way to be pointed directly at service, ever-expanding service. Service to all parts of the creation.

"And as our service has been needed, whereas before we were not capable of discovering the means to perform the service that we saw as our service.

"In this manner, we have developed abilities which you may call miraculous. We have the ability to transcend what you know as time and space. We have access in a conscious manner to knowledge of which you have access only during meditation, in a sub-conscious manner. The freedoms which we enjoy, my friends, are there because we have begun to see that we are all one. Realization is all that is between planet Earth and the planet Hatonn. On your planet as on our planet, each blade of grass is alive with the knowledge of the Creator. The winds sing His praises. Trees shout for joy in the creation of our infinite Father. If you are not able to see the Creator, my friends, it is a matter of seeking, and seeking, and continued seeking. And then, my friends, you will begin to realize, and to understand, that the Creation of the Father is all around you.

"Planet Earth, my friends, is indeed a lovely planet. It will soon be vibrating in a vibratory manner which is far more associated with realization of the Father's creation. Begin to realize, and move with your planet, as we moved with ours. There is only that which is in your mind, and within your consciousness, and within your faith, between the pain, the lack, and the limitation which you experience, and the complete freedom which in our vibration we experience."[13]

Here we find the Hatonn identification once more and another reference to seeking. When they speak of their vibrations, they are saying in another way that they are not within our physical reality. There is also an indication here that the planet Earth may be moving into a different vibration or area of reality.

We have aided many other planets within this general vibratory level. The aid is given to this level by us because we are, shall we say, at the next level of awareness, and are best able to communicate to those people who wish to enter into understanding which we share.

We have dealt with many planets who are beginning a new phase of vibration. We have aided many a graduating class, and we have done so successfully. We have also failed, not once but several times. It is completely possible for us to fail if it be the will of the people of the planet we are attempting to aid.

We come because we feel the desire that brings us here. And we give what aid we can to those who wish it. Our thoughts are available to those who desire them. However, we attempt to do this in such a way that no individual is ever in a position where he cannot accept or deny our thinking as he so pleases. Those who are vibrating within the level that will appreciate the information that we give surely recognize that which is truth.

At the present time, we are far behind where we had hoped to be at this point while helping planet Earth. We had hoped to have been much more successful at reaching the people of this planet. It is possible that there will be a smaller graduation than we had hoped.[14]

The reference to a graduation concerns the transition from our present reality to the reality in which many of the UFOs normally exist, one which is a comfortable environment for our higher bodies. These graduation and transition references are found in many and various places:

> Our purpose in coming at this time is to help speed up these reactions so you will be prepared for the change-over in the Earth's frequency. This is taking place over a number of years. Many of your people are being affected mentally and spiritually in a discomforting way, and some of them in a very spiritual way.[15]

> The program that is in operation is to prepare the Earth for a major rise in consciousness, to what you call Christ awareness but what we term communication with Universal Energy.[16]

> They are making themselves known to the world as a whole to lead mankind thereby into a New Age as the Earth enters the more intense vibrations of Aquarius.[17]

> To sum up just what Flying Saucers are, we would say that they are mechanical devices intelligently controlled by men like ourselves. These men originate from many planets and planes and although they are different from one another in spiritual evolvement, they are banded together in an Interplanetary Brotherhood or Confederation of Solar Systems in this area of the Universe. The purpose of this organization is to aid their brother-man on the planet Earth as the New Age dawns. The Saucers constitute the "Host" which is the forerunner of the promised "Second Coming" of the Elder Brother. The ORIGIN of the Saucers, however, is not the important consideration—but their MISSION is![18]

> The … most important reason for their visitation to Earth at this time is that our whole solar system is at this time in transit into a new area of space, a new density, and that this is changing the vibratory rate of the nucleus of every atom in our planet, raising it to a higher frequency.[19]

> "Q. Why do they come here—what is their purpose?
>
> "A. To try to awaken within us a yearning for higher understanding so we can help ourselves in preventing any further destruction of

our planet, which could conceivably have a bad effect in our solar system. It is about time we grew up as a humanity."[20]

Of course UFO sources are not the only ones to sound the graduation theme. The Book of Revelation in our Bible discusses it in detail, as do the Edgar Cayce readings and that odd book, OAHSPE. In SECRETS OF THE ANDES, a contactee entity called Aramu-Meru says, "Upon the horizon Armageddon is shortly to come to pass."[21] Occult analysis of the Great Pyramid at Giza seems to predict a transition period, as do the ancient predictions of Nostradamus. These references to "the end" of things as they are, are certainly not a new thing. We devote a chapter to this subject later in this book. For now, I'll just say that basically the theory has all of us moving into a new area of space, a new vibration. It will be a higher vibration. The higher body of each of us will be our basic body, just as the physical body is here. This higher vibration, in which many of the UFOnauts already dwell, allows for a much more direct control of the environment by mind. Back in the '50s, contactees were talking about that time in the near future when telepathy, telekinesis, and other paranormal abilities would be commonplace due to the advance of our solar system into the higher-vibration space. As G. H. Williamson's contact, Brother Philip put it,

> … the messenger shall come unto you, even as it was in the days of Pentecost. And the living tongues of fire shall descend upon you. The gifts of the spirit will come unto you. And some shall manifest the gift of healing, and some the gift of tongues, or discernment, and the others.[22]

❧

> Man has the capacity to express the full spectrum of creation in all of the variations and harmonies of the Divine Thought for man was created as a creator. He has only to learn to express these harmonies from his Creator, and there is no end to the extent and the beauty of the expression of life which he can manifest.[23]

❧

> You are beginning to know things. You are beginning to hear things. You are beginning to sense them and to use mental telepathy. You are beginning to see beyond the physical vision. When you close your eyes, pictures form; colors that you do not see in the three-dimensional, or in the Earth plane, begin to flash before your eyes. You do not know where they come from, because you are going into the fourth dimension.

> Man has always been in the fourth dimension, because man always has contained an etheric body while he lived in a physical body on this planet. But that physical body is now being transmuted into the etheric body, more closely attuned so the etheric body can be the operating or dominant body while on this planet.[24]

One can only wonder if the continually increasing number of children now beginning to display these abilities might not be the promised harbingers of the new vibration.

So the UFOs are here, they say, for a specific purpose, at this specific time. There are like a "red alert" to our inner self: an alert that it is time for us to remember who we are, and why we are here.

> Behold a fairer time is with you than any men have dreamed of; behold there is a gladness again in the heavens when a host not of earth is seen of all shepherds."[25]

> We of the Confederation are here, as I have said, in great numbers. We are allowing your people to see us: at present we are allowing more of your people to see us. You can see us, as this instrument has. I will appear to you in the very near future. I will be seen in your skies. It is only necessary that you continue in your seeking. You see, my friends, it is truly written that, in order to find, you must seek. That is the scheme of things at this time. All of our efforts have been directed towards fulfilling this simple phrase: "Seek and ye shall find." Why do you think we have been so elusive? This was wisdom, my friends, that it is necessary to seek in order to find. You will understand this wisdom, if you think about it. It is a very old and tried system of producing an increase in the awareness of an individual, for only he himself can produce this increase in awareness. We cannot impress it upon him. But he can very easily increase his awareness many, many-fold. But the seeking is necessary.[26]

> And we will always continue to learn, for, take away curiosity and take away the thrill of living and seeking and man could not exist. There would not even be a creation. So we shall never reach the end of that road. We shall always seek.[27]

Boiling this basic desire of the UFOs to help us down to a workable plan seems to entail first of all the requirement that the UFOnauts have a great deal of patience. They want to help us without pushing us around. In advertising jargon, one could say that they're giving us the soft sell of all time.

> I am aware that many of the people of your planet consider that we have wasted too much time in our attempts to awaken the slumbering population of your planet. We would greatly prefer to act much, much more rapidly, but the speed and the degree of our activities must be regulated, not by us, but by you. The acceptance of us by the total population of this planet is the only governing principle that controls our activities.
>
> We will, very shortly, increase these activities. More and more of our craft will be seen by the people of your planet. This can be done because they are willing to accept us. We will do this, in order that their curiosity will be stimulated. This curiosity will then lead them to seeking the truth of our presence. This truth is what they desire, even though they do not consciously realize it.[28]

❧

> Give help without obligation. Lead without dominating. This is the Mystic Virtue.[29]

The UFOnauts report that they have quite a bit of experience at making contact with populations such as ours. Their technique seems to be gradually acclimatizing the people of this planet to their presence. From the days of the first widely-publicized sightings, and Orson Welles' historic radio broadcast of THE WAR OF THE WORLDS that caused such panic, we have come to a time when there is a high degree of acceptance of the UFOs among young people, with little indication of fears of attack. We may think that, OK, if they really are here, they should get on with it! Land! Make contact now! But in the light of their statements about the speed of their actions being regulated strictly by our acceptance of them, we can begin to understand their elusiveness. For though the young do tend to accept them, many of the rest of us do not. Also, we occasionally find indications that their lifespan does not have the limitations of ours. As the contact "Hoova" tells Puharich, "We occupy our physical bodies for about a million years at a time."[30] This would definitely make a time difference of fifty or a hundred years much more acceptable.

> We of the Confederation of Planets in the Service of the Infinite Creator are here to serve you. It is a great privilege, yet we must remain aloof. This is our understanding of proper service, for in serving your fellow man, it is necessary that you serve his exact wants and needs. You cannot determine for him what these are. Therefore, if his wants and needs lie outside the limits of your ability or your

desire to serve, it is best that you remain aloof, as we. There are, however, many, many of your people who desire exactly our service. For this reason it is impossible at this time to come among you. For this reason it is necessary at this time to act through instruments such as this one.[31]

It is necessary that if an individual is to make progress in a spiritual sense, that it be a result of an inner-directed seeking of his own, rather than an outer-directed commandment given to him by an organization of a religious or other nature. For this reason, it is necessary that we do not make ourselves too generally known and accepted by the people of your planet. If we were to do this, then the inner direction of their seeking would be for the most part lost. This is the basic reason for the conditions that you experience in your present physical environment. These conditions have been selected by yourselves, and by others, and they are a natural consequence of the creation, so as to act upon the consciousness of the individuals and create an atmosphere which will produce the inner-directed seeking for truth of which I spoke.

Unfortunately, many of the people of this planet at this time are so involved with activities that are of an extremely transient and unimportant nature that they do not have opportunities for experiencing the growth of an awareness that is necessary in order to accomplish the seeking that they actually desire.

We of the Confederation of Planets in the Service of the infinite Creator have attempted to balance between too much exposure of our craft to the people of this planet and too little exposure. If we were to become too much a common phenomenon, so that our presence was beyond question, then we would eliminate, at least in part, a large interest in seeking for spiritual truth. This may seem to be a strange or unusual point of view, but we have observed this in the past, and since the basic reason for the physical isolation of a people such as yourselves is to cause an inner-directed seeking, then it is evident to us that we should follow, as closely as possible, this plan.

Our craft and our people have visited this planet many, many times in the past. This was done only after the civilization that we visited was ready to accept us. This was done only after the civilization had reached a satisfactory level of inner-directed seeking of the truth of the creation, and therefore it was displaying the principles of love and brotherhood that are the product of this seeking.

We are at this time forced by conditions over which we have no control to visit the civilizations of your world, even though they have not reached a state of spiritual awareness satisfactorily high enough for our contact. This presents a problem. The problem is that we must approach a part of the peoples of this planet without distressing the rest.

We are attempting to do this. It is necessary that the evidence of our visits and our communications be of such a nature that it can be rejected or accepted by anyone who is exposed to it. There will be, unfortunately, a degree of infringement upon the people of this planet who do not wish to accept our contact. This is an unfortunate condition, but it is one with which we must deal, since at this time it is necessary that those of the people of this planet who are seeking truth be given truth.

It will not be necessary to prove to these people that what we are giving them is truth, for if an individual has reached an understanding of truth through the inner-directed seeking of which I spoke, then he will recognize this truth when it is given to him. It is therefore only necessary that we, by some means that will not disturb those who are not seeking our contact, give to the rest of the people of your planet that which they seek in a form that is suitable.

This, then, is our service: to lend a helping hand up the ladder of spiritual evolution to that part of the people of this planet at this particular time, a time that is unique in the history of this planet, a time that must be dealt with in a more direct and forceful way than previous times and experiences in the history of this planet.

We are extremely privileged in being able to offer this service to those who seek it: and our service is largely given to them through the process of their daily meditation. If they are to avail themselves to this service, it is necessary that they do so through meditation.[32]

❧

It is not our policy to fraternize with the natives of any of the worlds we supervise. We did that in eons past and it brought disaster to all and gave rise to fantastic legends in your own world.[33]

❧

Karmically we cannot overrun or overrule, as you would put it in your parliamentary terms, your mass desire. We could not do that. Don't you understand that? You are there to set up the desire and to help them have the desire for us. But we cannot interfere, or cannot overrun them. Please understand this basic rule of the universal law. Please, it is very important. Don't expect us to come down and force you into seeing us or accepting us. This must be accomplished from the Earth plane level. Please understand.[34]

❧

We must remember that according to Universal Law, our space visitors cannot interfere with our progress on Earth. Since the Earth is only a classroom in the Father's many mansions certain lessons must be learned before Earthman earns graduation to higher spheres. An eighth grader doesn't enter the first grade to make fun of the students because they do things more simply than himself. Likewise, spacemen aren't going to step in and dictate to us; they are going to let us learn our lessons in our own way, even though they will undoubtedly be painful lessons, for the history of the Earth has proven this to be always true on this sorrowful planet![35]

❧

The Space People themselves state that by Universal Law they cannot interfere with man's progression upon the Earth.[36]

The one thorniest question asked of ufologists is "Why don't they land?" Or, put another way, "Why don't they contact our governments?" If you accept these contactees' messages, then this thorny question is thoroughly laid to rest.

The UFOnauts in this particular group look upon planet Earth as a place with one function: the growing of people. Not their bodies, but their spirits. Hence they are concerned only with this people's spiritual growth. They are celestial gardeners here to enrich the etheric soil of mental communication which is available to everyone through meditation.

We cannot come directly to you, and land upon your surface and speak with you. For it would do no good. We must provide a spark, a clue, something for a start, a start of seeking. Seeking that results in finding the truth that is within you. This, my friends, is the only way to help the people of your planet. For they must help themselves. They must find the truth that is within them. They must initiate the seeking. All that we can do is to provide a stimulus for their own initiation of this seeking.[37]

❦

We of the Confederation of Planets in the Service of the Infinite Creator avail ourselves to this knowledge through meditation. For this reason, we do not come among your people, giving them our service directly, for we are aware of detrimental effects upon them in doing this. Our service is aimed at what they actually desire. What they actually desire is an ability to realize truth. In order to give to them this ability, it is necessary that we bring about a condition to cause within them a personal seeking of service and a personal seeking of knowledge of the truth of the creation. Only through this process can they understand the truth that is within them. It is something that cannot be too effectively given to them in an intellectual manner.[38]

❦

Allow people to read transcripts of these transmissions only when they ask. And only *if* they ask—never at any other time. We cannot stress this enough. Never force either our, or your, opinions on anyone. People will come to you when they are ready to accept what we have to say.[39]

❦

Each man, and hence each world, must learn the lesson and make its own progression.[40]

❦

… they look upon us as younger brothers whom they love dearly, but whom they know must solve their own problems in order to learn the lessons well. … Growth and progress are individual matters. The way may be pointed, but each must travel it for himself. He may choose to travel the main highways, meeting and mastering the lessons brought by each moment, or he may choose detours. The choice lies with each one alone.[41]

At this point, we can see fairly well the reason that the craft are here, according to the contactee messages. The UFOnauts want to help us, if we want to be helped, by sharing with us their philosophy, if you will, or their concept of truth. Or call it their religion, if you must. I personally hesitate to use any of these terms, but especially the term "religion." There is a good deal of feeling caught up in the word itself.

Many scientists think that the studies and beliefs of religion are unscientific. And many clergymen find science to be unreligious or even sacreligious. I would like to remove this discussion from both camps, and refrain from getting tangled up in semantics. Whatever your bias, just look at this data with an open mind. Remember that there are always problems encountered in the communication of both scientific and religious concepts.

There is another consideration, too, in studying these contactee messages. We must make allowance for the limitations of vocabulary and religious and scientific expertise of the telepathic receivers of these contactee messages. They could only repeat that which was to some degree comprehensible to their own minds; therefore, we receive largely simplified versions of the original UFOnaut's concepts. Yet these views are most provocative. Here, an entity from Hatonn blends science and religion in a discussion about life itself:

> Life is composed of two materials. One of them is what you might call consciousness. The other is light. But my friends, consciousness is love, and light is its physical manifestation. All that you are able to experience in the way of a physical universe is composed of one ingredient. This ingredient we will call light, since this word is closest to what we wish to express, and it is the only word that we have available in your language to express the basic building block of our Creator.
>
> Originally, the Creator expressed a desire. This desire was expressed in a state of consciousness that is best described in your language using the word, love. The Creator, then, expressing desire through love, caused the creation of all matter. He caused the creation of light. This light was then formed in its infinite configuration in the infinite universe to produce all of the forms that are experienced. All of these forms, then, are molded or generated through the expression of consciousness that is love. They are composed of a fabric that is light. For this reason we greet you each evening, with the statement "in his love and his light." For this, then, encompasses all that there is.
>
> The consciousness that creates, and the fabric that is love and light.
>
> The love that produces the configuration of light occurs in what we term various vibrations, or, using a word in your language that is not sufficient but somewhat descriptive, "frequency"—love occurs, then, in various vibrations or frequencies. These vibrations or frequencies are the result of free will. When the Creator produced this original concept, the concept included the gift of freedom of choice to all of the parts that he created. These parts are then totally free to change

the original thought. In doing so, they change what you understand to be the vibration of some portion of the original thought.

Each of you here this evening have a vibration. This vibration is yours, and you have control over it. Your freedom of choice has created the love that manifests the light that is the fabric molded into your physical form.

This is the simplest analysis of all created forms of all of the creation. Each part of it is able to utilize its own consciousness, through the principle of freedom of choice, to vary or change the original vibration. The creation, therefore, continues to be self-generating, in an infinite variety. This was provided for in the original thought of the Creator. It was provided that he might generate, in an infinite way, in an infinite number of forms.

Through this use of freedom of choice, man upon planet Earth has generated many forms. Some of these forms were never envisioned by the Creator with the original thought. However, they were allowed for, due to the principle of freedom of choice.

This is perhaps the most important principle in this creation: that each of the Creator's parts be able, throughout eternity, to select for themselves what they desire. In experimenting with this desire, there has in some instances become a slight problem in straying away from thoughts and desires that would be most beneficial. In experimenting with these desires, some of the created parts have lost contact with the original desire.

This has occurred in many places in this creation. We are here at present to communicate, to those who desire to find their way back to the original thought, information leading those who desire the path back along the path to the original thought. It is necessary that we act in such a way so as to lead only those who desire this pathway along it; therefore not violating the important principle of total freedom of choice.

As I was saying previously, each of you, as do all parts of this creation, have a particular vibration or frequency. This vibration or frequency is the only important part of your being, since it is an index of your consciousness with respect to the original thought.

When an individual is aware of life in its infinite sense, he is also aware of the benefits of matching this vibration with the vibration of the original thought. It is our effort to match our vibration with that of the original thought. This is the reason that we of the Confederation of Planets in the Service of the Infinite Creator are here now. For this service that we perform is a service that would be in harmony with the original thought. This, then, produces within us a vibration more harmonious to the original thought.

We are attempting to give instructions to those of the planet Earth who would seek the instructions how to produce within themselves the vibration that is more harmonious with the original thought. This, as I have stated before, was demonstrated upon your planet many times before by teachers. The last one of whom you are familiar was the one known to you as Jesus. He attempted to demonstrate by his activities his thinking. His thinking was in harmony, much more than those about him, with the original thought. His vibration was, therefore, much more in harmony with the original vibration.

For this reason he was able to work what were called miracles. However, the original thought was that all of the parts of the consciousness that were of the original thought should be able to generate by thought and consciousness what would be desired. The man known as Jesus desired, and therefore created, since the vibration which he generated was in harmony with the vibration which the Creator used to form the creation.

It is only necessary, then, that an individual become in harmony with the vibration that formed the creation in order for him to act within the creation as did the Creator, and as does the Creator. This was demonstrated to you by the one known to you as Jesus. Not only did he demonstrate what could be done in a very small way, but also how to think in order to do this.

Unfortunately, man upon planet Earth has misinterpreted the meaning of this man's life.

At this time we wish to point out the true meaning of this man's life. It was desired that those who were aware of his thinking and his activities then follow the example, and as he did, become more in unison and in a harmonious vibration with the thought of their Creator.

We are here to bring you information and to impress upon you in a nonintellectual way during meditation the idea that is necessary for you to increase the vibratory rate of your real being so that it is harmonious with the original thought of our creator. Our teachings will be simple, as were the teachings of the one known to you as Jesus.

> It is only necessary that you attempt to understand these teachings. Understand them in depth. Understanding in depth can be done only through meditation.
>
> And then, once these teachings are understood, it will be necessary that they be applied, and that the individual so desiring to apply them demonstrate in his daily activities and in his daily thinking the concept that was the original thought. The concept that we have spoken to you as being love. We have used this word, as I have said, because it is as close as we can come, using language, to the original thought.
>
> However, this word is miniature compared to the original thought. The original thought can be obtained in your intellect, only to a very small degree. It must be obtained in your total being, through the process of meditation.
>
> Once this is done, and once your activities and thinking reflect this thought, your vibration will increase. At this time you will find the kingdom that has been promised to you. It is truly all about you. It is only necessary for you to grow in order for you to receive it. This growth is simple: spend time in meditation and learn of its simplicity.[42]

All exists, then, in the love and light of the Creator, or to say it another way, all that exists is made of light, directed by love. The concepts of love and light are not exact, the space contacts tell us, but they are the most appropriate words available in our language. Here are correlating passages from several other sources, which repeat the basic thought: some use the word "love," some the word "light," and one the word "energy," but they all are aiming at the same concept.

> But until all men agree about the principle taught by the collective prophets and principal teachings, you can have no equation by which to work all your difficult problems. The equation is that God is love, and love is all; and love is the key, or Spirit is the force, by which all love is possible between men and between planes, planets and forces of nature.[43]

❧

> Love is the essence of all creativity. Without love, there would be no life. For it was through love that God received the spark of the idea of creation and conceived the vision of creating man to be a part of Him.[44]

❧

> ... attune the frequency of your own individual being nightly, calling upon that being by whichever name you know that being—the Infinite One, God, the All-Knowing One, Our Radiant One—to send forth His light to assist you in attuning with those frequencies of Light which are being sent forth now at this time into the very core of your own beings.[45]

❧

> My friends, remember that you are living in a universe of energy. Even you, yourself, are pure energy.[46]

This concept of a vibration forming light is in precise agreement with the findings of Dewey B. Larson's revolutionary unified field theory which he calls the Reciprocal System. Larson says:

> If this is a universe of motion in which matter is a complex of motions, then motion is logically prior to matter.[47]

Let's take a look at a further application of the UFO concept that consciousness is prior to matter:

> The creation was initially conceived by our Creator to be of a property so as to reflect the impressions given to it by man. It was so designed as to express his desires in any way that he chose. There are various levels or densities in this creation: levels and densities that are not yet suspected by your physical scientists. Each of these levels is expressing the desires of those of the Creator's children who are acting within it.
>
> Each level or density is moldable or may be acted upon by the thoughts of the individuals within it to a greater or in some cases a lesser extent than that appreciated by those who dwell upon the surface of your planet at this time. It is only necessary to desire an effect to create it. This is what the Creator of us all provided for us. This is not understood at present by the population of the surface of your planet: however, it is in actuality the truth of the Creation that they are experiencing at this time. The conditions that you experience in your daily activities are a result of your thinking and the thinking of those about you and others on your surface.[48]

And again:

> ... Thought can also be transmitted on many frequencies ... The effect that these frequencies will have in the envelope of your earth will depend on the frequencies of thought. Now you say, "What

> determines the frequency of the thought?" There are several things there too; the motive back of the thought will determine somewhat the frequency—also the type of thought. For instance, thoughts of resentment, of hate, of fear, each has its frequency, and this frequency has its effect, and will eventually seek out the same vibration or level of vibration in the envelope. As this builds up in the earth's envelope and becomes greater and greater in quantity, it will have its effect upon the earth ...[49]

It is interesting to note, in the context of these messages, that all of the people who are currently able to produce Geller-type effects are generally of the opinion that the way they cause the direct alterations in their physical environment is to want those alterations to occur. They desire that the metal change its shape, or whatever, and this change happens. I speculate that the mechanism of this bending and breaking of materials by mind has to do with the mind's affecting an alteration of the basic vibration or space-time mismatch which Larson identifies as the most basic building block of the material universe, the photon, or light.

A much greater refinement of this ability would theoretically allow the individual to create his own reality by arranging the vibration of the fabric of space-time as he desired. As he thought, so would it be. It is the reported condition in the finer planes of existence, as reported by astral travelers too numerous to cite. Indeed, the ability to cause changes in our environments by our own efforts of will seems a desirable talent to cultivate. The UFOnauts tell us how to go about achieving fantastic abilities. The instructions are seemingly simple, yet because of their need to put their concepts into our language, there is always the big question of whether we are able to fully understand what they mean.

> Seeking, my friends, is, as we said, extremely important. First, I would like to explain why seeking is important. Seeking is a way of growing. It is in truth for the people of this planet at this time their only way of truly rapidly growing; growing, my friends, in a sense that is spiritual.
>
> The people of this planet at this time are almost all children, in a spiritual sense. Most of them are not at this time seeking spiritual growth. This is very important, if an individual is to rapidly grow, spiritually. All of us throughout all of space are growing, in a spiritual sense. However, some of us are growing much more rapidly than others. The reason for this growth is simply that these are the ones that are seeking.

It is written in your holy works that it is necessary to seek if you are to find. This is with reference to finding spiritual enlightenment. This is in reference to developing the awareness that is necessary for man on earth to develop if he is to take his rightful place in the creation.

We of the Confederation of Planets in the Service of the Infinite Creator are aware that seeking is necessary if one is to get where he wishes to be, and he wishes to be at a higher state of awareness. Look about you, upon your planet. There are many conscious beings, in many forms of life. There are the animals, and birds, and the fish, and man on earth. And each has a state of awareness. But it seems that man has the higher state of awareness. And yet we tell you that this awareness is very minimal. And the awareness of man on earth can be raised to an awareness that he would consider godlike.

But, my friends, this is what was meant for man to have. This is what was the original concept of the Creator: that this awareness would be possessed by all of his children. This is what it is necessary to seek, if you are to find this awareness.

The reason that it is necessary to seek this awareness is that it cannot be given to you. It is something that each individual must find for himself. It is not a difficult thing to find. It is a very simple thing to find. It is only necessary that the individual go about seeking in a proper way. We are here to attempt to aid those who desire our aid in seeking our awareness, to find it. We will not attempt to confuse those whom we wish to aid with complex lectures on various problems and concepts. We will simply give to them the simplest of the Creator's ideas. For, my friends, His ideas are not complex. It is man, especially man on earth, who has made a complex set of rules and conditions for spirituality. The Creator's concept, my friends, is extremely simple. This we are here to bring to you. It is only necessary then that you seek an understanding of this simplicity. Then, upon understanding it, demonstrate it in your daily lives, and in your activities and associations with your fellow man. Then, my friends, the awareness that was meant for you will be yours. It is an extremely simple process. It is only necessary that, first, man on earth seek.

Seek, my friends. This is what is necessary. This is the first step. Seek awareness. Seek the spirituality that was meant to be yours, and surely you will find it. For this is the Creator's plan: that all of his children should have this.

> Seeking, my friends, is extremely simple. And yet, through the powers of your intellect, with the best of intentions it is possible to make it seem complicated.
>
> There is the complication in your vision of the concept of time; and there is the complication in your vision of the concept of space. And you say "Where, and when, may I seek? In what place may I find holy ground? And at what time may I seek the Creator?"
>
> My friends, you are the Creator. For the Creator is you. And, my friends, as it is written in your holy works, the place whereon you stand is holy ground.
>
> There is no complication in time, for all time is here and now.
>
> There is no complication in place, for all place is here and now.
>
> My friends, there is naught but seeking: there is naught but the Creator. It is only necessary for you to turn inwardly, into the light, and enter the light.
>
> These words are poor, but they lead the way to a new understanding. It is not necessary to have the most perfect meditation or the most proficient spiritual moments in order to be seeking. It is necessary only to turn your will.[50]

❦

> So we must desire, we must have the desire, and then we must be willing to work for it, to practice, to develop. You see, we have many powers within us, greater powers than you can imagine, but we must develop them, you see, and as we master one, we become aware of others and we master them, and so we do, on and on, but it requires great effort especially in the beginning. As you gain more confidence in yourself and in your powers to do these things, you see, it becomes easier and easier, for it becomes, it's like it's natural to do this.[51]

So we are supposed to seek. But how do we go about seeking? And what is the object of our search?

> There are many ways, my friends, of gaining what you seek. However, what you seek now will change. It will change as you seek it, for this is the nature … of seeking. For as you seek, you find, and as you find, you understand. And as you understand, you continue in seeking, but at a different level.

So do not attempt to understand that which at present seems to be beyond you. Simply go within, and you will be led to an understanding that will place you upon a new plateau, from which you will be able to view much, much more of reality.

Seeking, my friends, is not a direct attempt to understand each intellectual question which crosses your mind. Seeking is the attempt to know one's Creator. There will be in your seeking an unfoldment of understanding. Each step will show itself to you. When it does, raise yourself upon it, so that you may find the next one.

We bring to man of Earth understanding, and yet we cannot speak to him and cause him to understand. We cannot communicate through channels this understanding. We can only point out directions for his seeking. For it will be necessary for him to change his point of view, and to change it, he must understand; and to understand, he must seek.

There will be many paradoxes in your seeking, for this is the nature of seeking. But as you continue, these will dissolve, for you will reach a new plateau, and a new understanding. And the seeming paradox that you have bypassed will appear in its true light. Meditation, my friends, is the only method of which we know to allow an individual to rapidly form this new basis for his understanding. For this is not dependent upon preconceptions. It is not dependent upon the definitions of a language that was never intended for spiritual seeking.

Redefine that which you experience. Redefine it through your seeking, and through your growing awareness of the creation and our Creator.

And then, my friends, you will not question, for you will know. For you will have grown in your understanding.

It is sometimes frustrating to be unable to find answers to those questions that seem paramount, and directly in the path of your seeking. But these too will fade, as you pass them by, and become more and more aware of the single truth that permeates all things, and answers all questions. We will continue to aid you in any way that we can, but primarily we will point out to you the wonders and the joys of the creation that you experience. And we will attempt to bring to you an understanding that will be the result of your meditation.[52]

They realize that they cannot really express themselves fully through our words:

> This is the sad part of their contacting us on this earthy plane of expression, where we are very limited in interpreting mental impressions and meanings into words.[53]

But they are not hampered critically by this communication handicap, because what they want us to do more than anything is meditate and get in touch with our own higher awareness:

> ... we should consider the highest state of spiritual harmony, love, an awareness of which we can conceive and so make this state of consciousness our own personal goal. We should keep revising our goal upward as our concepts and realizations of the nature of our Creator grow and blossom within us.[54]

How can we seek this higher awareness? The UFOnauts refer again and again to a quotation from our own *Holy Bible*:

> Ask, and it shall be given you; seek and ye shall find; knock, and it shall be opened unto you. For every one that asketh, receiveth; and he that seeketh, findeth; and to him that knocketh it shall be opened.[55]

Once we begin to come into this higher consciousness, say the space brothers, we begin to learn a new way to live, a way focusing on service to others:

> Service, my friends, is very natural. It is the way of the Creator. It is the plan of the Creation. Everything in the creation is performing a service. The vegetation that is abundant upon your planet performs a service. But your people ignore this. The animals upon your planet perform a service, but this is largely also ignored. The flowers, the very air, the water perform a service, but this is ignored. If it were taken fully into consideration, it would become obvious that everything in the creation is there to perform a service. This includes all the Creator's children. Each of you is here to perform a service. This is the plan of this infinite creation. This is how it works. It is only necessary to understand this, and then all things are possible. Unfortunately, upon the planet that you now enjoy, this principle is not understood. Very, very few of those who inhabit the surface of this planet understand the simplicity and totality of this plan. It is the way the creation functions. It is only necessary that you understand this, and then perform with the best of your ability. Perform these services to your fellow man, and then you too will be functioning the way that the Creator of us all planned.[56]

❧

> … we must learn in spiritual work to be flexible, to be open, to be of service to one another.[57]

❧

> It is because all things are interrelated and all parts of the whole must cooperate with each individual segment of the whole; giving, flowing to one another the priceless energies and the goodwill of love and comradeship which must bring forth the highest in each part of the living creative force field on the planet at this time, and with those who work in and through the planet at this time.[58]

❧

> The Lord answered: Serve thy Creator by doing good unto others with all thy wisdom and strength, and by being true to thine own highest light, and all knowledge shall come to thee.[59]

❧

> You cannot grow by taking in all the truth and beauty of the inner life which you can find and just holding it there. You must bring it forth into your daily life and live as best you can by its tenets and share it with others who ask to know. We may only grow by being agents in the great river of life which flows into our world from our Creator. We must let our Light shine forth. If we do not give of that which we receive to those who seek, in the same spirit that it was given to us, we become a full and stagnant pond and we can receive no more.[60]

❧

> I gave thee Light of Life that you might extend My action; that others might feel the joy of Me that are in darkness bent, who are trouble-blinded and cannot see that I am there.[61]

All right, we understand that we should attempt to be of service to others. But that is not as simple as it might seem! How are we supposed to go about determining what "service" is?

> Service, my friends, is an extremely difficult task to perform effectively. It is necessary first to define the objectives of true service in order to understand how one may serve. There are two classifications under which all services may be divided. The first classification includes those services that are of a transient or unlasting nature. These are the services that you perform in your daily activities for your fellow man, and they are truly services.

But there is a test that may be administered in order to determine whether the service performed is of a transient or unlasting nature, or whether it should fall into the second classification, which includes all services of a permanent and not-transient nature. The test is to determine whether or not the service is of such a nature to cause spiritual growth for the one served.

This, my friends, whether it is known to the individual or whether he has forgotten, is in truth his only real objective.

The people of your planet are, for the most part, in a state of ignorance with respect to their real objective, which is the evolvement of their spiritual awareness. This, then, is what must be served if the second classification for service is to be met.

Each of these two classifications are desirable, and we would like to perform for the people of your planet acts which would be classified under both classifications. However, since we are aware that the second classification is by far the more important of the types of services that may be performed, it is necessary at this time to postpone performances of services of a direct way, to aid in a physical or more transient nature. We are quite fortunate that we are able to act as we are doing now, to provide the people of this planet with information that they may use in order to augment their seeking in a spiritual sense.[62]

❧

Fragapatti said: Quick, now, seize the goal; go forth practising thy light for others, and it will grow, giant-like. And Hoab was strong in faith, almost mad with the delight of such wondrous change; and he rushed forth, commanding, in the name of Jehovih, raising up hundreds and thousands, even as he had been raised, crystallizing.[63]

❧

Love is mental or spiritual and can be done with your thinking. Love through your thinking is the only way. Outward expressions of your love do not mean anything unless they have love in the thinking behind the expression.[64]

❧

The reason for life in the physical sense is to experience service. For this is very effective in creating a deep and complete understanding of the Creator's plan for the creation. In this plan was the concept of service. Through His love, He instilled in each of the parts of this creation the desire to serve. This desire to serve is within everything that exists. It is within the planet that you walk upon. It is within the vegetation. The atmosphere itself. Everything about you exists to serve, and unless an entity becomes involved too deeply in thoughts generated as an action of his freedom of choice, he will maintain his awareness of his desire to serve, as does the vegetation upon your planet, as does the atmosphere that you breathe, as do we of the Confederation of Planets in the Service of the Infinite Creator.[65]

❧

This is really your purpose, service to your Creator and your fellow man.[66]

❧

For know ye all, that whoever aspireth to Me shall come to Me; but the nearest way for many is round about. Ye being above grade fifty are already more to Me and for Me than against Me or from Me, and in equal degree are cast upon your own responsibility. For such is the light of My kingdoms, from the first to the highest: To the child, no responsibility; to grade twenty-five, one quarter; to fifty, one-half; to seventy-five, three-quarters; but to the emancipated in my etherean realms, responsibility not only to self but to all who are beneath.

Wherein My highest worlds are responsible for the lowest, being bound unto one another through Me for the resurrection of all.

In this day am I come to deliver My Gods down to the earth, to walk on the earth with mortals, raising them up in My name.[67]

❧

You have desired our presence, and we are with you. We are of the Confederation of Planets in the Service of the Infinite Creator. We are always with those of the people of this planet who desire our presence. This is our service to the people of this planet at this time. This is our technique of seeking. It may seem strange that we would seek through service, but this is our understanding of seeking.

It is stated in your holy works that it is necessary to seek in order to find. We have found many ways of seeking. One of these is to serve your fellow man. And this is our form of seeking at this time. We are seeking understanding of the Creator. For this is our desire. We are seeking this understanding through service. Through serving our fellow man on Earth, and aiding him in his desire to understand the Creator.

And through aiding him, and fulfilling his desire, we aid ourselves in fulfilling our desire. For in doing this, not only does man on Earth perhaps learn more of this creation and the Creator, but also we: for it is a law of this Creation that only through service, may one be served. In serving others, we serve ourselves, as even does man on earth. For this was the original idea that generated the entire infinite Creation: the idea of mutual service. The idea of mutual understanding. And the idea of mutual love.

This we are bringing to man on Earth: an understanding of that that is within him. An understanding of that which created him. An understanding of our service and the need for his. It is unfortunate that there are so many that do not understand the true principles of this creation. We are attempting to help them realize this truth. It is within them, and this is our service: to help them find what they desire to find: the realization of the thought that generated not only them, but all that there is, and the thought that provided that all that there is act in such a way to serve all that there is.[68]

We wish to help you find the Father and His blessings as we have done. Sharing with others is one of the great pleasures of life. You will never know great happiness until you can share the love of the Father with someone else.[69]

We are all one, beloved ones: and to serve others is only to serve yourself.[70]

The ideals of both our churches and our statesmen are very much in line with this "space brother" philosophy of service to others. It is just that on Earth, we seldom manage to put these ideals into action. Missionaries and diplomats alike want some return for their service. Indeed, the UFO concept of foreign aid is a revolutionary one!

Chapter Six
The Development Of Man

According to the communications from space contacts, man on earth has something to learn about long-forgotten abilities. According to some of these communications, we all should be able to work "miracles." The problem is diagnosed as being the atrophy of Earthman's basic mental muscle. Therefore, we see a lot of contactee material on how to regain the natural abilities which at present we now call psychic or paranormal.

Their general attitude is that this mental muscle is not synonymous with the intellect as we know it. Instead, it is a process whereby the basic personal consciousness or vibration of the individual is strengthened through expanding the awareness in an intuitive or non-thinking sense. This process is achieved by means of very simple mental exercises and then is distilled by what you might call the subconscious. The mental exercises have to do with daily meditation.

> Much can be said for the magnificence of silence, for in silence one may hear the musical voice of God. Listen just for a moment and feel life as it exists. Look into your brother's eyes and see the love of God in the reflection. Don't look *up* for God, look *in*, for it is within each man that He exists with powers unlimited.[1]

> It is necessary, in addition to practicing this form of meditation, for you to become aware of the original creation, and not creation of man. Pay attention to that which is natural. Become aware of it. People of your planet are not aware of the original creation. They have created a very false illusion. Therefore, they are not in awareness of reality. If you think that you are totally aware of the original creation at this time, then you are mistaken. For, if you were, you would see us, for we are part of the original creation. There is a technique for increasing your awareness. This technique will be given to you a little at a time, so that you may employ each step. The first step will be to seek to understand each thing that you see that is a portion of the original creation. Take these things one at a time, and consider them in detail, and try to establish in your mind a totally detached understanding of them.
>
> If this part of the creation happens to be a leaf, then study it with care. Become aware of it. Do not rely on old impressions. Develop an awareness of each thing. This will be the first step.

> This instrument receives my thoughts, and relays them to you. These thoughts are not my exclusive property. They are the thoughts of an entire creation of our infinite Creator. It is not necessary for this instrument to be used for you to know these thoughts. They are available to all people in all places at all times. For they are the thoughts of the Creator. And these thoughts were meant for all of mankind, in all places. These thoughts are the thoughts with which the Creator created us.
>
> These thoughts are very simple. They are a simplicity that is unique, for they are the very foundation of the creation. This is what we are attempting to give man on earth: this original thought. This is what he needs at this time. This thought can only be approached using pure language. It is not a common concept among the people of your planet. This is the reason for their difficulties. The Creator never imagined difficulties in his creation. They are the product of man's erroneous thinking.[2]

Meditation begins with a simple increase of awareness of the natural world around you.

> As you move down the corridors of time, let your awareness grow. Observe the beauty that lies about you; observe the handiworks of your Creator in His Creations. Observe Nature in the raw, in your plant life, your animal life; and then peer into the heavens and truly see the great works. Observe closely, allow your consciousness to open wide and really take in the beauty that lies therein, and soon a realization will begin to dawn in your consciousness of the true greatness of creation[3]

❧

> It is important that we see the beauties of creation and begin to catch glimpses of the Creative Consciousness behind it. We recognize that the ability to sense these qualities of life is the direct verification that these properties exist within ourselves. Otherwise we could not respond to their qualities. It is only by mutual resonance that we experience.[4]

❧

> Thinking is not something one does. Thinking is the act of becoming aware of what already exists. One does not try to think to become aware. One only has to remove his own thoughts and the Universal Mind rushes in to fill the void.[5]

❧

It is evident that all creations throughout this infinite creation are the works in either a direct or indirect sense of the creator of us all. It is unfortunate that the people of this planet are unaware of the principles that were provided for the extension of the principle of creation. Our creator provided each of his children with abilities quite similar to his own. Each of you has within you these abilities. They are not possible to be removed. They are within all of the children of the Creator, and will always remain with them. It was so designed by our Creator. He wished for all of his children to have and to use the abilities to govern and mold their environments at will. Unfortunately, the people of this planet have forgotten the principle that was within each of them. It is only necessary that this principle be remembered for each of the children of our Creator to fully manifest them. The teacher that was known to you as Jesus was able to use many more of the abilities than the people of this planet. He was no different from any of you. He simply was able to remember certain principles. These principles are not at all complex. They are very simple.

And an understanding of these principles is what we of the Confederation of Planets in the Service of our Infinite Creator are attempting to give to the people of this planet who would desire them at this time.

These principles are not necessarily of an intellectual nature. They are of extreme simplicity, and may be realized by anyone at any time. It is only necessary that you avail yourself to our contact through meditation in order to begin to re-realize that which is rightfully yours; the truth of the creation and the truth of your position in it.

Unfortunately, on this planet there is what we might term as interference. This interference occurs because of erroneous thoughts that are manifested in most of the areas of your planet. These erroneous thoughts are of a nature so as to cause a problem in the realization of truth.

These erroneous thoughts must be totally obliterated from the thinking of an individual if he is to be successful in returning to the original thinking with which he was created.

We have attempted many times to suggest to you that this original thinking is one of total love and brotherhood. This is not enough. It is very difficult for the people of this planet to understand these concepts in an intellectual way. They have for a very long period of time been mentally conditioned by erroneous thinking, so that they cannot easily become intellectually aware of the principles that are simplicity and truth themselves.

It is therefore suggested that the intellectual mind be circumnavigated, and the principles be directly communicated to the soul or spiritual mind through the mechanism of telepathic impression in a non-intellectual or a conceptual sense. This we have found to be highly effective with respect to any attempt to get from an intellectual thought to a deeper understanding and awareness of the truth of the principles of our infinite Creator. It is for this reason that we have asked that the individuals who wish to understand these truths avail themselves in daily meditation, so that these impressions may be analyzed by them at a deeper level, and therefore a true and complete understanding be arrived at.

If this process of daily meditation will be continued, then each of those who avail themselves to this will find that they begin to become aware of things about them in a new sense, and that they find that they begin to appreciate the true creation in a greater and more beautiful way.[6]

❧

Pluck from your mind all resentment, fear, hate, anger; leave not one stone unturned to take these things from your mind and close the door—close the door tightly against them—for where these things exist, the seeds of Truth do not grow well.[7]

❧

As our world is bathed in the violet frequency, only Truth will be able to exist; all falsity will fade away of its own accord. That which has blinded man's eyes to reality will pass away before the Pure Violet Fire, like fog passes away before the dawn.[8]

So meditation is a process of becoming aware of the creation about us in a new way, of quieting the preconceived and negative impressions of our world and letting the higher reality of the true creation take its place in our conscious awareness. This is decidedly not an easy thing for most of us to do.

It is very difficult for man on this planet to look about him and realize the truth for what it actually is. He has been conditioned, through his thinking and through the thoughts of others, for a very long period of time, to see things as they are given to him, rather than as they really are. The way that they really are, my friends, is extremely simple.

> This simplicity is within each of the children of the Creator. Each of them possess all of the knowledge that was the original creation. It is only necessary that they avail themselves to that knowledge. And this is very simple. It is done through the process of meditation.
>
> When this is done, all the truth and beauty of the original creation become apparent. And then it will not be possible for the individual to be fooled by the illusion. He will not see his fellow man in any form but perfection, even though within the illusion he has been taught to disdain. This was not planned by the Creator. The Creator only planned that each of his creations should express itself in any way that he chose. This, my friends, is perfection. If man on Earth could only realize this, he would once more think in total harmony with the original creation. This may be done on an individual basis. It is not necessary that this be understood in an intellectual sense, or by anyone else than the individual endeavoring to reach this understanding.
>
> This has been demonstrated upon your planet before. The man most familiar to you having demonstrated his understanding is known to you as Jesus. He made the simple realization, and then demonstrated it by his activities this understanding. It was not necessary that he be understood by his fellow man, for it is impossible to force externally upon another individual this understanding. It is only possible that this understanding be attained from within.
>
> But yet this man demonstrated this understanding, pointed out a pathway, a guidepost for others, so that they too could find the original creation, and once more lead themselves from darkness to light.
>
> For light, my friends, is eternal and infinite and real. The rest is illusion. Go within. Become aware of reality. It is within each of you.[9]

> ... it is not in complexity that we find the Father. It is in simplicity that we find him.[10]

Contactees who are members of the different cultures of Earth receive messages about the spiritual leaders in their particular culture. In our Western culture, the messages most often relate to Jesus.

> This man known to you as Jesus was born into the physical upon your planet. He was able to realize the truth of the creation, and then he was able to demonstrate this truth to those about him. This man came into the physical on your planet as have many teachers in the

past. Each of these teachers came into the physical for the purpose of serving the people of this planet. However, it was up to them to carry out this service. Each of them did it in his own way. This is within the limits of our understanding of the intent of our Creator.

These teachers were limited: limited by the same conditions that each of you and that each of all the people on the planet experience. The people of this planet have misinterpreted the meaning of these men. The people of this planet are at this time misinterpreting the meaning of the man known to you as Jesus. His purpose in his life was to demonstrate that it is possible through an awareness of the Creator's truth, to experience what the Creator planned for each of us. This man worked what was called miracles. These were truly miracles to those who thought of them as miracles, but this was given to each of the Creator's children. He was simply demonstrating the result of thinking in the original way as planned by our Creator. He was also demonstrating that it is possible for anyone, at any time, to demonstrate this type of thinking, and therefore, the abilities that accompany it.

Unfortunately, the people have very much misinterpreted this man's life and teachings. He was attempting to provide an example of understanding so that each of the children of the Creator could seek the same understanding.

This is the task of any teacher upon this planet or any other place in the Creation. This is our task at this time.[11]

This man Jesus taught brotherly love of one another, and love of the Father. Through His understanding of the Father and His creation, He was able to demonstrate miracles, as you call them. These were not miracles but normal, natural things that man can do when he realizes his kinship with the Father, and expresses this love of the Father. ... All mankind are the sons and daughters of the Father, not just one. We respect and love this man Jesus because He, out of many, was able to realize and demonstrate His true relationship with the Father, as all peoples of this planet are capable of doing if they would but learn the truth. ...[12]

There was a teacher once known to you as Jesus. This man had desire. His desire was to serve his fellow man by demonstrating a knowledge of the Creator's love. Through this desire he accomplished things that

> you know as miracles. This man had true desire. It is only possible to achieve true desire by initiating this yourself. If you are able to initiate a desire that is a true desire, then you will achieve what you desire, just as the man known to you as Jesus achieved what he desired. He achieved what he desired because he desired to serve his fellow man in a way that was in harmony with the desires of the Creator, for he realized his unity with the Creator.[13]

The master known as Jesus, then, was demonstrating the understanding that he was one with the Creator. His vibration thus came into harmony with the vibration of the creation, a vibration of total love. This vibration of the Creator was understood by Him, and he desired that we understand it also. Hatonn speaks to us also on this theme:

> At this time I wish to speak to you upon our understanding of truth. We could give to you many things. We could tell you of many mysteries that … would interest you. However, we consider that it is first necessary to first provide for the peoples of this planet a simple truth, that is in reality all that anyone in this creation needs to know. After this truth is understood, the rest of the mysteries vanish, for this truth is the key to a total understanding of creation.
>
> This truth is the pathway to all truth. I shall at this time speak upon this truth. I and my brothers, who are with me in the name of the infinite Creator, understand a simple truth, that is *the* important concept in this creation. This simple truth is that the creation is one thing. Everything that you can imagine; everything that you can see; everything that you cannot see; all that there is, is one thing.
>
> This is not realized by most of the people of this planet at this time. Due to this, they are experiencing conditions that they do not desire. It will be necessary, if an individual is to find the pathway that he desires, for him to realize the truth of this simple statement: there is no separation. Separation is an illusion. All things are one thing: the creation. To effect one part of the creation is to effect the creation.
>
> We are here to aid the people of the planet Earth, but we are here to aid ourselves. It is impossible to give service to others without serving yourself. For you and those whom you serve are the same: you are one.[14]

❧

> Man continually progresses up the ladder toward perfection, and though a rung may break under the weight of his many errors, still his goal is to reach the top and one-ness with the Infinite Father.[15]

❧

I am Oxal. My friends, this is of no consequence, for I am the Creator. Yes, my friends, you are listening to the voice of the Creator. You hear the voice of the Creator each day, my friends, as you go about your daily activities. It is only necessary to recognize it. As you meet your fellow man in your daily activities; as he speaks, then you hear the voice of your Creator. Birds singing in the trees, my friends, speak with the voice of the Creator. The very winds that blow through these trees speak to you, my friends. And this noise that you hear is the voice of the Creator.

For his expressions are infinite. It is only necessary that you hear and see these expressions. And then when you hear and see them, it is then necessary that you understand them. To understand that these are the Creator.

This is what is missing upon your planet, my friends: the simple understanding that all of these things are the same thing. They are the Creator. This knowledge is self-evident. It does not require a complex analysis. It does not require that I prove to you that what I am saying is true. Truth, my friends, speaks to you. It is all about you. It is the Creator.

It is only necessary for you to recognize this, totally, with no reservation, and then you will think as the Creator thinks. For the Creator recognizes himself, and there is no part of himself that he does not accept. For it is him, and he is one thing: the creation.

It is impossible to separate yourself from the creation. It is impossible to isolate yourself from the creation. You are it, and it is you. And all of its parts speak to you, saying, "Be of the creation." It is only necessary that man on Earth listen to this voice, and then understand its words. Understand and then demonstrate this understanding, and then man on Earth will take his rightful place with those of us who roam through this infinite Creation.

For this is our privilege. And this is your privilege. For we are all the same thing. We are love, and we are light.[16]

All of the children of the Creator throughout all of the universe, all of this infinite Creation, my friends, are truly seeking only one thing, whether they realize this or not. They are seeking understanding. For this is all that is necessary.

For once this understanding is accomplished, then all things are possible, for this is the way that the Creator designed it. This is the way that He provided. It is only necessary that you realize this. It is only necessary that you demonstrate in each thought this realization. And then, my friends, you and the Creator are one, and you and the Creator have equal power. For this is truth. Each of us is the Creator.[17]

❧

For I can only Be, through you.[18]

❧

As you serve, remember each and every one of your fellow-men is deity. Think of each one that you meet not as this man or woman or child but that each one that comes before you *is the Father in essence.* If you would think on Earth of each one as part of the Father, with due respect in that degree, then the Earth's problems would dissolve instantly.[19]

❧

Man is limited but God is unlimited, infinite, expressing in all men, all forms.[20]

To see the Creator in every man is a beautiful idea, but exquisitely difficult to accomplish from day to day. Yet the Confederation contacts say that this message of "love and brotherhood" is the only reason they are here: they truly want us to have this truth before us. They do not seem to care whether we believe that they are who they say they are; they care only about getting the message of love out, to those on Earth who want to hear it at this time.

Earth's last mile, we sad.[21]

❧

(The UFOs) … are orbiting your planet in answer to the many prayers for help from your population of many beliefs, colors, creeds, races. We would not come to the aid of Earth unless there was a call for help on a mass scale.[22]

❧

We of the Confederation of Planets in the Service of the Infinite Creator have used this method of contact in many, many places, with many, many people. Upon your planet at present, there are people in almost all areas that are receiving our communications. There are many of these people who do not understand what is happening to them. They do not understand who we are, as do you. They simply receive communications. The reason they have no idea who we are is that they have no concept of people coming to them from the stars.

This is unimportant. The only thing that is important is that they understand the message that we give to them: the message of love and brotherhood. There are many other people who receive our messages who do understand our identification. In this case, it is also only important that they understand the message that we bring to them. This is what we are here for: to bring this simple, single message. This is what is necessary for the people of your planet to learn at this time.

We of the Confederation have lived an example of this knowledge for many, many of your years. We are totally aware of the results of living the type of life that results from the understanding of the principle of love. We are not unwise in our attempt to give these principles to you, for we have experienced the effect of using these for quite some time.

I am aware that these principles are not understood by the people of your planet, not even the people who have been given them directly, through channels such as this one. There seems to be a barrier to this understanding that has been generated through thousands of years of an ignorance of these truths. This barrier is so solid at this time that it is very difficult, even for those who desire this knowledge, to accept it and put it to use. They are able to hear the words and understand them, and even though they agree totally with the concepts that are present, they are still unable to assimilate them into their own thinking. We have suggested many times that in order to assimilate this knowledge into your thinking it is necessary that you meditate. But this is something that is also misunderstood.

It is extremely difficult for the people of this planet to remove their thinking from the hypnotic state that has been created. Everything that they experience is created by their own thinking. You cannot experience something that you cannot think, because this is all that there is: there is nothing but thought. It is found in many forms and expressions, but thought is the source of all that there is: the thought of the Creator.

And this is what you are. And you are able, like the Creator, to generate thought. The thought that you generate is your responsibility. The people of this planet each generates thought, and communicates these thoughts to others. If the thoughts that are generated are of a low quality, then they will in turn generate low-quality thoughts in others. This is a self-perpetuating action. And this is the reason for the strife and confusion that is so abundant with the people of this planet. It is erroneous to say that you cannot do anything about a situation as complex as this one which has been created by millions and millions of minds through thousands and thousands of years. It is only necessary that the individual remove himself in thought from this sea of confusion and express himself in the true love and light of the Infinite Creator. This may be done at any time. It is up to the individual. If he desires to do this, then it is only necessary that he do it. This has been demonstrated to the people of this planet many times in the past by the teachers who were here to demonstrate to the people of earth life and the expressions of the Creator as they were intended. It is a very simple lesson, but man on Earth desires to ignore this. Very few accept these teachings, and stand in the light and express only the love and understanding of the Creator of us all.

This is unfortunate. It is a situation that we who are in the service of our Infinite Creator are attempting to remedy, by giving instructions which are not only verbal, and which have difficulty in penetrating the barrier which the mind has erected, but instructions of a nature that will bypass this intellectual barrier and reach the spiritual self directly. This is done, of course, during the process of meditation. This is why we have stated, for so many years that meditation is extremely important. It is only necessary that you avail yourself to these concepts for these concepts to begin to cause the individual to realize once more his proper stature and position in the Creator's scheme of things. It was stated by your last great teacher: "Know ye not that ye are Gods?" This man understood the true created purpose of all of mankind. Why is it necessary for people, especially people who have been made aware of truth through their seeking, to stop short of achieving the knowledge of their true created purpose and being?

We have been puzzled, at times, by the inability of the people in general of this planet to be awakened to this simple truth. We suggest that it is necessary to maintain a continual awareness of your objective. We suggest that that objective is to realize your true position in the creation, and then to act in a manner intended by the Creator. In order to do this, it will be necessary that a considerable effort be put forth. We find that the state of hypnosis brought about by the evolution of thought of the people of this planet is so great that if an individual is to free himself from it, it is necessary for him to maintain a constant awareness of his spiritual nature and purpose, and to augment this awareness with meditation. The effort put forth to do this will be much more rewarding than any other activity that the individual can engage in.

This step must be successfully made by each individual of this planet at some time or other. Wouldn't it be reasonable to do it at the earliest possible time? For it is an extremely beneficial step. We would suggest that if progress is seemingly slow, then additional meditation may be necessary, for only in this way can the people of planet Earth free themselves from the erroneous thoughts that have been impressed upon them for so very long.[23]

Each part is a portion of the Creation. Each holds equal rank.

I am aware that there are many upon your planet who would not understand this concept. They feel pain, if it is within their individual being, but they do not feel the pain of others.

This is not so with the Confederation of Planets in the Service of the Infinite Creator. We feel your pain, and this brings us to you at this time. To serve you. For in doing so, we serve ourselves, since you and we are one. Your pain is felt throughout all of the creation, and for this reason there are many, many here to serve you at this time. We serve you in the very best way that we can. To eliminate this pain. We give to you the information that you need in order to eliminate this pain. It is something that may be done in the twinkling of an eye. It is the way that the Creator planned. He did not, however, anticipate that his children would create from their own desires the pain that we now feel emanating from your planet.

This is a result of the desire of the people of this planet. Unfortunately, these desires affect not only the ones generating the desire, but also others who live on the surface. It is what you call a contagion. It requires an extreme degree of understanding to live upon your surface and not experience this contagion.

It can be done, my friends. It is only necessary that you know and demonstrate the Creator's truth in every thought and deed. And then you will be freed from the effect of the desires of your brothers who live about you on the surface of your planet.

At this time, very few of the people upon this planet are seeking anything outside of the physical illusion that so constantly busies their minds with trivialities.

We of the Confederation of Planets are aware of the trivial nature of the things that involve most of the people of your planet. These things seem of great importance to them. However, the importance of their activities is a function of their inability to still their active minds, and return to the awareness of reality that is possible through meditation.

The activities that seem so important to the people of this planet at this time are so very transient as to be in reality negligible, as are all activities within the physical, except for that activity of service to one's fellow man. For through service, one builds one's awareness of truth. This is the reason for life, as you know it, in the physical.[24]

Truth is all about you, very obvious to those who have stilled themselves for the very short time that is required to become aware of it. It is very obvious, to those of us who view the creation of the Father in its original form. All of its parts act to support all of its other parts. All that sustains each of us is a gift of our Creator. All of the joys and experiences that come to us are gifts of our Creator.

It is only man upon this planet who has become lost in a complex creation of his own, with many thoughts of a complex but trivial nature that keep them very busy, in an effort to reach that which is of no value—a minor creation that will last only the shortest period of time—which has no value, once it is attained, for he will lose it, and once again return to the creation.[25]

Never allow your mind to be your sole ruler. A man who allows his heart to think will not perish.[26]

The thing is that Man of Earth, in so many cases, has a distorted idea of what is necessary and he becomes rather controlled—under pressures that he feels are necessary and are required by his environment, rather than controlling it. It becomes difficult to withdraw and bring about the realization of his true I AM. When man becomes truly conscious of his oneness with Creation, this takes precedence over all other things, and as this becomes more and more a part of his consciousness, it becomes easier and easier to have a true realization of this.[27]

One of the larger questions which faces the entity who claims that the Creator is one universal thing, that God is Love, is the question of evil. How can it possibly exist if the universe is all one thing? Here are some thoughts from the space contacts on this.

There are groups who express themselves in ways that were never conceived by the original thought. The original thought, however, provided for no limits on expression. It is possible, therefore, for any of the Creator's children to express themselves in any manner that they desire. For this reason, throughout the creation, there are individuals and groups expressing themselves in infinite numbers of ways. You, at your present state of understanding consider some of the expressions to be evil. We consider them to be expressions. We find that for our purpose, certain expressions to be of a more beneficial nature to our own enjoyment than others. There are, however, expressions of an infinite quality and an infinite quantity occurring throughout the creation. We attempt to serve those within the creation who desire our service. They desire our service because they are interested in our concept of truth. We believe that our concept of truth is correct. In our understanding, we know that our concept is correct. There are many who would disagree with what we understand. This is their privilege.

They do not desire our service. We would freely serve them in any way that we could. However, they do not desire this. Therefore, we do not serve.[28]

❧

Evil does not exist. It was not created in the beginning by the Father. It has been created in the mind of man, and can only be gotten rid of by man, through a change in his thinking.[29]

❧

For evil is not of My creation, O man. Evil is brought about by those who falter on the way to Me.[30]

❧

There are many, many myriads of populations throughout the cosmos. Many of them are extremely advanced, and a few of them are not only advanced but also of a nature which you might call evil.

The Creator is at the end of your path. Your faith is far stronger, if you indeed realize it, than any evil. Remember this, my friends. It is completely within your power, through meditation, to gain the love of the Creator that conquers all lack, limitation, and pain. But my friends, be aware that the only true nature of evil is separation from the Creator. It cannot touch you if you maintain your contact with the one who is all. Nothing from the outside may come in to harm.

> From the universe of truth and understanding you may show love and light upon all who come into your view.
>
> Do not fear, my friends. There is nothing to fear. Never waste time in fear, or in hatred, or in anger, for it is only another opportunity at such a time to experience and to demonstrate the love and the light of the infinite Creator.[31]

There is one last thing to be said about evil and our perception of it:

> This is one way of designating in your own consciousness who is of Christ force and who is of the anti-Christ force. You will see many, who will cry out that there is no God, come and fight shoulder to shoulder with you for peace and love and brotherhood equally for all men for all time. This is truly one who is of the Christ force. Yet you will see others, who profess to be of God, speaking words of God, who will say that some are to be saved and some are to be damned. These you will know are not of the Christ light, for the Christ light speaks of brotherhood first and foremost and will defend the right of all men everywhere to share equally with their brothers.[32]

It is not just evil in the abstract, but all sorts of troubles of every kind that seem to surround us in the physical plane. As Israel Regardie, a practitioner of white magical arts, says:

> … early in life an impenetrable barrier is erected within the psyche itself. A barrier of inhibition is built up between the unconscious and the conscious thinking self—a barrier of prejudices, false moral concepts, infantile notions, pride and egotism. So profound is this armored barrier that our best attempts to get past it, around it, or through it are utterly impotent. We become cut off from our roots.[33]

There is a reason for this, according to the UFOnauts:

> Every person creates their own world—whether they want to be or not, they are creators. We create our own situations, surroundings. The conditions that we find ourselves in today are a result of past thinking. That is why it is so necessary, so very, very necessary to weed these things out of what you call the subconscious.[34]

Hatonn on this subject:

> You are aware upon your planet of night. This darkness is real to you within the illusion that you know as life. There is a simple physical way in which you can intellectually imagine that darkness to be only a local phenomena. The method of that understanding is to imagine that you are observing the solar system from the standpoint of the

> object that you call your sun. From the standpoint of your sun, there is no night. There is no darkness. There is no lack. There is no limitation. There is only light: an enormously wasteful amount of energy, infinite, self-perpetuating, a type of light that expresses itself in all directions with all of its heart and strength. The concept of darkness, lack, limitation or any petty restriction of any kind is quite foreign to the point of view of the inhabitant of the sun. It is for this reason, my friends, that we often describe to you the love and the light as being like sunlight or some form of light. This light, this phenomena called light, is a spiritual Phenomena. It is one of the two building blocks of your entire universe. Light, with no limitation of any kind, vastly energetic and infinite in its capacity, is the basis for all that is in a physical sense. The shaping, the creating, the molding force is the Consciousness, the Thought which we call love. Love shapes light into the vibration that we know as the physical world. The Creator's love is completely, down to the very smallest detail, a spiritual thing. The lack, the limitation, the darkness and the want is the creation of that most chief of the Father's creations—that being mankind. Mankind is a creator even as his Father wished for him to be. He has created. And those things which he desires are things which he does not truly desire. He has invented a great many different ways to experience lack, limitation, and want. This, my friends, is only true thought from the point of view of the dweller within the illusion who rotates with the planet and sees the sun go down and disappear. A simple shift in point of view, from the point of view of the planet, to the point of view of the Source of light for the planet will enable the understanding of the conditions of the planet upon which you now enjoy the physical existence to come into much clearer focus. We are aware that this is a far more generalized statement than requested. However, there are many things which do not have the spiritual answers themselves, but deal only with the illusion. The ability to change one's point of view will often banish a question and replace the question with understanding simply by the realization of a shift in point of view.[35]

So the basic distinction which separates the experience of wealth from that of poverty is the inner orientation either towards a state of love and oneness with the Creator and man, yielding abundance, or towards desires and emotions within this physical illusion, which yields lack and limitation. Here the contactees say this in two more ways:

> Earthman … must learn to distinguish between love and emotion. Emotion is a desire—love is a state of consciousness where you realize

a state of oneness with Creation and all mankind, and you see all mankind in a consciousness of love. Not a possessive love, nothing to do with sex, not a state of desiring but a state of giving, a wanting for another that which is for the highest good and rejoicing in them receiving, with no thought for self.[36]

❧

There was a man upon your planet who had great wealth and in this wealth, he saw much power. For his fellow man would eagerly do his bidding to share part of this wealth. And, for this reason, many of those who dwell upon this planet, known to you as earth, require vast quantities of material wealth. And, therefore, acquire what they consider to be much power. What is not understood by these men is that in acquiring this wealth and in attempting to possess much power through this wealth, they are giving up an infinite amount of power for that which is in actuality no power at all.

The man of which I spoke, who had much wealth, used it to satisfy his desires. And his desires were for things which he thought that he wanted and needed. For he saw in this wealth, not only a great happiness which would come from possessing those things that he desired and having dominion over all of his fellow man about him, but also great security in that he would need nor want for the rest of his days. And, therefore, he coveted greatly his accumulation of wealth. And had at his command everything that he desired and great status.

But he lacked one thing. He lacked love. For it was not given to him by those about him, and this he did not understand. And he became aware of his need for this experience that he called love and he set about to discover how to obtain it. And he questioned those about him, and asked them why he was not given love. And they could not answer for they did not know. And he went to a wise man and offered to pay him much of his wealth if he would but tell him how to obtain love. And the wise man gave unto the rich man all that he possessed, for all that he possessed was but a pitiful small amount. And the man of great wealth accepted it. For he had long ago resolved never to turn down a gift. And he left the wise man and went to his home and pondered this gift, leaving the wise man penniless. For he had not paid the wise man. For the wise man had not told him how to find love.

And as the days passed, he returned to the wise man, for he could not understand why he had been given all that was possessed by the one who was said to be so wise. And when he asked him he was answered by the wise man, who said, "It is because I have a great love for you and you desire wealth. Therefore, I give you that which I have to add to your riches for this is what you desire."

And at that moment, the man of great wealth looked at the wise man and said: "And in turn, I, for the first time, know love."

And he gave to the wise man great wealth. And in doing so, he felt an even greater love. For, for the first time, he had learned the truth of the Creator's gifts to his children. And this man was very fortunate for he had been able to discover a way of generating love. And yet, man on earth continues to seek within his material illusion. Continues to seek that which is of no real value. For he lacks faith. He stands upon the surface of this planet and experiences all of the gifts of his Creator. He breathes the air and smells the fragrance of the flowers and is in the company of his fellow man and finds many things provided for him; and, yet, he does not understand. He does not have faith that within this Creation, he is supplied, and due to this lack of faith, he finds hardships, for he does not understand faith. Therefore, man, in many instances, does not seek the knowledge of the wise man. But he seeks a security and a power that is not secure and is not power.[37]

Again and again, the contactee messages stress the basic technique for acquiring the spiritual understanding of which they speak: meditation. There are many forms of meditation already long in use upon planet Earth. Christian contemplation has yielded many mystical revelations from the saints; yogic meditation techniques have produced yogis who can baffle scientists by their abilities to control supposedly non-controllable bodily processes such as breathing, temperature of the body, the rate of bleeding of a wound, etc. The contacts which I have seen do not urge the adopting of one or the other techniques of meditation; they simply suggest the basic process. We can choose the technique we find the best for us.

If there is dissension amongst you we will not contact you. Be calm and quiet.[38]

❧

Unfortunately, there has been much misinformation about us, and much misunderstanding, even of the ones who are aware of us, of our real message. We have attempted to maintain a simple message, for man on earth has confused himself for many generations with complexities. We have attempted to maintain a simplicity in our teachings, in order to remove man on earth from the web of his entangled complexities. What we here present to those of the peoples of this planet who would desire it is the simplicity of truth itself. The truth of this creation, and the truth of man's part in it.

It is, my friends, very, very simple. It is not necessary to get lost in the complex web of intellectual seeking that man on earth seems to be so fond of. It is only necessary that he avail himself to an understanding that is not of an intellectual nature. And this he may do in daily meditation. It is only necessary that he raise his awareness, so that he grasps the understanding of his unity and oneness with the creation and the Creator. This we bring to man of earth. This we offer in hopes that he will accept it.[39]

❧

Many of you are very much aware of the fact that words themselves are traps, for they mislead you and you go into a state of argument over the meaning, the finer nuances, of words and of phrases.[40]

The contactee messages emphasize again and again that we should not put our reliance in the fruits of our intellect, which expresses itself in words, but instead should become silent and begin to listen for that "still, small voice." Like Thoreau, they ask us to simplify the way we think our life, so that our reactions to circumstances are not totally dependent upon our mentations, but instead have their grounding in the awareness of the Creator that can only come from meditation and contemplation.

I am the voice, O mortal man, that whispers in the silence of your Being.[41]

❧

Allow your mind to stop. Think of nothing. It is difficult to change quickly, in the confusion that you meet during your daily activities, and the intense use of the intellect that you experience. This is one of the great problems on your planet.

It is not necessary for man to use his intellect in such a manner. Everything that man desires is provided. It is only necessary that he realize his true relationship to the Creation. It is only necessary that he realize that he is the creation.

And this is not done by intellectual complexities. This is done through a simple process; a very simple process of becoming aware. We call this process meditation, but it is not necessary that it be so formalized. It is only necessary that man realize that this may be done

> at any time. Relax, and allow this awareness to be with you. I and my brothers will help you. We are here for that purpose.[42]

> The human mind is like a sponge that can be saturated with every impression that comes along. When it is habitually concerned with its own personal interests, it is impossible for it to receive a message accurately, regardless of its source. To do so requires total elimination of all personal interests. In other words, the line must be clear.[43]

In order to get our minds clear, we need to slow down our intellectual mind until it allows us to listen, really listen in silence not just of the outer world, but of the inner mental world. The mental wheels need to stop for a while. Hatonn takes another look at why this is so:

> My friends, your minds are stayed far, far too strongly upon those illusory goals of the intellect which your conscious awareness makes such advanced company of. These intellectual pretensions, my friends, are no kind of advanced company to be in. Their group name is complexity, and, my friends, understanding is simple.
>
> Let us examine this concept. Understanding, my friends, is simple. It is unitary. It is not logical. It is not intellectual. It is not necessary that you understand understanding. It is not necessary that anyone around you understand what you are understanding.
>
> It is necessary only for you to seek the understanding of the true creation within, and this we will attempt to give you in a simple way. With the intellect and with words, my friends, we can only approximate understanding to you. And your attempts to examine it on an intellectual level can only be a type of subterfuge, camouflage, and misdirection. You must not depend upon the tools of the physical illusion, in order to build for yourself your bridge to eternity, for that which is of the illusion will vanish and be no more before you are able to cross that bridge.
>
> Let go of the preconceptions which are imbedded deep in your intellectual mind. Allow yourself simply to seek, and then to have faith in the seeking. What you seek is simple. The creation is simple. There is only one understanding which we can offer you, my friends, and that is that the creation is one great being. The creation is you; the creation is me; the creation is all that ever was and ever will be. The creation, my friends, is the Creator. As you look into the eyes of another upon your planet, you are looking at the Creator. As he looks at you, my friends, he also is looking at the Creator.

> If you may achieve this simple understanding, then and only then you may live in harmony with the understanding of the Creator, who created each portion of his creation in order that it may be of service to every other portion of the creation.
>
> This is our understanding; this is our simple understanding: all is one. We cannot speak to you in any complex manner, for we do not have a complex statement. We sincerely hope that you may heed our caution, and allow that portion of yourself which is stored with the knowledge of all of the creation to come into life within you. Allow it to do so by exposing it to the love and the light of the Creator through meditation.
>
> Seek, my friends. Seek understanding, and through meditation, understanding will be given.[44]

> You are the manifestation of the Father's creative force. You are surrounded and engulfed by the light of the Father. Your thoughts are the thoughts of all. All thoughts are one. We are all one. We are all perfect manifestations of the Father. We are at one with everything in the Creation. When you can realize these things and know these things, then you will be expressing the true you, the Creator.[45]

> The Chinese philosopher Wang Yang-ming said, "My nature is in itself sufficient. To search for principles (li) in affairs and things was an error."[46]

This sort of sublime self-confidence is echoed very much, and in the same spirit, by the entities making the UFO contacts:

> Those of the people of your planet who do not desire the thoughts of those of us who now surround your planet are not obliged to receive them. This would be a great effort on our part. Those of the people of your planet who desire our thoughts receive them. Whether they may be translated into a verbal form or not is of no particular consequence.[47]

Which brings us back to the basic concept of the primary validity of free will. OAHSPE puts it this way:

> … the highest wisdom is to suffer all men to have full liberty to think on all subjects in their own way.[48]

This point, of total free will's sovereignty, is one of the mainstays of the Confederation message:

> ... thou art thine own master, even as all men are self-masters.[49]
>
> ❧
>
> I judge not, neither do I hold regrets, for all are given right to choose.[50]
>
> ❧
>
> ... we dare not interfere in the form of force or control in any way. This would not conform to the Father's laws to which we adhere.[51]

And so, in the end, we get a picture, not of "Gods" coming to help a planet of benighted heathen, but of brothers who have heard our call for help, and have come to give us what aid we can receive in free will. But no matter how much help we receive in the form of this information, it is our own will, and ours alone, which must turn to the path of seeking, before we can begin to gain an understanding of truth. The nature of this search for understanding is so well expressed by the poet T. S. Eliot, that I close the chapter with it:

> We shall not cease from exploration
> And the end of all our exploring
> Will be to arrive where we started
> And know the place for the first time.[52]

Chapter Seven

A Solution To The Mystery Of Uri Geller

One of the most controversial books currently in print is URI: A JOURNAL OF THE MYSTERY OF URI GELLER, by Andrija Puharich. Puharich's background is impressive. After graduating from Northwestern University Medical School in 1947, Puharich completed his residency in internal medicine at Permanente Hospital in California. In 1948, he established the Round Table Foundation in Maine. There he conceived and developed a series of experiments to enhance ESP in sensitives by means of electronic systems. His subjects included Eileen Garrett, Dr. D. G. Vinod, Peter Hurkos, and Harry Stone. In 1958, he moved his laboratory to Carmel, California, where he continued his research and served as consultant to industrial corporations, foundations, and universities. In 1960, he moved to New York and founded Intelectron Corporation, with J. L. Lawrence, to develop electronic systems for aiding hearing in nerve deafness. After 10 years of research in this area, he held 56 patents for his inventions.

During this period, Puharich led several medical research expeditions to Brazil to study the healer Arigo. It was while he was in Brazil that he first became aware of UFOs, for he saw and photographed a number of them there. In 1971, he went to Israel to investigate seriously the phenomena of Uri Geller. He was able to confirm claims that these phenomena were caused by Geller's psychic abilities, and reported that Geller could actually break metal by mind alone, communicate telepathically, and perform many other seemingly impossible feats.

Shortly after confirming Geller's abilities, Puharich subjected Geller to age-regression hypnosis, and touched off a long series of incredible events. These events make up the body of the narrative of the book, URI. Puharich reports that he and Uri received dozens of communications from UFOs. The method of reception was quite unbelievable: Puharich's tape recorder would run, by its own volition. When Puharich would play the tape back, the messages would be on it.

My personal reaction to the book was immediate acceptance, since so much of the information in Puharich's messages had been independently compiled by my researches and one confirmed the other. I felt certain that Puharich was reporting exactly what had occurred. I can, however, understand the reaction of those who, although experienced in the methods of science, are novices to ufology.

It has been my experience that many of today's scientific community err on the side of caution to the point of excluding any new evidence that doesn't neatly align with some accepted theory or practice. Even if this evidence remains stubbornly before him, he keeps killing it off. And, like the phoenix, it keeps rising again. A radical in any field is ill thought of unless history proves him correct. These correct radicals then become known as the true leaders. Dr. Puharich had made solid advancements both in medical electronics and parapsychology before writing URI. I suggest that what he records in that book did happen, and that he takes the radical step of writing a careful report of it as a service to us all. I think the years ahead will spin out a story that casts Dr. Puharich as one of the true leaders.

I will not dwell on the contents of the book, except for certain of the UFO messages which find correlation and clarification in the material from contactees which I have been collecting.

Here is the account of the beginning of the tale of UFOs and Uri Geller. Puharich is speaking.

> When all was quiet, I explained to Uri that even though he was going to be hypnotized, he would remember everything that happened in this first session. We would only explore things of interest to Uri that had happened in this lifetime.
>
> We started. I simply had Uri count backward from twenty-five. He said, "Twenty-five, twenty-four, twenty-three, twenty-two, twenty-one, twenty, nineteen, eighteen," and he was in a deep, hypnotic trance. I asked him to look around and tell me where he was. He said he was in a cave in Cyprus just above Nicosia with his dog, Joker. I asked him what he was doing here. He said, "I come here for learning. I just sit here in the dark with Joker. I learn and learn, but I don't know who is doing the teaching."
>
> "What are you learning?"
>
> "It is things like I told you last August when we first met. It is about people who come from space. But I am not to talk about these things yet."[1]

I recognized this "sitting in the dark" technique as the meditation which is recommended by the contacts. It is their standard technique for learning.

> Seek understanding, my friends. Seek through meditation. Seek to know the reason that the master teacher known as Jesus retreated from time to time to a place where there was silence. There was

> something he was seeking. Seek for the silence, where there is much understanding awaiting you.[2]

To change the subject from basic philosophy to a particular item, note the message from Puharich's contact, Spectra about a power blackout:

> AP: Did you cause the blackout in Israel on January 14 of this year?
>
> The power failure in Israel is from us.[3]

There have been other mysterious blackouts, notably the New York blackout of 1965. UFOs were sighted before and during the blackout at strategic locations like the Niagara Falls power complex. The events seem to correlate well. This is, of course, completely within the realm of speculation. Their motives for doing such a thing are also widely open to speculation.

There is another motive which should be considered also, and that is the basic desire of the Confederation of Planets' ships to attract attention, to suggest to people who are on the verge of seeking answers that lie without the physical that there is indeed an extra-physical side to reality.

One of the strangest correlations between the Puharich contacts and my own research began for me in 1968. My research partner and I received messages which asked us to get into the movie business. We responded to this by writing a story, and turning it into a script, which we hoped to produce as a motion picture. The story we wrote had as its hero a Dr. Padeyevsky, a medical doctor with expertise in telepathy and paranormal research who did a good deal of consulting with various agencies in the field of medical electronics.

His co-worker was a real magician. The plot of our story revolved around their involvement with a UFO contact. After Carla and I had read URI, we were dumbfounded by the similarities between Padeyevsky and Puharich, and between our magician, Joshua Starr, and Uri. We visited Puharich in Ossining, where we were further amazed to note that the house we had described as Dr. Padeyevsky's in our story was identical to Dr. Puharich's real house. The estate seemed to match, tree for tree; the only difference was that in the story, the curve of the drive had been graced by a hedge. Carla could not resist asking what had happened to the hedge. It turned out that there had indeed been a hedge, which had been cut down in 1972. The story was written in 1968 and '69. We did not meet or know of Dr. Puharich until his book was published early in 1974.

To this pile of coincidences we begin to add Puharich's own instructions from the UFO contact:

> Do a movie on Uri. Melanie is the one to do it. Work at it; it will come out at right time. You are not to entrust anyone with the secret of our existence—no one. Do not interfere with our educational Israel army program. We will contact you once more before you leave Israel. We showed ourselves to you in the sea by the hotel on April eleventh.[4]

Our instructions in 1968 were not recorded and so cannot be compared word for word. And there are various other details, like the "Israel army" reference, that we have never received. But the instructions to enter the movie business in order to do a motion picture about UFOs and real magic are quite similar.

When Puharich asked Spectra with whom we should work in these contacts, he was told, "Only three. Uri, Shimshon, you. We cannot use your full powers unless you and Uri and Shimshon are together."[5] This preference for groups of three or multiples of three is often seen, in UFO messages such as this one:

> Q. How many people are aboard a flying saucer?
>
> A. I have never seen more than six in one craft; however, they can travel in units of 3-6-9, or 4-8-12, depending on the planet from which they originate, or the polarized balance of the people in connection with the mechanics of the craft traveling through space.[6]

❧

> YOU must have a group for contact. Band yourselves together.[7]

And of course, the concept that "when two or three are gathered together in my name, I will grant their requests," is as old as the teachings of Jesus.

Puharich's contact talks now about the coming time when they hope to be able to land on planet Earth:

> Uri and Andrija, listen carefully! We hope to land on your planet in a few years. We are seen more and more by people. We will enter your orbital system through (word lost) transformation and be able to enter your environment.[8]

The expectation of a mass landing of extraterrestrials is shared by many contactees. The Hatonn source devotes many messages to their desires to land during the cycle change. George Hunt Williamson's contact, Brother Philip, says:

> Beloved ones, from the hosts of Michael the Sun, the golden-helmeted ones sweep toward the Earth—those of another dimension

> and another time. And yet, they are here to add their light and their love in the program now manifested upon your earth-world.[9]

And again:

> On the day of the "Great Telling" millions of citizens of the civilized parts of the world will know beyond a shadow of a doubt the fact that space visitors are here and they will know why they are here.[10]

In the same message as the one in which the reference to the mass landing appears, Spectra tells Puharich:

> One of our failures is that we cannot contact you directly. We can only talk to you through Uri's power on the tape recorder. It is a shame that for such a brilliant mind we cannot contact you directly. Maybe in time we shall be able to contact you directly.[11]

They are speaking here of direct telepathic contact. They say that any person who sincerely wishes to contact them can accomplish the contact:

> All are capable of direct communication. You merely have to ask, then be receptive. We do not set the time. We work through your teachers. Your own teachers and spiritual aides and guides will let us know when we can come through. Of course, remember too, spiritual guides and teachers are your own Christ-aware Self as well as those who are assigned to your development.[12]

It has been my experience that the more used to intellectual thoughts and cerebrations a mind is, the more difficult it is for that mind to display telepathic ability. However, it has also been my experience that with the proper training, anyone who has the desire to achieve this telepathic contact will eventually succeed in doing so. Dr. Puharich's busy and mentally challenging life has so far not left him with time to work at stilling his intellectual mind for this purpose. But if he could find the time, I think he or anyone could succeed in getting this type of contact.

As Spectra finishes this message, it talks more about the proposed movie which Puharich has been working on:

> It is a brilliant movie, but not the story we want. We want you to prepare the earth for our landing, a mass landing on earth. We landed in South America three thousand years ago, and now we must land again. We want you to tell our story—what you call the UFO experience. Use all the collected data and literature.[13]

Again, this message is quite congruent with our instructions to make a movie.

I am going to talk next about IS, which is a dubbed name, standing for Intelligence from Space, and refers to the entities aboard the ship Spectra. Spectra, like many UFO-related names, sounds totally fake, right out of science fiction, and many readers of UFO literature have objected to this seeming comic-book flavor. Uri asked Puharich, "Why the Hollywood name?" Williamson's book, THE SAUCERS SPEAK, is especially full of these strange names. I realize these names are strange, but on the other hand, I'm quite sure that people like Dr. Puharich and Williamson, who have extensive educational and professional backgrounds, could make up far more convincing sets of identity if they were intentionally creating falsehoods. I think the problem here lies in the limited ability of the UFOnauts to understand our language. If they have been monitoring our communications systems, it might be quite reasonable for them to choose these names as being good for recognition in our language. I would not have been surprised to find their ship named the "Star Ship Enterprise."

To find my way back from the digression: when Puharich asked IS when this mass landing would take place, the reply was, "We will not reveal to you our timetable in landing on earth in your local time. It may be some years, or sooner."[14] This coincides with the Hatonn source, which says that the exact time of the cycle change will be dependent upon the consciousness of all of us, as we help or hinder that change, and that the time when landing will be possible is dependent upon the degree of acceptance of them which they find on earth at the time of the cycle change.

I had been given a fairly exact date for the desired mass landing, and when I talked with Puharich in 1974, I asked if he had such a date. It turned out that we both had the same information. However, there may be a delay from that desired date, due to the slow dissemination of information about the UFOs' purpose and the acceptance of that information by man on Earth.

IS tackles the question of why the UFOnauts don't contact our government:

> Andrija, many people in the U.S. Government and the Russian Government know about our existence. We do not give them any breaks to know us better. They only know that UFOs are real, nothing more.[15]

Their lack of interest in our politics is due to their own feeling about governments:

> But we do not desire your world, the Earth, but we desire instead that you should develop it.[16]

The UFOnauts view all of the Earth's peoples as being the same. They are not interested in our government, science, or any facet of the normal mechanics of our civilization. To them, all of these are of a very primitive nature. They are interested in the development of man himself, and care far more about the nature of his manifested higher body or aura than his scientific or political credentials. For this reason, many of the contactees are persons of no great importance to the society, though their vibrations are exemplary. It is easier to see why they do not contact government or other officials if you consider what would happen if they had been in the skies in the time of the Caesars. Do you think they would have been keen to contact Rome's top scientist, or the politicians of the day? No, their interest in us, their service to us, is not societal or indirect, but personal and individual.

> AP: May I now take Uri to Captain Mitchell to start experiments?
>
> You were not given permission to do this.
>
> AP: Since you indicated two days ago that I may tell everything, may I reveal your presence to any outsider now?
>
> Not yet. You may start a motion picture and reveal everything. You may go ahead with everything but do not reveal to anybody yet that we are truly so near to you.[17]

The UFOnauts desire a dissemination of information about their presence, but they are aiming for a method of advertising that does not bully the customer. They want Earthmen to be made aware of their presence and their message in a gradual way, and they are in some instances not quite sure just how much can be tolerated by the public without producing difficulties from adverse opinions and fear.

In URI we see again the UFOnaut's attitude towards contact with us. Even though it seems cumbersome to deal with the seeming hocus-pocus of contactees instead of just landing in plain sight of all and dealing directly with us, yet still this indirect way is preferred. Because not all of the population of our planet, by any means, wants this forced addition to their sure knowledge. Not everyone wants their world to expand. As IS put it:

> We have been checking out all the human race, and we came to the conclusion that only panic and disaster may appear when we will land on your earth in a few years. We wanted to give you, and test you,

> how deep in conscience you can go in telling the human race that we people exist—we creatures, as you call us in science-fictioned terms—on earth. ...
>
> ... the human race is an anxious and unacceptable race. Andrija Puharich, Uri Geller, and Shimshon Strang, we still need your will of mind for our purposes, and we shall keep on using you. From today ... you will be completely independent. You shall decide for yourselves. You shall go on with work. The way you figure out, that is the best. But you must stay in close contact with us.[18]

G. H. Williamson also suggests that, to the UFOnauts, we are an "anxious and unacceptable" bunch:

> Many people today are asking: "If spacemen are here, why don't they land and contact our leaders? Why don't they explain their mission?" Did these same individuals ever stop to think that no sane Earthman would descend into a pit of crawling rattlesnakes? With all Earth's strife, with bloody wars that carry thousands of men, women and children to slaughter worse than any Circus of Nero or Medieval inquisition, is it any wonder that spacemen have not landed here?[19]

Although from our own point of view this seems a rather harsh thing to say about man on Earth, from the standpoint of our own ideals of behavior, our wars and other negative acts do seem indefensible. So that, from the unflinching standpoint of our own ethical standards, we would have to say the same harsh thing. I personally do not have the answer to how we can stop wars, for each time we see men do things to people we care about which are harmful, they become our enemy, and it seems right to defend ourselves. To get from where we are to the point where there are no wars will take plenty of meditation!

I have stated earlier that the only real result of our lives on Earth is the evolution of our essential selves, call it the evolution of mind or progression of spirit. The UFOnauts want us to arrive at a more evolved state of thinking by the only process which is effective in causing real evolvement: our own independent seeking of the truth of the meaning of our existence. The visitors to our planet are very willing to help us, but always they back off before a contactee can prove his source. Always they let the contactee tell his story at second-hand. Then the stimulus of other life in the universe will occur only to those who are ready to hear it. As the UFO contacts say, the knowledge of all truth is within everyone. Meditation can stimulate the memory of our true nature and relationship to the creation.

There are strict rules of Confederation contact with planets such as ours. The non-interference rule which governed the STAR TREK crew covers it very well.

There is another problem in dealing with this "anxious and unacceptable" people of Earth: many in our society do not desire mental evolution in the direction of these particular UFOnauts. The Confederation is a group strongly polarized in philosophical or spiritual terms towards the "good," towards unity of all things, towards merging in oneness with the Creator. In sharp contrast, many of our people are on a path of separation, of self as set against the rest of the universe.

The Confederation sees this line of separation as an error but respects the right of each man to choose his own direction. You can see that, although the message of these Confederation brothers is spiritual, there is nothing of religion proper in their approach: they do not believe in the "hard sell" type of conversions! When Puharich asked IS whether the mass landing would still take place, if the Earth's people remained "unacceptable," IS replied, "There shall be landings on Earth. But the landings might be invisible, and only visible to you."[20] Many contactees comment on this ability of the craft to seemingly appear to some and not to others, and to appear and disappear from our skies instantly:

> But there is another way too in which we are capable of working. That is in projecting our astral bodies into the third dimension. In other words, fourth dimensionally we can project into your third dimension. The experience would be extremely real to you, and of course real to us, but it is not the physical body that you would see at that time.[21]

> Not all will see the spaceship because some of them are etheric in nature ...[22]

> It has not been seen in the physical, but it shall be seen by those who have eyes to see. And then, when it is necessary, after most of the cleansing has been completed, it will take on material form. But nothing would be accomplished by materializing the ship at this time. Other ships have been seen coming from the etheric into the material and then dematerializing, and little has been accomplished except to make a very, very few think and spread the word.[23]

> That is why some of you see spaceships and others do not. They are actually vibrating at a different frequency. Sometimes they can change their frequency to correspond with your visual or your physical sightings or senses. Then you or a group can see them. But for the most part they are in operation at another frequency and you cannot see them. Those with the higher senses can see them, even when they are invisible to others, because their senses are tuned to it. Those people are often scoffed at because they say there is something to be seen and others see nothing with the physical eye.[24]

> If we chose to remain unseen, we could do so easily and, in fact, we have done so almost without exception for hundreds of years. No one sees us unless we want to be seen.[25]

The Hatonn source gives a slightly different slant to the details of this visible/invisible characteristic:

> Each person has a vibration from eternity to eternity. At any given moment, each person vibrates in an individual manner. Therefore as we vibrate in our individual manners, from dimension to dimension, there are some who, with their higher vibrations, may see us. We are able to appear to some, or to others, by adjusting our rate of vibration. This is, as we say, usually done for a purpose, that purpose being to alert individuals who are ready to receive this stimulus.[26]

So, IS advised Puharich that he should teach people, but not "people who cannot accept happenings."[27] "Do anything that produces energy, good works."[28] Then, IS bid them adieu: "Although we are always with you people, we shall stay away from this human race for a couple of years."[29] The one exception was that they would continue to work through Uri: "We are not interfering in any way. We are just letting things happen sometimes for Uri."[30]

I had an interesting demonstration of this last statement while returning from a UFO research convention on October 19, 1975. I was piloting a Beechcraft Baron, which is a light airplane, and I experienced a total malfunction of the artificial horizon. This is the primary instrument used to maintain level flight during bad weather, when there are no visual references that the pilot can see. In cloudy conditions, the real horizon disappears, so the artificial horizon is all-important.

The artificial horizon is similar in its malfunctioning to a flat tire, in that it never fixes itself. You either replace it or repair it. But, after being inoperative for over an hour, my artificial horizon started working perfectly again just when I became in need of it. This was so unusual a thing to happen that I doubted whether I could convince the maintenance mechanic that it had malfunctioned at all, and for this reason I took a witness to the phenomenon when I talked to the technician back at the hangar.

Five days later, I was visiting Uri Geller in the Las Vegas Hilton, and just happened to mention the strange occurrence with the gyro horizon. He immediately became very excited and started looking for a manila folder. I noticed the corner of a manila folder sticking out from some other papers right beside me and fished it out. "Is this it?" I asked. Note please, skeptics, that the folder was only a few inches from me, so that Geller had no opportunity to write in it. Since I had not been in previous contact with him or any of his associates for about a year, it is highly unlikely that he would have found out about the malfunction.

"Open it, open it up," he shouted. I did, and found the following notation scrawled across the first page:

> Horizon went out!!
>
> Plane?

Comparison of our activities showed that when I was having my troubles in the air on the 19th, near Evansville, Indiana, Uri had been listening to stereo music on his headset in his New York City home. Over the music, Uri suddenly heard a voice say, "Horizon went out." He didn't know what the statement meant, so he wrote it down on the folder. Then he felt energy flow through him, like when he fixes something. But this made no sense to him, and he forgot about it. Until he heard my story.

"I guess I fixed your horizon," he said. "It sure looks that way," I replied. We then noticed an ashtray in the middle of the floor that had not previously been there. As I commented on this, a small bottle flew spontaneously from the desk across the room, sharply striking a window some ten feet distant. The bottle hit glass with such a resounding crash that I was surprised that nothing was broken. "I fixed it, I fixed your horizon," said Uri. "That's how they tell me." When Puharich reported his dog vanishing instantaneously, articles appearing and disappearing due to Uri's presence, people found it hard to believe him. I suppose you still find it hard to believe my story. When it happens to you personally, you have no choice but to witness to the truth.

The book URI contains a description of the state of meditation from a more physiological point of view:

> Molecules in brain cells are only positively open when excitement is not strong. Normal excitement overcomes the vibration to our powers. Brain should be in a very relaxed state to receive messages from us.[31]

This is the same state with which I have experimented, as have many others, in producing telepathic contact with UFO sources.

One last tie-in from URI to the body of contactee data occurs unexpectedly. Puharich reports a string of odd occurrences having to do with some pens on his desk which had flipped up out of their holder and fallen in a pattern which spelled out the word "WHY":

> At 3:45 P.M. I returned to my study, where I found Uri doodling at my desk. I looked at what he had just doodled. It was a set of very advanced tensor equations describing the nature of the gravitational field. Uri did not know what he had just doodled, and he asked me where this came from. Since I recognized the equations as being of the form written by Albert Einstein, I replied, almost facetiously, "Einstein." As I said this, there appeared a piece of paper on the floor some ten feet away from me. I walked over to pick it up. It was a newspaper photo of Albert Einstein! I remembered seeing such a photo in the NEW YORK TIMES MAGAZINE some ten years earlier. I had clipped it out but had not seen it for several years. At this vantage point I was looking at my bed across the hall from where I was standing. In front of my eyes there had appeared a book on the white bedspread. I walked over to examine it. It was a book I had last seen in the basement; it was by Edwin F. Taylor and John Archibald Wheeler, entitled SPACETIME PHYSICS, published by W. H. Freeman and Company in 1963. I looked through it carefully, but the equations that Uri had doodled were not in this book, although the general subject matter was there.
>
> Throughout all this activity I had left the nine pens on my blotter pad intact spelling out the word "why." I returned to my study with Uri—holding the book. As we approached the desk, right in front of our eyes the nine pens flipped simultaneously in the air and settled down into a new pattern as follows (though I did not understand the symbolism or meaning of the configuration[32]

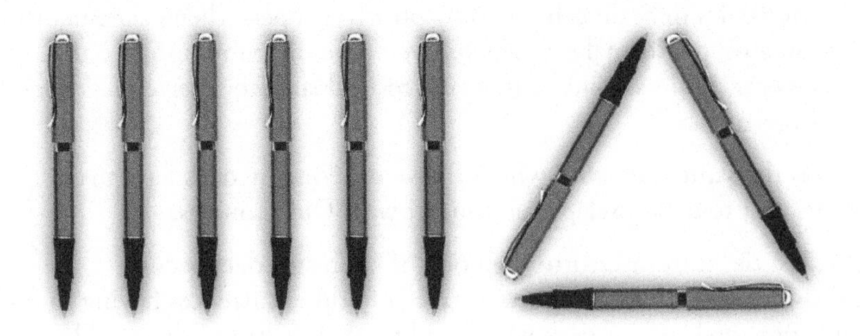

After I read URI, I decided to see if I could get a response from the UFO source on this arrangement of pens. I used two of my best telepathic subjects to try to discover the possible significance of this pattern to the UFOnauts who had sent it to Puharich. They came up with the following answers, quite independently of each other:

1. The six straight lines are the Creator's house, the triangle represents the Creator.
2. The six straight lines represent the three dimensions of time plus the three dimensions of space; the triangle represents the Creator.

So, in both cases, the triangle was said to represent the Creator. The subject who received the impression that the six upright pens symbolized the Creator's house was not a scientist; the other subject was one.

I immediately referred back to Dewey B. Larson's analysis of the physical universe as possessing three dimensions of space and three of time. And I have to agree that, translated from the mathematical language of dimensionality, three dimensions of time and three of space are the same as saying, "the Creator's house" in Larsonian physics.

Here is Hoova's statement concerning UFOs:

> Most of these reports by humans are due to hallucinations and aberrations. But some of our units have landed. But most of the reported landings have been from other visitors from space—some of whom we do not see, but which you can see. They are of different vibrations, different spaces, different velocities. We are the only ones who are mostly here. The other visitors come and go. We stay.[33]

This is precisely our understanding of the situation as communicated through telepathic receivers.

I'd like to look again at the essence of the anti-dogmatic yet spiritual type of message which telepathic receivers so often report. Note the characteristics: a desire to help people, a fitting in with the religious belief of the culture to which the contact is made, a desire to help prevent wars, and a strong motivation to open peoples' awareness:

> Ah, we know the past of the human race. But this is one of the secrets—we cannot tell it to you. As to the future we are not permitted either. But remember all that people need to do—God has written on stone, the ten commandments. Thus shall it be done. Remember you are working for us in ways that are important to us, and which we have not yet explained. Actually, there is no special message for you to pass to the human race. It is possible that should there be a war impending, as between Russia and China, there may be a message to prevent it. But you may try to open their minds with things like telepathy and psychokinesis—things which we have almost forgotten. Yes, they are to be helped.[34]

There's one more interesting correlation between a statement by IS and material in OAHSPE. Remember this passage:

> We want you to prepare this Earth for our mass landing, a mass landing on Earth. We landed in South America 3000 years ago, and now we must land again.[35]

With it in mind, look at these passages from OAHSPE:

> And Jehovih caused the earth, and the family of the sun to travel in an orbit, the circuit of which requireth of them four million seven hundred thousand years. And he placed in the line of the orbit, at distances of three thousand years, etherean lights, the which places, as the earth passeth through, angels from the second heaven come into its corporeal presence. As ambassadors they come, in companies of hundreds and thousands and tens of thousands, and these are called the etherean hosts of the Most High. Not as single individuals come they: not for a single individual mortal come they.[36]

> First the earth plieth in a circuit around the sun, which circuit is divided into four arcs called spring, summer, autumn, and winter.
>
> Second, the sun, with his family, plieth in a large circuit, which is divided into one thousand five hundred arcs, the distance of which for each arc is about three thousand years, or one cycle.[37]

Here is the idea of the cycles, with a more specific discussion of how long they are. Just what are these cycles? How do they affect us? And why must the UFOs appear during the cycle-change? One general reason for the

UFOs' appearing is quoted by researcher Brad Steiger in his book, REVELATION: THE DIVINE FIRE:

> The craft that contains the instrument in which I am recorded is four and three-tenths miles in length—by your method of measurement—and two and one-tenth miles in circumference. This craft also contains others of us who are in human form. I have passed the phase of human form. My knowledge and mind processes were long ago recorded into an instrument you would liken to a computer.
>
> I was brought to the vicinity of this planet approximately thirty thousand years ago, by your method of time measurement. Your planet and the living forms upon it have a specific value to us. Your form of life has a particular value to us.
>
> For this reason, at about the time I was brought to the vicinity of your world, we interfered with the natural development of the species of man that inhabited this planet. Our purpose was to shorten the cycle of development necessary for the human inhabitants of this planet to be of use to us.[38]

Interestingly enough, in URI we read that IS also reports a computer or computer-like state:

> Andrija Puharich, you must understand, in this state we are computers.[39]

But, be they computers or humans, or entities of an unknown and novel kind entirely, the question remains: why do they appear at the cycle's change? And what is a cycle? These are questions important enough in the space contactee message to deserve a chapter to themselves.

Chapter Eight

The Wanderers

George Hunt Williamson, an anthropologist of considerable reputation, began reporting UFO contact in the early '50s. He published several books about his contactee experiences, none of which were seriously given credence or consideration by his peers. The books contain much that we still consider untrue: the UFOnauts had told Williamson that the Sun was not a "hot, flaming body" but a cool body, and that we had two moons, one a "dark" moon which was unseen. He was told, moreover, that the moon we already know about had an atmosphere and water. Obviously, none of these statements make sense.

But let us back up a bit and look at these statements again considering not our third density alone but also those densities which interpenetrate ours. Since most of the UFOnauts are in a reality displaced from ours, it is quite possible that they are experiencing these described conditions. In fact, if the Williamson book, THE SAUCERS SPEAK!, is read keeping the physical and mental variants of these displaced realities in mind, the material makes quite a bit of sense.

In the SAUCERS SPEAK, Williamson quotes the UFO source as saying, "To apples we salt, we return." No explanation is given of it here, but in a later work, OTHER TONGUES, OTHER FLESH, he interprets the statement as a promise made to a certain type of individual on Earth. It seems that throughout the history of Earth, people have been born into our planetary vibration who are not Earth natives; that is, they have not incarnated into the physical from Earth's spiritual densities, but from elsewhere. They are true extraterrestrials in that their previous experience is of places elsewhere in the universe; they are true Earth natives in that they have gone through the process of birth, entering first the spiritual realms of Earth and from there incarnating into our physical plane just as any Earth entity would do. During the birth process, the "apple" usually loses the memory of his extraterrestrial past. He is truly of this planet as he enters its physical plane.

His purpose in coming to Earth is twofold. First, he hopes to advance his own vibration or thinking by experiencing the strong catalyst of our physical world. It is a sort of trial-by-fire approach, the chance to advance more rapidly than is possible in less dense vibrations. Secondly, he hopes that he will be able to reawaken the dormant memory of why he came to Earth, and so be able to carry out his mission of service to Earthmen by helping to increase their awareness of universal reality.

It is not a foregone conclusion that the "apple" will remember who he is and what his mission is, but most "apples" have at least a strongly developed tendency towards meditation and contemplation, so that gradually many are indeed able to recapture at least a portion of that memory. Here is the portion of OTHER TONGUES which deals with this:

> There were several statements made in THE SAUCERS SPEAK that are significant in connection with these "Wanderers" or "Apples." "Seeds may be planted but they can rot and never reach maturity." This means that the people of outer space knew what was going to develop on Earth. They "planted" some of their own people here; "salted" them away like "apples." But every seed that is planted or "salted away" does not grow and reach maturity; it may rot in the ground because of many conditions. Therefore some of the "Wanderers" now on Earth do not know who they are—they are lost in the ways of the Earth, and on physical death will return to their own worlds. They will be none the worse for their experience, except that their mission will not be accomplished.
>
> Space intelligences knew that a certain percentage of the "apples" would fall by the way, therefore enough of them incarnated into Earth bodies to make up for this inevitable deficiency.[1]

The source who channels through Nada-Yolanda says much the same thing:

> You have people who have come from other planets who know no such thing as life on other planets, who even may not believe in life on other planets. Yet, they are in your Earth's atmosphere waiting, living the life—normal, so-called average, everyday, prosaic lives, according to you who are studying—and they still are receiving.
>
> Their teachers are around them. Their high Selves know who they are and what their destiny is. Not everyone will succeed. Many will go through the life experience and never be aware, and waste or not make gain. But they are neither to be judged nor condemned.[2]

The concept of there being entities from other worlds is an intriguing one to many people who indeed have never felt at home on this planet, living the Earth life. In general, "apples" are said to be poorly suited to the third density vibration, and have problems adjusting to the socio-economic web of our culture; indeed, often they also have persistent health problems. But they do not appear alien or extraordinary: they are just people:

> ... there are many people on Earth that don't really belong here! This doesn't mean that they came here aboard a Flying Saucer, disembarked, put on a tweed suit, polished up their English language and moved into the house next door. It does mean, however, that there is a special class or order of beings in the Universe that are different from the rest because of the fact that they wander from one world to another, and from one system to another.[3]

These people, however, tend to be set apart by their inherent bias towards the kind of love and brotherhood-oriented message that the Confederation is bringing. That is what it is hoped will happen to the "apples": that they will awaken and remember that they are here to give light to Planet Earth.

From the early Williamson book, THE SAUCERS SPEAK:

> Ponnar speaking. There are now many young people in your world who understand our message. They will accept it quickly for they are of the New Age. The Great Awakening is here. Many of our people are in your world now. ...[4]

And, from Nada-Yolanda:

> We have contacted key units because they are teaching this new understanding or Aquarian development now. That is why we come through in this way. Why do we not come through to your government heads or your very educated scientists; education, to your way of thinking, of course? Because they could not change the temperature of the mass consciousness, for they do not believe in thought transference or thought control or thought power.
>
> But your key units do, and that is why we contact them primarily; secondarily, because they are us. Many of them have incarnated purposely from our realms, dimensions, and other planets to do this work, knowing how to do it.
>
> We ask you to remember it. We ask you, and stimulate you through our control and through our interest in you and through our mental communication and spiritual education with you, to do this. That is why we have concentrated for so many years—twenty-five years, to use a loose segment of time—in teaching these New Age thoughts to those already planted, so they could begin to regulate the thought temperature of mass-consciousness. It takes time. Now is the time for us to show ourselves and to make the project a physical manifestation.[5]

The extraterrestrial source known as Ishkomar adds its footnote on "apples":

> By mutual agreement between a planetary dweller and an inhabitant of our craft, the knowledge and the memory of one of us may be blended with the planetary without the loss of the receiver's identity. The one from our group adds only his knowledge to the planetary dweller, and the abandoned body is disseminated. This blending may not take place without mutual agreement between the beings involved, and the planetary dweller must fully agree and desire this blending. We seek, therefore, not to take, but to give.
>
> We, however, are not alone in our interests in your world. There is in existence with us another group. Their interests are not necessarily harmful toward you, yet their methods are in direct opposition to ours. They also have interfered with the development of your planet. They wish to reach their ends, not by cooperation, but by control and domination ...
>
> You must reach a high level of mental development and knowledge to be able to understand our purposes. We have attempted to gain your cooperation for thousands of years. We have been vigorously opposed by the other group. We must achieve our goal by guidance of your kind, but we must desire guidance for us to be of assistance to you.[6]

This source describes a type of "apple" which is no doubt very heavily in the minority; there must be very few of these around. But I do think they exist.

However, our main interest in this chapter is to explore the concept of the "apple" developed by Williamson and others, for I do think that there are very many of these "apples" among us today. As I said, few if any serious researchers paid any real attention to Williamson's and others' contactee information, since it seemed to be unsupported in any way and quite unverifiable. It may be that this situation has changed now, to some extent, for I have found interesting evidence which supports this contactee information about "apples."

I started doing age regression hypnosis in 1955. The general technique is to produce the deepest state of hypnosis possible in a particular subject, and then suggest a retrograding of memory, back through childhood, and then to birth. Most people are able under hypnosis to remember and describe in exhaustive detail not only the exact environment into which they were born but the details of the delivery, sensation by sensation. The subconscious mind seems to store memory independently of the normal functioning of conscious perceptions.

The subject is now at the point of birth into this world, and the suggestion is made that he go further back in time, and remember what has occurred previous to this birth. Most subjects relate several Earth lives as the guide patiently listens and asks questions of the subject. Many, many people are true Earth children in the spiritual sense, and in age regression you find their trail as it leads through tinker, tailor, merchant, thief, etc. However, every once in a while I have come across subjects who, when regressed beyond birth, leave our Earth planes entirely. These seeming "apples" that I have uncovered give information that correlates substantially with Williamson's "apple" data. I have selected material from my files on three of these "apples" because they independently claimed to have known each other as extraterrestrials, and thus their testimony forms a fuller picture, one story fitting into the next. I have edited out the parts of the regressions having to do with this life.

I have deleted the names of the three subjects and substituted the initials "A," "B," and "C" to indicate the identity of the speaker. As you follow this story through, please remember that I am not suggesting that all the "apples" come from this one place described by these three subjects. "Apples" come from many places. Their cultures and personal details vary widely. What they have in common is their motive and mission here on Earth. I am including the personal details concerning this one small group's life in another world, however, because it adds a depth to their fascinating story.

We start with the physical appearance of these people. They look quite human and rather Nordic:

C

OK, YOUR OWN SKIN, YOUR OWN COLOR WOULD BE DESCRIBED MOST CLEARLY AS WHAT?

Very light. Blonde.

WHITISH?

No. Yellow.

A

They are … I keep seeing just one man there.

PICK THAT MAN OUT AND JUST CONCENTRATE ON HIM.

He is tall. There is much bright vibration coming from him. It's very hard to explain appearances. He has long hair.

IS HIS HEAD COVERED AT ALL?

Just by vibration, by white ... we see each other and he smiles.

HOW DO YOU FEEL ABOUT THE EXCHANGE OF GLANCES AND THAT SMILE?

I feel that he is somehow important to me, but right now, he's ... he's just a good man. We are wearing robes. That is my impression, white robes. Appearances don't mean anything, but there's vibration. But he has such a kind face, all full of light.

IS HIS FACE BEARDED, SHAVEN?

No, it's ... he has no hair on his face.

AND THE COLOR?

It is a golden color.

HIS HEIGHT WOULD BE ABOUT WHAT, IN TERMS OF FEET AND INCHES?

About seven feet.

IN TERMS OF POUNDS, HIS WEIGHT WOULD BE ABOUT WHAT?

He is so slender ... very light.

YOU JUST PASS HIM, AND CONTINUE ON YOUR WAY.

Yes.

One great difference between our Earth race and theirs seems to be the aging factor: they count "time" in quite a different way.

A

YOU ARE ABOUT HOW OLD?

(Pause) It doesn't mean anything.

HOW LONG HAVE YOU BEEN THERE?

My body's size is not as tall as this one. But mine has been there for a long time. Age is a hard thing ... I cannot see age. I feel old. I feel young. I feel wonderment at what I've seen.

VERY WELL. ARE THE OTHER PEOPLE OLDER OR YOUNGER THAN YOU ARE?

They seem to be perhaps a little older. Once again, age here doesn't show. Well, it shows, but it's not connected with numbers. It is simply physical appearance.

I feel very old and yet when I saw myself I was not old. Today we simply have a different physical appearance.

C

LET'S GO BACK TO AGE 26 THEN. ONE, TWO, THREE, (snap).

All right. I seem to be rather old.

THEN YOUR YEAR IS DIFFERENT FROM AN EARTH YEAR, THEN, ISN'T IT?

Yeah, must be.

AND YOUR APPEARANCE? AND YOUR MATE'S APPEARANCE? HOW WOULD YOU APPEAR TO BE?

Just the same. But old.

YOUR APPEARANCE DOES NOT CHANGE, BUT YOU JUST PHYSICALLY DETERIORATE, THEN?

It's a slowing down of energy, as much as anything.

The normal mode of person-to-person communication seems to be telepathy:

A

DO YOU COMMUNICATE VERBALLY, BY SOUND?

Not very much. No, most of it is mind-reading. Telepathy. There is not much use for words with the teachers.

B

YES. WHAT ABOUT COMMUNICATING WITH ANOTHER INDIVIDUAL. IS IT BY VERBAL COMMUNICATION, BY VOICE FORM. DID YOU TALK OR LISTEN?

There was some of that, but mostly minds.

YOU HAD MOUTH AND VOICES AND EARS? SO YOU COULD COMMUNICATE IF YOU WANTED TO?

> Yes, but much was done with mind. The ... the importance was done with mind.

These otherworlders seem to enjoy considerably more freedom than we as regards the boundaries of consciousness. They have the ability to move out of the physical body in consciousness, very much at will. There are many on Earth who have had such experiences, but it is not common here; it seems to be common there. One "apple" mentioned by George Hunt Williamson, Nikola Tesla, certainly used the other dimensions while he was here. He is reported to have been able to visualize his inventions in precise detail. He would say to someone, "Here is my experiment. Can't you see it? I've been running it for three days. Tomorrow I'll disassemble it and inspect it for wear." The observer could see nothing. Yet with these invisible experiments, Tesla made significant advances in science, and is the father of alternating current theory and application. Tesla was using the power of his mind to create devices on the finer planes of existence. "C" talks about these planes:

> Well, in the body, there is a great difference in the potential there. It is known to be greater, so that there are many more different kinds of people there than here.
>
> AM I TO TAKE IT THAT YOU ARE TALKING ABOUT LEAVING YOUR BODY?
>
> Not exactly. It is an extension with oneness with the body yet the dimension extra other than you can work in and affect you here, and it is real, and it is a lot of fun. It is not a leaving of the body, it is not a dissociation from the body; it is an extension of intelligence, not through the body but the other way around. First the dimension which means you can move in and out of the body into the extensions of the body into different dimensions, then by these it is much more easy to be helpful. It is difficult to be of use when kept within the body, without the other dimensions. Yet there were dimensions there that we could not enter although we knew of them.

To these "apples" on their home planet, death does not seem to pose the threat it tends to on Earth. Life and death seem to be perceived with some clarity as one flowing substance.

> C
>
> ALL RIGHT. I BELIEVE YOU ARE GOING TO LEAVE THE LIFE HERE SOON?
>
> Yes.

YOU WILL NOT APPROACH THE AGE OF THIRTY?

No.

IS IT A TRAUMATIC EXPERIENCE?

Not at all.

ALL RIGHT. WILL YOU GO TO THAT POINT?

My heart stopped. That's all.

IS YOUR MATE WITH YOU?

He was, yes.

HE WAS? AND WHAT HAPPENED TO HIM?

I don't know.

HE'S STILL ALIVE?

He stayed by where I was for a while.

AFTER LIFE HAD LEFT THE BODY, IS THERE A SOUL AS WE KNOW A SOUL AND WHAT HAPPENS TO IT?

Yes. I stayed there for quite some time.

WHICH WOULD MEAN FOR A FEW DAYS, OR A FEW WEEKS, OR ... ?

I waited for my mate. He taught for some months.

YES. IS HE AWARE OF YOUR PRESENCE?

Oh, yes.

B

YOU LEAVE THAT PLANET? WHEN YOU LEAVE WILL YOU DIE A DEATH, OR WILL YOU JUST TRANSFER OR MOVE ON? HOW WILL IT WORK OUT?

It has to do with the ship, but ... I will have to leave here, but I don't understand about the death. When it ... I just know ... I believe the leaving takes place without the body, but it has to do with a ship. But there will ... there is a body, but it is not the same as a tangible one. That one is ... I believe ... it is unnecessary for the journey.

THEN HOW DOES THE SEPARATION TAKE PLACE? WILL YOU GO UP TO THAT POINT, AND TELL ME STEP BY

STEP? HOW DOES THE SOUL GET INTO THE SHIP AND LEAVE THE BODY? IF THAT'S WHAT HAPPENS.

I'm ... ss ... I'm on a ... I look ... looking, over the temple can see it ... The time ... somehow the leaving is connected with that. With the ship ... I see them ...

HEROTA, WILL YOU GO ON UP TO THE DEPARTURE, AND DESCRIBE IT VERY CAREFULLY FOR ME.

I am old. Old ...

HOW DOES IT TAKE PLACE? HOW DO YOU GET THERE, HOW DO YOU GET INTO THE SHIP, DOES THIS TAKE PLACE—

It seems ... it seems that the old beloved shell is no longer needed and, as we go in the ship, we become new. We become new and young, but not with physical bodies at this time, but new and young. (sigh) Spirit bodies like—bodies, but not the same. But the sadness of leaving disappears with the old shell that was much loved. And we're new and ready. (sigh).

So we begin to get a picture of the tall, fair race of people that live a many-dimensioned life, whose basic consciousnesses dwell less on the things of the body and more on the things of the finer planes than perhaps do ours on Earth. What sort of environment do these "apples" enjoy? First, it is definitely stated that the planet is not Earth:

A

DO YOU KNOW WHERE YOU ARE? ARE YOU ON MOTHER EARTH?

No.

DO YOU HAVE ANY IDEA WHERE YOU ARE?

No ...

B

UNITED STATES, OR EUROPE?

No, no, it's no place that I've seen on Earth. I don't think it's part of Earth. It's no place that I've seen here. But I don't know.

Though the planet is not Earth, it seems to be quite Earthlike:

A

OK. IS THERE AN ATMOSPHERE?

Yes.

C

DOES THE PLANET HAVE AN ATMOSPHERE? IS IT SOLID, LIKE THIS ONE?

The Planet's a lot like this one.

SAME GRAVITY?

No, not quite. Slightly easier to get around. But very similar. Very similar.

WHAT IS IT LIKE?

Nice. Much water, little land, great riches in the ocean, great minerals. Ah, that's it. That's why they're all metal.

"They" refers to the buildings the subject had just talked about.

B

DO YOU HAVE LAKES, RIVERS, STREAMS, OCEANS?

There is water.

OK. DO YOU HAVE FISH?

I don't know. There is much water.

Their planet, call it Otherworld, has the same day-night that we do, suggesting that they also revolve.

A

DO YOU GET TIRED, AND REST AND SLEEP?

Yes.

IS THERE ALWAYS DARKNESS, OR IS THERE LIGHT AND THEN DARK?

Light and then dark.

THERE IS DAY AND THEN NIGHT.

Yes.

B

NOW, YOU MENTIONED, HEROT, THAT IT WAS DAYLIGHT, AND THE SUN WAS SHINING. IS IT ALSO NIGHT TIME?

There is. I don't see that there is night now but I know that there is.

There seem to be cities and country, though apparently not like our rural areas:

B

ALL RIGHT. NOW, WHERE DO YOU LIVE? WHERE IS ALL THIS TAKING PLACE?

This place is removed from a city, but it's perfect. It's not like wild country, it's perfect. It's harmonious.

Not in the city. Like the country, but ... there's a sidewalk that goes from down the hill up the hill. I'm up the hill. There's ... almost a circle where I am. And then down the hill again.

HOW MANY ENTITIES WERE ON THAT PLANET?

I don't know.

THOUSANDS?

I don't know. I have impressions that there were cities. This was not part of it, exactly.

MILLIONS?

Many, but I ... I don't really see the rest. I see our part, here.

Here is some description of the cities on Otherworld: streets, people, metal buildings.

A

DO YOU HAVE A HOME?

It seems like I am just walking down the street, down this long ...

OK, TELL ME ABOUT THE STREETS. AND ABOUT THE PEOPLE, AND THE TRANSPORTATION.

I don't see any transportation. People are out on the streets. I am just walking, and there are children. I play. They all wave. A very happy time.

C

It seems like what I saw was a lot of metal, like metal buildings, something like that.

GO AHEAD WITH IT.

OK. It seems that I am a young boy or girl of apparently another world.

GO AHEAD WITH IT.

And the world has metal buildings.

A

NOW AS BEST YOU CAN, TELL ME ABOUT THESE BUILDINGS ... WINDOWS, ROOFS, WALLS, LIGHTS—

They've got glass tops—domes—just smooth. I can't see them here, windows or anything like that. There seem to be roads—wide roads that wind around through the domes. On the right there's some tall structure, I can't ... I don't understand—at least that's where the things that are going up in the air are coming from.

AS WELL AS YOU CAN, DESCRIBE THE TALLER STRUCTURE.

Well, it seems circular on the very top, but it's much taller than the rest of the city. It's like a long diamond shape except that it goes in in the middle instead of out. It's circular at the bottom and at the top.

IN OTHER WORDS, IT'S LIKE A BIG HOUR GLASS?

Right.

OK. NOW THE FORMS GOING UP IN THE AIR. ARE THEY COMING FROM THE TOP OF THIS STRUCTURE?

I don't know. At first I saw something go up, maybe two things go up; now I don't see them.

THINGS? LIKE WHAT?

Objects.

SOLID OBJECTS? BALLOONS?

No, solid objects, round ...

A CRAFT?

Most probably. It's too hard to say.

WAS THERE ANY SOUND INVOLVED?

No.

OK. BUT THERE WAS A LIGHT THAT WAS IN THIS?

Yes.

Here is further information on the craft which seemed to be coming out of the tall structure:

B

WHAT ABOUT TRAVEL? DO YOU HAVE VEHICLES?

Hm ... somehow ... from the ...

HOW DO YOU TRAVEL FROM ONE CITY TO ANOTHER? ON THE GROUND, OR UP OFF THE GROUND?

I saw, from the top of this, I can't tell if it's the temple, I think ... I, no, I can't tell if it's the temple, but its a rounded building from the top of which metallic, round vehicles come and go. I just see the glimmer in the night.

OK, DESCRIBE THOSE VEHICLES. DO THEY HAVE WINGS, LIKE AIRPLANES?

No, no, no. They ... (pause).

HOW DO THEY LIFT UP AND SUPPORT THEMSELVES? AND HOW DO THEY GO?

It has to do again with these things. ...invisible conce ...

THE ELECTROMAGNETIC WIRES.

It's invisible, but it has to do with that.

YES.

Um, but it's ... they're metallic. I can only see them from a distance.

HAVE YOU BEEN IN THEM?

At this moment I am looking from a distance. As ... There seems to be ...

THERE SEEMS TO BE WHAT?

The way of seeing out comes from the side. There is a ... a ... as in a brim of a hat, all around, sloping slightly upward to the windows around, and then a slightly sloped top, but mostly these that I see are,

> not flat but more round, more flat than elevated. They're round, with the lip of the hat going slightly upward, and windows around at that point where it meets. The top with nothing on, the top is smooth, and silver, blank. It has almost a white light in the starlight. There are more than one, they, they are to be used.

The craft sound suspiciously like what we would call flying saucers—a very painstaking description from a subject who had not previously pored over pictures of such vehicles.

"B" also tells us about what communications are like on Otherworld:

> WHAT ABOUT COMMUNICATIONS FROM ONE CITY TO ANOTHER? DID YOU COMMUNICATE?
>
> Invisible wires. Wires—that comes to mind. They were wires but they were not visible.
>
> DID YOU COMMUNICATE WITH ...
>
> Mag ...
>
> YES, GO AHEAD.
>
> Ah ... not ... magnetic ... I don't know the concept, I know, I can't—it was through hidden wires, wires hidden, they were not visible. Um, but they had to do with ... something magnetic—Electromagne ... ?
>
> ELECTROMAGNETIC?
>
> I don't know what, but they were ours, the communication of the power from the temple, and any communication needed came from those. Came from this. But it was like invisible lines going out that had, that had power.

Although each subject was questioned to some extent about the political and governmental setup of their country or planet, no information was forthcoming from these people, who in their Otherworld life must have been quite uninvolved in politics, either because of their place within their society allowing them freedom from the day-to-day politics of the culture, or because their culture was not a politically structured one. It seems possible that people who have mastered the extraphysical dimensions described earlier, and who are telepathic, might well be able to function as a society without the ponderous bureaucracy and decision-making machinery of our political systems.

The Otherworlders had a good deal of trouble trying to express where their planet was in relation to Earth:

C

CAN YOU GIVE ME ANY IDEA OF WHICH PLANET WE ARE TALKING ABOUT?

No.

ALL RIGHT. NOW, IN TERMS OF EARTH TIME, ARE YOU AWARE OF OTHER PLANETS IN THE SOLAR SYSTEM OTHER THAN YOUR OWN?

Yes.

ALL RIGHT. ARE YOU AWARE OF PLANET EARTH?

No.

ALL RIGHT. WHICH PLANETS ARE YOU FAMILIAR WITH? DO YOU KNOW ANY OF THEM BY NAME, OR DO YOU CALL THEM NAMES?

I don't know.

ARE YOU OF THE SAME SOLAR SYSTEM AS THE EARTH? DO YOU HAVE THE SAME SUN?

No.

A DIFFERENT SUN?

Yes.

A DIFFERENT UNIVERSE, THEN?

Same universe, different time. Different dimension.

ALL RIGHT. SAME UNIVERSE, BUT IN A DIFFERENT DIMENSION OF THAT SAME UNIVERSE?

Yes, that's right.

ALL RIGHT, I UNDERSTAND. IN TERMS OF TIME, HOW WOULD YOU DESCRIBE THAT AS RELATED TO EARTH TIME OR UNIVERSAL TIME.

Time. I see more ... I see time easily. I am not as able to move about, yet I can ... time is more like water. It is more easily penetrated.

SO YOU DO HAVE AN UNDERSTANDING OF TIME, AND A WAY TO DEAL WITH IT, THEN?

Yes.

NOW, THE FACT THAT YOU ARE TEN YEARS OF AGE. WOULD THOSE TEN YEARS RELATE TO TEN YEARS OF EARTH TIME?

It is of the body.

There is more room in time. We can move about and live and be in more depth.

A

HOW FAR IS EARTH FROM WHERE YOU ARE, IN ANY TERMS OF MEASUREMENT THAT YOU USE?

There is no measurement. It is just there.

IT'S A DIFFERENT DIMENSION? CAN YOU SEE THE EARTH FROM THAT PLACE?

No.

One last note about the Otherworld environment: their relationship with the animals:

FISH? BIRDS? ANIMALS?

They are there, but they ... They are there, but they are there as a guest when they are there. They are not always there but they will come and visit.

B

BUT YOU HAVE AN ANIMAL KINGDOM THERE?

They are there, but I don't see them now. But they are there and they are our friends.

FROM YOUR MEMORY ARE THEY SIMILAR TO EARTH ANIMALS?

I ... I don't see them. But there are animals there, that are ...

CAN YOU COMMUNICATE WITH THEM?

Without words.

On this slightly whimsical note we turn to the question of what the family life is like on Otherworld. The three subjects report a kind of extended family setting which is often attempted these days by communal groups.

C

NOW YOUR STRUCTURE, FAMILY. DO YOU HAVE BROTHERS, SISTERS?

It's not like we understand here.

OK. AS BEST YOU CAN, TELL ME THE STRUCTURE.

We're born like here. We're all of the same kind, but our people form attachments to those of natures which are harmonious not in a single but more in a community … very close, like a clan. We make no difference. I have many, say, seven or eight parents.

YOU DON'T KNOW WHICH ARE YOUR REAL PARENTS?

Yes.

YOU DO KNOW.

Yes.

BUT YOU HAVE SEVEN OR EIGHT PARENTS?

Yes.

NOW, DO YOU ACCEPT THESE AS BEING REAL PARENTS OR ADOPTED PARENTS?

They are parents.

NOW YOU WERE BORN TO ALL OF THEM?

We know who planted the seed, but the bonds between the community are completely more real than the body. Each of my parents would do anything for me. Each of my brothers and sisters make no difference about the body. We are all of a home.

NOW, YOU WERE BORN FROM ONE MOTHER.

Yes.

BUT MANY FATHERS?

No. Mated. There are mated relationships in privacy. And also each has privacy.

ARE YOU IN RELATION TO EACH OF THOSE?

What you say, "blood"—with only my Father and my Mother of the body. But I am of a family bond within the clan.

B

ALL RIGHT. HEROT, LET'S GO ON, NOW. LET'S MOVE UP LATER THAT DAY, OR ANY DAY, TO THE EVENING. ONE, TWO, THREE, (snap).

I see a smaller dwelling that's round, of the same material, that is somewhere near the temple. I think there are other of these houses also. We gather ... I believe this is where we eat. There are shining floors there.

WE? YOUR FAMILY?

Not in a tight sense. It's ... a purpose. Family of purpose. But I believe actual parents are there.

We go on now to take a look at "B"s evening meal:

B

YOUR MEALS WOULD CONSIST OF WHAT?

No animals, no animals we're eating. It's like a broth, but it's not of animals. It's a gold ... white dishes. Dishes not like dishes. Warm ... anyway, there are no animals in it. It's not harming anything. And the things we eat out of, they're ... these bowls. It's almost like a marble, they're like with ornate things around them, I mean, ornate, the same material, they're not like bowls, here.

COULD YOU DRAW A PICTURE OF ONE IF I GAVE YOU A PIECE OF PAPER?

They're like on a stand, with things coming down and holding them onto the table, and they're white, almost like marble, but not as heavy. It's like a ceremonial bowl. And all of us, there's a large one in the center from which we all eat. Someone serves us.

THE BROTH IS MADE OF GRAIN AND VEGETABLES?

I don't know. It's thick almost like ...

PORRIDGE?

But it has nothing granular in it, you can see it's smooth and fairly thick and golden.

UM HUM. SOMETHING LIKE CREAMED POTATOES OR PUMPKIN? THAT TEXTURE, THAT DENSITY?

Yeah.

BUT YOU DON'T EAT FISH.

No.

"A" and "C" also talk about food:

C

THE CROPS OF YOUR PEOPLE ARE?

In the body, the crops are grain, and a type of root, like the potato, and other—many other—things familiar to those who are like us everywhere.

A

TELL ME ABOUT THE FOOD. WHAT FOOD DO YOU EAT?

It seems that ... that you can think it, (Words inaudible) ... teachers ... Everything seems to be a lot by thought. I can't see people growing food, or making clothes—

Everything is just there, if you want it there.

DO YOU WORK, EAT, AND SLEEP LIKE HUMAN PEOPLE DO?

I am being trained not to do so much of that. Other people do more.

The clothing which these three wear is very simple and monklike:

B

I'm just waiting by the temple for something.

VERY GOOD. LET'S JUST WAIT THERE. WHAT ARE YOU WEARING?

White robe. White, loose garment.

A

ALL RIGHT. WILL YOU TELL ME ABOUT YOUR MANNER OF DRESS AND CLOTHING?

It is like ... with robes.

OK, THOSE ROBES ARE MADE OF WHAT?

(Pause) Cloth.

DOES THE MATERIAL COME FROM THAT PLANET?

Yes.

Presumably the Otherworlders have other garments which they can use when they need to be more active than they are in this temple life. One of the subjects has mentioned to me, not while in hypnosis but afterwards, that she had seen herself in a sort of jump-suit or ski-suit, comfortable and form-fitting, while she was on duty working off the planet.

Earlier I mentioned that I could not find a political consciousness within these three people. However, they do seem to have a government, but one which is dedicated totally to service, rather than to the running of a governmental self-perpetuation machine:

> C
>
> I am of a certain clan of persons that takes a special training to serve in government. We are like monks, and give all our energies to helping society. We start very young. I'm ten.

In this particular case, "C" had been born into the government-service clan. But she was not required to remain within that "caste."

> C
>
> I am studying to be helpful.
>
> VERY WELL. IS IT FORMAL STUDY, ORGANIZED STUDY?
>
> Yes.
>
> My clan asks each to decide. Each of us who do not desire this life may join another clan. This is done at the age of 8.
>
> YOU HAVE ELECTED TO STAY WITH THIS CLAN, THEN?
>
> I am very happy with this clan.

The clan trains its youngsters in a place which these subjects describe as a temple. "B," who seems to have spent more of her life within the temple atmosphere than the other two, has a great deal to say about it:

> B
>
> It's like a ... a white building there, big building. I'm outside. It's very beautiful outside. There are steps going into the building. It's different looking, and ... it's not a square building, it's more rounded.
>
> THE MATERIAL IS WHAT?
>
> On this building it seems like a kind of stone, but not stone. It all is one piece. It's not pieces, it's all one piece.

ARE YOU SAYING THAT THE ENTIRE BUILDING IS JUST ONE PIECE, OR IS IT LIKE WINGS STACKED ONE ON TOP OF THE OTHERS?

It's a rounded building, but there is a ... some kind of design ... a glyph or something on the front, the same materials that this is made of, but it stands out. It's ... like a temple. I don't see any ...

(Turning tape over, loses continuity. Pick up on side two of three total sides.)

... a leaf on the outside of the door ... that uses flowing things and it's in relief above the door, but it's not words.

OK. IS THIS A SYMBOL OF SOME KIND?

Yes.

WHAT ARE YOU DOING NOW? LOOK BACK OVER THE PAST YEAR, AND SEE WHAT HAS BEEN GOING ON.

I can't see. Initiate comes to mind. Initiate. I have been one. Am one. *Am* one.

CAN YOU GO BACK TO IT? LET'S GO BACK TO YOUR INITIATION, THEN, ALL RIGHT? ONE, TWO, THREE, (snap.)

Inside, inside. Candles round inside. Beautiful dark, candlelight, light, and golden light at the top. Altar, there's an altar, and a ...

Robes. There are other people besides me ... in the same robes, and there are at the altar teachers, teachers, priests, teachers. And there is music as though from voices, but it's not ... there are no people making it. The music is there but I don't see what causes it. That is all I see.

DOING FINE. TELL ME ABOUT YOUR INITIATION. WHAT WAS IT? YOU BECAME A WHAT AFTER YOUR INITIATION?

A servant.

YOU BECAME A SERVANT? TO WHOM OR TO WHAT?

A servant of God, I don't know how, what to ...

ARE YOU ON THE ORDER OF A PRIESTESS?

No, not yet.

OK, HEROT, LET'S MOVE ON. LET'S MOVE UP ONE TENTH OF YOUR LIFE TIME. ONE, TWO, THREE, (snap).

I just saw that I was older and carrying a cup at this point.

THE SAME CUP?

A cup. A different one.

NOW, ARE YOU STILL IN THE TEMPLE? ARE YOU STILL A STUDENT?

I help with it now.

OK, YOU'VE MOVED UP SOME, THEN.

There's so much still to learn. I know very little. But I'm helping with it.

GOOD.

That's what the challenge has to do with.

AS A GENERAL THING, WHAT DO YOU TEACH? RELIGIOUS THINGS PERTAINING TO SPIRITUAL DEVELOPMENT, OR DO YOU TEACH OTHER THINGS ALONG WITH IT?

Of the spirit.

LET'S MOVE UP TO HALFWAY, THROUGH THAT LIFE. ONE, TWO, THREE, (snap). NOW LOOK BACK WHERE WE'VE PASSED. WHAT ARE YOU DOING NOW.

Earlier, it had to do with the temple, sending out love and energy. We didn't actually depart physically, I don't, I can't see, later yet, but earlier, I do see that earlier the temple was used for service but it had to do a lot with things that weren't accomplished physically. It sent out help through thought and ceremony and ... I think ritual, but it was very, it was all with love, it was as a center.

DID THESE THOUGHTS ORIGINATE FROM THE TEMPLE ITSELF OR FROM THE PEOPLE WHO WERE IN IT?

All together. Left all together.

DID THE TEMPLE SERVE SOMEWHAT AS A PYRAMID?

It was not a pyramid.

YES, BUT ON THE SAME ORDER?

It was a holy, holy place, and it sent ... it was a center for sending—strength, love, for ... energy, energy sending, energy.

WHERE DID THEY SEND ALL THIS ENERGY TO? THROUGH THE ENTIRE UNIVERSE? OR JUST TO THAT PLANET?

It was not limited to that planet, but it encompassed that planet. It ... it was a protection ... and more ... more. It protected, and it healed, and sent out also where needed, but it was ...

Here is the temple through the eyes of "A" and "C":

C

WHERE DO YOU GO, AFTER THAT POINT?

I went to a place. I don't know where it was, but it was very beautiful.

TELL ME EVERY IMPRESSION OF IT.

I wrote about it once. It is a temple. We walked across the most beautiful grass. Beautiful trees. Beautiful place. We went into the temple, a great big white marble ... and no one was there, but we could hear very clearly, and we rested there until we were ready to find out what we were to do next. And we went to a temple.

A

WILL YOU MOVE ON NOW TO YOUR TEACHER, YOUR DESTINATION.

I seem to enter a beautiful house, a temple, like, with columns.

AS YOU APPROACH THE TEMPLE, WILL YOU GIVE AN OVER-ALL VIEW OF IT, AND THEN MOVE ON UP, AND DESCRIBE THE ENTIRE ENTRANCE THAT YOU ARE GOING INTO?

There are two columns, one on each side. Three or four steps. It glitters smooth. It is round, with a dome-like top. There is ... it is hard to explain ... there is, it is like music but it is not note-music, it is like air-music, dancing in sparkles. Everything is transformed to glitter.

TELL ME ABOUT THE CONSTRUCTION OF THE BUILDING. DO THE SIDE WALLS HAVE JOINTS IN THEM, OR DO THEY ALL HAVE ONE PIECE, OR ...

The walls are all one piece. They are about ten feet high and then the dome starts. The walls are smooth ... a dull, goldish color.

GIVE ME SOME ESTIMATE OF THE DIAMETER OF IT. HOW FAR IS IT ACROSS? IS IT A LARGE BUILDING?

On the outside it is not large, but on the inside it is. I am trying to remember why it is large on the inside but not on the outside ...

ON THE OUTSIDE YOU HAVE THE IMPRESSION OF PERHAPS A HUNDRED FEET IN DIAMETER?

Less. Well, that is about right. I am entering through the door. There is a cushion in the middle of the floor. It is dark outside. But not real dark, just shadowy dark.

A theme that is often sounded in these regressions is that of a certain and unique light which is encountered in the temple and about its teachers:

C

WAS THERE SOMEONE THERE TO ASSIST YOU, TO BE A GUIDE FOR YOU?

It was there, but not in the body. It was ... in the wind, sort of.

VISIBLE TO YOU?

No. Just light. Beautiful. It is really beautiful. You can see little wind that was speaking and it was with little flecks like ... little beams of light.

A

I kneel on the cushion. There is nothing else there but the air making music and I pray. And a light comes down.

It is at first very heavy gold bright light, a waterfall of light. It falls on top of me and is running like a river down on the floor, and it glows the whole room. I come here before I go see the teachers.

DO YOU HAVE A PHYSICAL SENSATION OF TOUCH OR FEEL?

Total warmth. Total oneness with the light. It is a dissolving of my whole body. I am washed out in the ocean. It is ... it is union.

The teachers who are spoken of by these Otherworlders seem to be a beautiful lot, much appreciated by their students. The job is filled by the members of the clan who have reached the age of what would presumably be retirement here on Earth. But on Otherworld, they begin a new career, passing on what they have learned to the younger clan members:

B

There is a teacher that is wonderful.

GO AHEAD WITH YOUR DAILY WORK WITH HIM. HOW DOES HE INSTRUCT YOU?

He's just blessing us all. He has much love, much love. It all … there's … oh, golden, golden, *golden* light, there. (Sighs).

BEAUTIFUL, ISN'T IT? IS IT WARM, COLD?

There is no cold or warm there. It is blessed.

A

THEN YOU MOVE ON TO YOUR TEACHERS? OR TO YOUR TEACHER, I SHOULD SAY. WILL YOU DESCRIBE AS YOU APPROACH YOUR TEACHER?

I am walking back out of the temple. The man is waiting for me.

THE SAME MAN YOU PASSED EARLIER?

Yes.

IS HE YOUR TEACHER?

He is not my old teachers. But we are both going there, to my teachers. He is … he has been waiting for me for the light to have come unto me.

THE TWO OF YOU ARE GOING ON, NOW, TO YOUR TEACHER.

Yes. We seem to … there is grass. We seem to go up to a cave, like the cave before. It overlooks the city.

YOUR TEACHER IS IN THE CAVE?

No. The back wall seems to open and we go through it, and there are the three teachers sitting in a semicircle, waiting for us.

CAN YOU DESCRIBE THEM? THEIR POSITION?

They are sitting down, cross-legged. They have white robes on, and their light illuminates the whole cave. They have long, white hair, and their eyes … their eyes just … twinkle. They have such power in those eyes. Such power and light in those eyes. We sit down facing them and we meditate. They are ... something is coming from their heads to mine. It is ... it is knowledge. I am ... I know all of this, and yet I will never ... I won't remember it for a long time. They have explained this to me, and we agreed. I am ... I am like a seed. I have been ... The word is being confused. I have been nurtured by them. I have ... been chosen to carry their information. We will be used, they say, in *time.* On the outside I am like a child. On the inside I am old and wise, and I see and understand everything that they see and understand ... I will not be able to speak for some time through this child. It is a strange combination. For now, all the teachers are feeding me. The child knows what's going on, but she will forget. But the old person inside will ... will be there always, with the information and the knowledge. I feel ... they do this all in love, love that is total understanding, total understanding of all that there is, and yet, I feel here a confusion because I am their seed. I am theirs.

ALL RIGHT. YOU ARE OBTAINING THE INFORMATION.

Yes.

HOW WILL THE INFORMATION THEN BE RELEASED? AND WHEN WILL IT BE RELEASED?

Very little at a time at first. Just enough to keep the child when she goes away secure and shielded from harmful environment. She will be sent away with other peoples to Earth. But that is some time from now. The child must go through a great deal of training first. When she is on Earth bit by bit will come ... but she will hide it from others. I do not see right now where, or even if all the knowledge will come out. She is most careful.

C

OK. CAN YOU MOVE ON FORWARD, NOW, MONTH BY MONTH. YEAR BY YEAR, HOWEVER YOU WANT TO MOVE. TELL ME WHAT'S GOING ON IN THE LATTER PART.

I'm teaching. I'm working with the younger clan. My mate goes out one more time than I do.

HE IS STRONGER?

Yes, and somewhat younger.

SO HE MAKES ONE MORE OFF THE PLANET JOB, THEN?

Uh huh.

HOW LONG IS HE GONE?

A year.

IS EVERYTHING ALL RIGHT WHEN HE COMES BACK?

He is beginning to be tired then, and joins the younger ones to teach.

YES. HE AND YOU TEACH THEM, IN GENERAL, WHAT?

Many things. I personally work with the younger members to try to help them with their personal understanding of themselves. That is my most primary interest. Others would be teaching other techniques and disciplines of the personality. This is the way of harnessing the dimensions.

That last statement strikes me as being quite central: "... disciplines of the personality (are) the way of harnessing the dimensions." This point is emphasized by the UFO contacts again and again.

After the Otherworld children finish their "schoolwork" with their teachers in the temple, they are eligible to enter the active service.

"A" spends nearly all of her time under hypnosis concentrating on the period when she, as an older person, was at the temple and then preparing to voyage forth to Earth after her "death" on that planet. So we can get no information about the service from her. "B" spends much of her time speaking of her work within the temple itself, and indeed she seems to have been more closely aligned with its functioning throughout her life than the other two subjects, remaining more cloistered. She does give a hint of her involvement with off-the-planet service:

I BELIEVE YOU ARE VERY HAPPY. YOU ARE A VERY HAPPY ENTITY. YOU ENJOY THAT LIFE, DON'T YOU? HAVE YOU TRAVELED WITH THOSE SHIPS, EVER?

I feel at one with them. I don't know if ... There is something ... It's part of our purpose there ... to use ... to do this ...

The subject known as "C" is the richest source of information about off-the-planet service by the clan. Their basic function is described well by Yolanda:

... not only did many incarnate on Earth so as to be part of the people and to lead them back gradually but also there were continual visits by those who came in their spacecraft, and otherwise.[7]

"C" tells of taking missions first on her own planet, and after passing this test, on other planets:

C

LET'S MOVE UP TO AGE FIFTEEN, THEN. ONE, TWO, THREE, (snap). NOW YOU'RE FIFTEEN. OLDER, WISER. LOOKING BACK OVER THE LAST FIVE YEARS, WHAT'S HAPPENED?

I had a darn good time.

A GOOD TIME WOULD MEAN WHAT?

Learned a whole lot. Started working with small amounts of responsibility, helping. First we have dealings with those of our own planet who are not as fortunate and do not have the ability to penetrate time and must dwell in the body. And we help them to find their way, without disturbing them. And that is very satisfying to see an actual success.

My first case was a tribe. The tribe was having a difficulty with a kind of predator which was eating their crops. And myself and two others found a way to enable the tribesmen to protect their crops. We fixed a more attractive prey by planting in wild land a crop which was more desirable to the catlike creatures. Therefore, the tribesmen had pride and protected their land, and we did not interfere. We found this a lot of fun, too.

THIS IS ON YOUR PLANET.

This is on my planet.

C

NOW, YOU'RE WORKING ON A DIFFERENT PLANET, AND THEY HAVE BEEN ALL BUT ANNIHILATED, I BELIEVE, BY SOME NATURAL CATASTROPHE.

Yes.

NOW HOW ARE YOU COMING ALONG WITH THAT?

OK. It'll improve in time. See, if you want to just come along and help them, that's fine, but then they'll never think it out for themselves. It takes time.

SO YOU HAVE TO DO GUIDE WORK FOR THEM?

That's right. Just put it where they can find it and—in the body, all of us have—so it will happen. It just takes time.

HAVE YOU DETERMINED THE CAUSE OF THE DISASTER?

Yes. That was easy. There was a … the plates of the planet went together abruptly and there was fire and then flood. Most of the people on the planet were living in the place where this whole area was inundated, and that's what put out the fire. Very few survived. And those that did survive were in isolated areas. It seemed that almost the whole civilization was …

THE PLATES WERE WHAT?

The planet, the surface, the earth, the rock …

AND THEY WENT TOGETHER?

They were together, and they crushed each other. They were side by side and there was heat within and it came out, and there was a shift, and one plate lapped over the other, a great—really two continents, you see, totally jammed up into each other. And it was like an eruption, and it was terrible. There was a great deal of destruction.

WHAT WAS THE REAL CAUSE OF THIS CATASTROPHE?

Oh. Well, I don't know.

WAS IT TOTALLY AN ACT OF NATURE?

The plates had always been unstable here. I do not know of the philosophy, why it happened; that it happened in such a way was because they were unstable in just that way.

THE PLATES DID PROVIDE STABILITY? DID THEY PROVIDE ANY FORM OF ENERGY?

This was the earth upon which the continents were … they were part of that planet's surface.

OK, VERY WELL. YOU'RE WELL ON YOUR WAY WITH RECONSTRUCTION NOW. YOU'VE GOT THEM READY TO HELP THEMSELVES?

Not yet.

YOU'RE STILL WORKING WITH THEM?

What we're doing mostly for them is just sending them comfort. They—we are still searching for records. Trying to find the records. We are going to have to bring them up from somewhere. We do not want to substitute records. There are surely some records left that were not either burned completely or destroyed by water.

WHAT TYPE OF RECORDS, AND FOR WHAT PURPOSE?

Any type of records that will give them back their language, their history, their culture.

OK. HOW DO THESE PEOPLE COMPARE TO YOUR OWN DESCRIPTION?

They are short, dark, very squat. They look like, well, they look like the cave people that they are, really, they're pretty messy right now.

HOW ABOUT YOUR RELATIONSHIP AND DEALING WITH THEM?

They do not know we are here. They suspect that there is something odd happening, but they do not know that we are here.

OK. HOW LONG DO YOU STAY THERE, IN TERMS OF MONTHS OR YEARS OF YOUR LIFE?

In the body, we stay a year. In the dimensions, we stay much longer. But we stay only a year, in the body.

OK. WHEN YOU FINISH THIS JOB, YOU ARE GOING BACK TO YOUR HOME PLANET, RIGHT?

Yes. To rest.

OK, LET'S GO BACK. YOU'RE FINISHED. ANYTHING YOU WANT TO TELL ME ABOUT FINISHING UP, OR THE TRIP BACK, OR THE RETURN?

Well, of course, when I finished, they weren't finished.

"C" goes on in her narrative to tell of her teaching the younger clan in her old age, and then of her death. We've read both of these portions earlier in the chapter. After "death" in the physical sense, "C" says she waits in another dimension for over a year, until her mate joins her. Why does she wait? All three Otherworlders begin a new part of the narrative at this point: they tell of their preparation for service on Earth as "apples." OAHSPE talks about these apples a lot, and even mentions the arrival of some from Hautuon, a planet whose name is remarkably like the chief contact of several contactees, Hatonn:

> Presently could be seen guardian ships, thousands and thousands, traveling beside the laboring sun, the hosts of Hautuon.
>
> And the guardian ships were themselves like stars, and carried millions of etherean souls who had been Gods and Goddesses on many worlds; and they formed wings for the Hautuon avalanche, to hold steady the course to the red star, the earth of mortals.[8]

Note that within the ships are "etherean beings."

Our people report that as they enter the ship that brings them here, they leave their physical body behind and have instead a new, lighter-density body. What is the ship like, and why do they need it?

A

OK. WILL YOU DESCRIBE THE CRAFT ON THE OUTSIDE, AND THEN DESCRIBE IT AS YOU ARE GETTING INSIDE OF IT.

It is sitting on its bottom. There are no legs. There's a door, that acts as a ramp. It has an edge around the middle.

IS IT ROUND?

Yes.

OK. IS IT THICKER IN THE MIDDLE THAN IT IS AROUND THE EDGES?

It is thick in the middle.

THE CRAFT APPEARS TO BE MADE OF WHAT, NOW? METALLIC? CERAMICS?

I feel as if it's a kind of metal.

SHINY, LIKE STAINLESS STEEL, OR ALUMINUM, OR COPPER, OR ZINC, OR WHAT?

Mmmmh ... flat. Not shiny.

ALL RIGHT. IS THERE AN ANTENNA UP THE SIDE OF IT? CHECK FOR ANYTHING UNUSUAL ABOUT THE EXTERIOR?

No.

ALL RIGHT. WILL YOU GO ON UP THE RAMP. AS YOU GO INSIDE, BEGIN DESCRIBING THE INTERIOR FOR ME.

It is round inside. I sit—there are seats around the windows. There are lights but I do not ... I am getting confused.

BEFORE YOU CAME INSIDE, WERE THERE ANY OTHER PEOPLE AROUND, GROUND CREW OR SERVICE PERSONNEL?

No.

FEEL ANY PEOPLE, OR ANYBODY ELSE.

No.

ALL RIGHT. YOU'RE INSIDE. THERE ARE SEATS INSIDE OF IT, AND LIGHTS. BUT IS THERE A CONTROL PANEL IN IT, A COCKPIT. HOW DO YOU CONTROL THE SHIP?

My impression is that there is no power—it is the minds that—I don't know if it's like just all our joint minds, or the teacher's joint minds, but just minds.

OK, THE SHIP'S CONTROLLED BY THOUGHT FORMS, THEN; THOUGHT ENERGY?

Yes.

BUT, NOW DO YOU CLOSE THE DOOR?

It is time to go. It closes.

ALL RIGHT. WHEN IT IS TIME TO GO, HOW DO YOU DEPART? NOW DO YOU START MOVING? JUST THINK?

Yes ...

B

HOW DO YOU LEAVE? WHO TAKES CONTROL OF THE SHIP? WHO FLIES IT? IS THERE A PILOT?

No, no.

A DOOR FRAME? COCKPIT?

There are lights within, but ... the control is ... we who are inside are as one, and that thought is at one with the thought within the temple. And that is how we leave.

A

LET'S MOVE FORWARD, NOW, ANOTHER TENTH OF YOUR EXPERIENCE. ONE, TWO, THREE, (snap). YOU ARE THERE. WHAT'S HAPPENING?

I am coming out of my cave, and going down the rocky cliff. I am going to go towards the city because they are starting to send off those who have been prepared, to help the Earth. I am very excited. There is a tall structure on the right, shaped like an hour-glass, very slender. And on top of this tall structure is a platform from where the crafts are leaving. There is a large one. It will hold many, many peoples from many places. They will unite here, in this craft.

WHAT'S IT SHAPED LIKE?

It is long shape, round.

LIKE A BIG CIGAR?

Yes. If it is like a ... we have trees here. It is like a very large tree, with a flat middle.

YOU MEAN THE TRUNK? LIKE A TREE TRUNK?

Yes.

NOT THE BRANCHES?

No. There are smaller crafts.

WHAT DO THEY LOOK LIKE?

They are light and silvery and they are circular, with a flat bottom and a flat top; wide around the middle. Like cupping your hands.

IS THERE ANY DOME ON IT?

I am getting the impression that if you want a dome, you can have a dome. I am trying to reach in for the knowledge of all of this. It seems that our powers of mind create the illusion of structures, just like all peoples on all planets. For some reason, those who were in control of creating the illusion of crafts chose these shapes. Perhaps they will have significance in another time. But all of it is not that important.

WHAT MAKES THEM TRAVEL?

Let me dissolve. (pause) It is power of mind, again, but it is not an activity of all our minds, but it is. All of this activity is put to work by a few, and yet because of our oneness, we are all doing it, but I am not thinking about the crafts or about ... thinking about the plans of travel. But there are others that do, and I am in full oneness with whatever they bring to us.

WHAT ARE YOU THINKING?

I am trying to find out how the crafts move through what is known as space. It ... there is very little reference I can make. It is a space and time that will finally be glimpsed at one Earth at a much later date. People ... one person, scientist, will say, will finally see that space and time are not rigidly held together. People will praise him, but they will not see it, and he will go ... There will be a few more who finally see that space and time are not held to a fixed line and that what they see in their space is only one space and one time, but it is not all space and all time. Therefore, what they call all space and their time, when they look into the sky, is an illusion. But they do not see but one kind of tiny space, as if looking into a room, and they just call that the Earth. Space and time will be difficult to explain in words to the humans, because they lack imagination. They lack the powers of mind. They do not have the training to see the reality, to know what space and time really is. Until they do, then their space travel will be a space travel of illusions. We travel by mind, and because we understand space and time, they mean absolutely nothing. They are not coated (?) with stars. There is no meaningful conception, no necessary conception, of time, through travel. Because that is pinpointing the infinite into two words. What we do is so far beyond the realm of ordinary thought that we would not be able to use words to convey any possibility of our progress. But someday, the children will understand imagination, and when they see the stars, they will see all that there is, because they will see the space. The concept of space and time separates us from those that we try to help, and it takes a long time to teach other peoples. And yet there is no time, but all of it.

"A" focuses on this point in her experience, getting on the ship to come to Earth. She repeatedly tells us that she feels sadness, for she will have to forget the truth of light and unity in order to come into the Earth through birth.

A

ALL RIGHT. WILL YOU GO INTO THE STRUCTURE NOW. FIND YOURSELF THERE. NOW, AS YOU GET TO THE STRUCTURE, TELL ME ABOUT IT.

Well, I don't go to the structure yet. I go back to the teachers' room for a while.

DO THEY KNOW THAT YOU'RE LEAVING?

Yes. They're standing, singing, when I come in.

ARE YOU SINGING TO THEM? WHY WOULD THEY BE STANDING WHEN YOU COME IN?

Because we will be separated.

ALL RIGHT. OUT OF RESPECT. NOW WHAT GOES ON NOW, BETWEEN YOU AND THE TEACHERS?

I turn to one, and he places his hands on my shoulder, and looks very deeply into my eyes. I turn to another one and he does the same. I am getting a great deal of strength and knowledge, but I don't know yet that it is knowledge. And when I turn to the third, he stares.

THE SAME WAY, INTO YOUR EYES.

Yes.

GO AHEAD.

It is very hard for me not to feel sad, but then all at once I sense it is all right, and I cry a tear and he cries one. I turn to leave. (quiet crying)

DO YOU KNOW WHY YOU HAVE TO LEAVE?

Yes.

OK. VERY WELL. GO AHEAD. ARE YOU GOING TO THE DIAMOND-SHAPED BUILDING? TO THE HOUR-GLASS BUILDING?

Yes.

WHAT ABOUT THE OTHER FOUR? ARE THEY COMING WITH YOU? WITH DIFFERENT TEACHERS? OR HOW DO THEY WORK?

I do not know about them.

OK.

I go the long way around.

WHY?

To meditate again on the way. I do know that this is a good thing. I am ready. I am going down the hill towards the hour-glass-shape. I am standing at the very bottom, looking up. I do not have the robes on now, I have something else on.

ARE THE OTHERS THERE YET?

They are coming within my view.

OK.

They are here now.

GOOD. THEY ARE READY TO GO TOO.

Yes.

ARE THEY DRESSED THE SAME WAY YOU ARE?

Yes.

ALL RIGHT. WHAT HAPPENS NEXT?

I do as the teachers did with me. I turn to each one, put my hands on their shoulders and look at them. And we exchange comfort and we exchange sadness and exchange love and knowledge and understanding. It is a time to feel our oneness. (Pause) Now, we are walking towards the structure. We are going up it like—I can't—it is called perhaps an elevator, it is going straight up.

GO AHEAD. YOU GET TO THE TOP. NOW, WHAT HAPPENS.

There is a craft, that is ... it is round.

DO YOU GET INTO THE CRAFT?

Yes. We all get in. For some reason I am thinking that this is a small craft, smaller than others that have left.

BUT IT IS BIG ENOUGH FOR FIVE?

Yes.

"B" describes this same scene:

ONCE YOU'RE INSIDE THE SHIP IN SPIRITUAL FORM, SPIRITUAL BODY—

Shiny.

DESCRIBE THE INTERIOR FOR ME. FIRST OF ALL THE SHIP UP CLOSER. DID YOU TELL ME IT WAS ROUND?

There are places to sit.

OK, BUT ON THE OUTSIDE, THE OUTSIDE APPEARANCE, IS IT ROUND LIKE A BALL?

No. I—I—I don't see this one close. When we go in it is as though ... it is as though there is a place to walk, from the temple right inside so you don't have an overview of this one at this time. The overview was before, from without. We walk within, from the temple directly into this.

YES.

There is a place to go in, not a door that opens, as ours do, but ... we walk up the door ... and our ... we're ... the sadness has been shed.

HOW MANY PEOPLE IN THE SHIP WITH YOU?

I don't know. There're ...

TEN?

No ... but—

A DOZEN OR—

No, no. I ... Under a dozen. I don't know how many. Wait a minute. There is one.

ARE YOU READY TO LEAVE.

Yes.

And so the little band leaves, and as OAHSPE puts it:

> Onward sped the ship of God, by the force of wills matured; and from its hallowed light displaying its purpose before other Gods and men, in other ships cruising, on adventurous paths in Jehovih's wide oceans of splendor.[9]

This sadness at the prospect of doing duty on Earth as "apples" has been reported by other investigators I've talked with, and seems quite common among those who under hypnosis report lives on other planets. It is certainly understandable. Volunteering for service on Earth is a bit like volunteering for service in the Marine Corps. The recruit knows the experience will be a rough one, but he believes that in the course of performing his duties he will become a more mature person. The Marines build men: an Earth incarnation builds Masters. As a space contact says through Yolanda:

> I see a very sad, but joyous, one. She is homesick, for she is far from her place. I understand this. I am also far from my home, in this ship. We do have deep understanding for such longings. Many of us volunteer a whole time of life to these missions. But you on Earth are so unfortunate, because when you volunteer you lose your memory of where you came from, for the most part.[10]

"B" and "C" talk about the sadness in their own way:

A

The child here will feel sorrow, for she will glimpse this and then lose it, and she will be pushed to an environment that will confuse her, and yet if she still wills, if she can still but remember, even her dreams, even the things she saw, that she will see, in the shadows of night, then in time she will remember.

NOW, TELL ME EVERYTHING THAT YOU CAN ABOUT THIS PARTICULAR EVENT. VERY QUICKLY, NOW, VERY CRISPLY. DON'T ANALYZE IT.

There are people there, but I cannot differentiate them. We are meditating, no words are spoken. We are just there, seems like. I am sad.

ALL RIGHT. THE MEDITATION IS IN ANTICIPATION OF WHAT EVENT? WHAT MAY HAPPEN?

Us leaving the planet.

AND YOU ARE SAD AT THIS PROSPECT ALSO.

In a way, yes.

ALL RIGHT, YOU ARE ANTICIPATING LEAVING THE PLANET, AND THE OTHER PEOPLE ARE TOO.

Yes.

ALL RIGHT. CAN YOU DESCRIBE THE OTHER PEOPLE?

No physical features. All I know is that they understand a little bit more than I and that I am more sad. I am sad because it is such a struggle. A long, long struggle. How sad that it has to be that way. The others know that they must leave. And they take some comfort ... I can't ...

ALL RIGHT. TELL ME SOME MORE ABOUT THE STRUGGLE. WHAT TYPE STRUGGLE?

The struggle of the mind, knowing all that we know. But we lose that, when we leave. We leave and we go back through ... back through the darkness again, and struggle ... struggle to the peace. I feel very light, right now. I am thinking, of all of this ...

B

VERY WELL. I'D LIKE YOU TO TURN BACK TO THE PRESENT NOW, ALTOGETHER, IN ALL DIMENSIONS. IS THERE A SPECIFIC REASON FOR YOU TO COME BACK AS NOW? WHAT'S GOING TO BE YOUR MAIN PURPOSE? WHAT IS YOUR ASSIGNMENT?

The blind closes.

WHAT DO YOU MEAN BY THAT?

When I come back here, the slate is wiped clean. It's hard to see.

(Pause) There is much sadness here.

WHY?

This planet ...

YES, BUT NOT ON THE SPIRITUAL DIMENSION? YOU JUST MEAN ON THE PLANET ITSELF?

I just see it.

YES. AND THAT'S WHY YOU'RE HERE? WHY YOU WERE SENT HERE?

It will be forgotten. We will forget.

WHY? WHY IS IT NECESSARY TO FORGET?

It's gone. (whispering) It's gone.

THE MEMORY OF THE PAST ON THAT PLANET IS GONE?

Off, off—it's gone. There is white slate. It's new—forgotten.

When the Otherworlder's spaceship arrives here with our group, it does not drop them onto the Earth's surface, but instead enters the finer or spiritual planes of our Earth and allows its passengers to enter the cycle of reincarnation on our planet. George Hunt Williamson says:

> If these Wanderers didn't arrive here by spaceship, how did they get here? They volunteered to come to Earth and go through the reincarnational cycle here. In other words, they were born here! They have birth certificates, they went to school, had the childhood diseases, drank soda pop at the corner drug store and made eyes at each other in school, or threw "spit balls" at the teacher. In brief, they were exactly the same as all the other people on Earth, except for one thing: they didn't belong here! They occupy physical vehicles and are born to parents of their own choice who they feel will best give them the advantages and training they need to fulfill their missions on Earth.[11]

And an entity known as Sut-ko gives this information:

> From time immemorial, teachers of Light came to planet Earth, incarnating from other planets, from other systems, even from other galaxies, and from the realms known to you as the nonphysical or supernal realms of existence; and great companies of Light came into incarnation, carrying with them the banner of Truth and Love and Light. In all the simplicity of these teachings, and in all dedication to

the One Creator and His Laws, these bands of Lighted Ones came down into incarnation and to the darkness and the degradation which they ofttimes found, and incarcerated themselves in flesh, not for their own experiencing—though much they did experience—but with a basic motive of service to the One Creator and His Creations, a motive of Love and Compassion.

At each time when the Great Ones, whom you speak of as Avatars, came, (there also) came many lesser teachers, many lighted souls, great in compassion and service. Often their tasks seemed small, yet they formed a chain, a pattern of strength, and each upheld the others; and as each company whom we have termed "the goodly companies" went forth, they went in groups of souls who had worked and known each other from lifetime to lifetime. These souls are incarnate once more upon planet Earth in many areas. These souls work for the upliftment of the planet and for the dawning of the Age of Reason at the end of this cycle upon the planet. These souls, who have come into incarnation, have formed what is known as the Lightlines and the Light Centers throughout the planet. Some there are who have gone forth on lonely ways, and have been cut off from their fellows and have worked alone in the materialistic world. They have sought to bring that understanding which is theirs, a glimmer of truth which they have remembered, wherever they have found themselves, and in whatever capacity they have labored. Now, many of these who have worked alone join with the others in order that strength may be given to all, that the pattern or web of Light, which is now woven around the planet may be vitalized to its highest capacity ...[12]

Here are "A," "B," and "C" describing their entry into the spiritual plane:

A

VERY WELL. ARE YOU READY TO DEPART?

Yes.

WILL YOU DEPART, AND FIND YOURSELF IN THE NEXT PLANE OR DIMENSION? ARE YOU NOW IN THE SPIRITUAL DIMENSION OF EARTH?

I am not sure yet where I am. I am not on Earth.

ARE YOU STILL IN THE SHIP?

No.

HOW DO YOU GET OUT OF IT?

Well, mind. It was time.

WAS THE SHIP ABSOLUTELY NECESSARY FOR YOU TO MAKE THE TRIP FROM YOUR PLANET TO THE EARTH'S SPIRITUAL DIMENSION?

In one way yes, and in many other ways, no. I cannot explain now, but that it is necessary to come in something like a craft to make that transition. Even though everything is one, and that the vibrations are infinite, and that we knew of all things that were going on on Earth, we could not do our task while still on our planet. That would be a confusion of our own development and Earth's development and our task. It was necessary for us to leave our vibrational level and that plane entirely, and to go through what is called reincarnation. We needed to learn as a soul the planes of the spirit, and all that Earthlings go through, for we do not go through these things any more.

VERY WELL. IS THERE ANYTHING MORE NOW?

No.

NOW, HOW DO YOU APPROACH EARTH? DO YOU JUST COME DOWN AND DO YOU LAND OR, WHAT HAPPENS WHEN YOU GET HERE?

No. We don't land. You can't do that.

WILL YOU DESCRIBE YOUR APPROACH, AND WHAT YOU DO THEREAFTER?

You simply leave the space ship.

DO YOU LEAVE THE SPACE SHIP UP IN THE AIR?

There is no longer any function. The … were turn to … we drop that body, we drop … we simply leave. We … are …

YOU SAID YOU LEAVE THE SHIP?

Yes.

AND YOU ARE ON EARTH, THEN?

Mnn … not on Earth. We are near, we are around, we are …

ARE YOU IN A SPIRITUAL REALM, SPIRITUAL LEVEL?

Yes …

NOT ON EARTH AT THIS TIME?

No.

OK. NOW WHAT IS GOING TO TAKE PLACE AT THIS LEVEL?

I know I must go through a thing called birth, but I don't know how.

IS THERE ANY INSTRUCTION FOR YOU? ARE THERE NEW TEACHERS THERE FOR YOU?

I find helpers.

B

YOU CAME TO OUR PLANET. NOW, WILL YOU TELL ME ABOUT THE APPROACH TO OUR PLANET. HOW YOU CAME TO BE HERE. DOES THE SHIP COME DOWN AND LAND RIGHT ON THE PLANET?

Mmnn, no. We're in the spirit.

YES. TELL ME WHAT HAPPENED. HOW DID YOU GET OUT OF THE SHIP?

We're just not needed in the ship any more.

AND WHAT HAPPENS TO THE SHIP?

I don't know.

DO YOU, DOES THE DOOR, DOES IT STOP AND—

We are, there is no need for doors at this stage.

SO YOU JUST DEMATERIALIZE FROM THE SHIP. DO YOU COME DIRECTLY TO EARTH THEN?

No.

WHAT HAPPENS? DO YOU STOP IN THE HIGHER, SPIRITUAL DIMENSION FOR A WHILE?

There is waiting. Watching.

CAN YOU MAKE ANY CONNECTION WITH ANYONE THAT YOU KNEW THEN AND ANYONE YOU KNOW NOW?

(Pause) I can only tell by … I don't see people … feel presences—

YOU FOUND SOMEBODY, DIDN'T YOU?

On the spirit plane.

WHO?

Mother and father. Mother.

BEAUTIFUL.

Spirit—dear soul. Dear soul.

SHE CAME TO EARTH BEFORE YOU DID. YOU WAITED FOR HER DIDN'T YOU? AND YOUR FATHER. THEREFORE, THEY KNEW EACH OTHER TOO, DIDN'T THEY?

It was planned.

IT WAS PLANNED THAT THEY WOULD COME TO BE YOUR PARENTS, IS THIS CORRECT?

I chose them.

OK.

They chose me too.

C

VERY WELL. I WANT YOU TO GO BACK TO THE SPIRITUAL PLANE, FROM THE OTHER PLANET, THERE BY ITSELF IN ITS ENTIRETY. WHO LEAVES FIRST, YOU OR YOUR MATE?

My mate.

AND YOU WAIT A WHILE?

I'm looking for the right people.

I was waiting for the correct challenge.

DID YOU MAKE THE DECISION ON YOUR OWN?

Completely.

A

I WANT YOU TO FIND WHO SELECTED YOUR MOTHER AND FATHER, AND WHY. WHY THIS PARTICULAR TIME, WHY THIS PARTICULAR LOCATION. FIRST OF ALL, THE PARENTS. DID YOU SELECT THOSE TWO PEOPLE BY YOURSELF, OR DID YOU HAVE HELP FROM YOUR HELPER?

It seems to have been my choice.

So our three Otherworlders come to Earth, having chosen their parents and gone through birth. It is apparently the plan that "apples" come to Earth in groups who, if they can recognize each other and remember their mission, will then be able to help each other and work together in harmony. It was quite amazing to me as I gathered the second and third of these regressions to find the same report of mutual acquaintance in the previous life. It is a story of at least five people, so I must fill you in on the other two. In addition to the three subjects, there is a man, named here "D," and a man named here "E." Perhaps the most amazing detail of these mutually agreeing reports was the fact that "A," who had never known "E," named him as an acquaintance, a member of her family on Otherworld. "E" is now dead, and there is no possible way she could ever have known him. She had, however, heard his name mentioned by "C." And from this slight knowledge she tentatively identified him in her regression.

A

LET'S LOOK AT THIS PLACE THAT YOU ARE LEAVING.

Let me come back down to the child. (Pause)

CAN YOU SEE THE ONES WHO WILL BE GOING? CAN YOU TELL ME NOW IF THERE ARE ANY MORE THAT YOU WILL KNOW UPON EARTH?

There is a male type standing beside me. He is happy with me. We are watching ... we are looking at the ships. They have not started to load the people, our brothers and sisters, inside yet. We ... I know him, he is my mate for a short time. I do not know him. I do not get to see him on Earth. And yet he will ... his presence will be everywhere ... he will be next to me when I have a new mate. He is working ... he will be working on a different level. Therefore I do not get to see him. And yet he will direct ... help watch over me and my mate.

IS THERE ANYONE ELSE THERE THAT YOU MEET ON EARTH?

I am trying to place the names ... the Earth names of "D" and "E." I am trying to see where they come from, if they are from my planet or from someplace else. (Pause) "D" is from my planet, though I do not know him. (Pause)

No. "D' is not from my planet. He will be a communicator between his peoples and all the peoples who are joining in this endeavor. He will be most necessary, most comforting to me on Earth. We will all be there. He is from someplace else. I do not know. And yet he will know about me. He will know about all of those who show him … who look into his eyes … he will be able to recognize … he will be like the watershed, that many of us will pass over, and go on to where we will be of most use. I see "C." She is grown now. She is very close to me. I … for some reason I feel that I should be much older … and yet age has been suspended.

DO YOU SEE ANYONE ELSE?

Not here on the platform.

DO ANY OTHERS TRAIN WITH YOU FOR THE SAME PURPOSE?

I do not see others doing what the teachers and I are doing. But there are others. There are others that will help me. We will help each other in bringing this knowledge out.

DESCRIBE THE OTHERS.

(long pause) ... I am sorry for the delay. I was dissolved. I am trying to see the others. The only way to do it while I am still in the cave is to dissolve. (long pause) … I do not see them yet.

IT IS VERY EASY FOR YOU TO SEE ONE OF THEM.

(Pause) … The man beside me, who came in with me, I am not sure whether he is going to be there, on Earth with me, for, as I am told, people cannot see invisible things, or they only see things that they want to see. I am trying to … but it's hard. I think … to go back and forth … he will be with me, and because I am still here on this planet and not on Earth, I cannot talk as if I'm on Earth. I know general things about Earth, for Earth is just one stage, and all peoples go through that stage, and it is an understanding. So therefore I know because of meditations I may or I may not see this person, but he is in reality always with me. I am not sure now of other peoples … I know I will have … I know we will have a group on this planet, but that will come later, much later. I am, as far as age go on this planet, which is simply an appearance, I am a child. These friends, I have the impression, will come later. Perhaps they are being trained like I. They do not know, either. But I am very split because I have the understanding of the universe, and yet I am dumb and unable to speak. I … speaking is not necessary here. But I accept all that the teachers give me here, because they are the reality and I am theirs.

LET'S MOVE FROM THE TIME YOU ARE IN NOW, FORWARD APPROXIMATELY ONE-TENTH OF YOUR EXPERIENCE ON THAT PLANET. YOU WILL MOVE FORWARD AT THE COUNT OF THREE, I WILL SNAP MY FINGERS, AND YOU WILL BE ABLE TO SEE. ONE, TWO, THREE, (snap). DESCRIBE YOUR EXPERIENCE.

I am with other people now. We are all sitting down. We are laughing. There seem to be five of us plus two teachers.

DO YOU RECOGNIZE ANY OF THEM?

I recognize vibrations.

DO YOU KNOW ANY OF THEM THAT ARE HERE ON THE EARTH-LIFE WITH YOU?

Yes.

WHO ARE THEY?

"B" and "C." They are on each side of me. We seem to have finished eating.

IS THERE ANYONE ELSE THAT YOU RECOGNIZE?

There's two male types, but I don't make out their impressions or vibrations yet.

IS THIS GROUP SIMILAR TO THE GROUP THAT COMES TO YOUR PLACE, TO THE CAVE, TO MEDITATE?

It doesn't seem to be ... It is hard for me to say. There are other groups ... Seems there are five of us. But it's hard for me to say if there are not other groups on our planet like us. It is hard to think of others than us.

THERE IS NO STRUGGLE ON YOUR PLANET?

No. It is a struggle within yourself, of your own knowledge of the task that is before us.

WELL, GO AHEAD AND TELL ME MORE ABOUT THE STRUGGLE, ABOUT THE TASK, HOW YOU LEAVE, AND WHERE YOU PLAN TO GO?

We must go there without our memories—people who have forgotten everything and will have to grow again. But these five people will go together and will know of each other.

B

WHERE ARE YOU GOING? DO YOU GO TO A DIFFERENT PLANET?

Uh hum.

WHICH PLANET.

We come to Earth.

WHICH OTHER PLANETS WOULD YOU HAVE HAD THE OPTION OF GOING TO? WERE THERE MANY OTHER PLANETS YOU COULD HAVE GONE TO? OR OTHER ENTITIES COME FROM? HOW MANY PLANETS ARE INVOLVED IN THIS SYSTEM?

Sand. Sand. As many. We ... (pause) ... we are needed here.

NOW, BY SAYING SAND, ARE YOU SAYING LIKE GRAINS OF SAND?

As many as sand.

AS MANY PLANETS AS THERE ARE GRAINS OF SAND. SO IT'S JUST INFINITE THEN.

YOU WERE ALL TOGETHER. ALL RIGHT. THE PERSON YOU KNOW AS "D." IS HE IN YOUR PAST?

He was one with us.

WAS HE ON THE SHIP?

N ... I don't know. He was one with us in the temple.

HE WAS IN THE TEMPLE?

In ... that—family. And I, I believe in the temple.

WAS HE THE INSTRUCTOR YOU WERE TALKING ABOUT? THE OLDER TEACHER?

I ...

NOW DON'T LET ME LEAD YOU. YOU BE SURE. DON'T SAY SO BECAUSE I SUGGEST IT. YOU CAN EASILY SAY HE'S NOT.

I know it. ... I think so. I think the love was the same.

WHO WAS ONE OF HIS ASSISTANTS, THAT YOU MAY KNOW?

I believe "C" ... was a handmaiden. I believe behind the altar the day that we all were there.

THE PERSON WE KNOW AS "A"?

I think "A" ... had to do with the place that we ate. The place that we gathered. I believe ... that she served us.

C

WAS YOUR NEXT SHALL WE SAY REINCARNATION ON EARTH?

Yes.

AS "C"?

Yes.

WHO WAS YOUR MATE?

"D."

I WOULD LIKE FOR YOU TO REMAIN ON THAT PLANE FOR A MOMENT. DIVIDE PART OF YOUR ATTENTION BACK ON THE PLANET THAT YOU WERE ON BEFORE YOU CAME HERE, PART OF YOUR ATTENTION TO WHERE YOU ARE RIGHT NOW, PART TO THE PLANE TO WHICH YOU WILL GO. "D" HAS BEEN WITH YOU ON THE SPIRITUAL PLANE AND ON THE OTHER PLANET. HE WAS YOUR MATE. IS THAT CORRECT?

Yes.

OK. LOOK AT OTHER ENTITIES, NOW. RELATE PEOPLE YOU KNOW NOW BACK ON THE SPIRITUAL PLANE OR ANY OTHER PLACE YOU HAVE EVER BEEN. DO YOU FIND OTHERS?

A whole lot of them, it seems like. An awful lot of people I know. "E"—he's dead. He was a brother. "B" ... "A"—"A," wait. "A" was my mother in the body.

"J" was a brother ...

"B"?

"B" I know. She was my sister.

WHERE?

In the clan.

A sixth person, "J," was mentioned by two, but not by the third, as being part of the clan and of this mission. It is possible that he was sent to take the place of "E," after his death, though this is never said by any of the subjects.

Now, this "mission" which has been talked about: what is it? Williamson describes it thusly:

> So there are several million people in the world that have nothing to do with this world as far as learning anything from it that they haven't already acquired. They either passed through many lives on the Earth planet itself, or they learned the same lesson on another world similar to our Earth. At any rate, they are far ahead of the average Earth man or woman. Why do they come back? The answer is, because they want to help; they feel that there is something far more beautiful for man on Earth to attain.[13]

And OAHSPE echoes this:

> To serve others, is to do good unto others; to help them; to teach them; to give them joy and comfort. This is the service of Jehovih. ... But good works alone are not sufficient to attain the highest grades, for they require knowledge and the capacity to unfold others. To accomplish which, those of the higher grades shall oft return to the lower and learn to lift them up. For this is that which calleth the ethereans in the times of resurrections. Wherein the righteous, who are yet mortal, begin at once lifting up their fellows. Which labor is to the spirit as exercise is to the mortal body, that which giveth strength. Judge then thyself, O man of the earth, as to the place thy spirit will rise in the time of thy death.[14]

And here are "C" and "B" talking about the mission:

> C
>
> YOU DECIDED TO COME BACK TO THE EARTH, THEN. FOR WHAT REASON?
>
> Two reasons. I knew that I wanted to help this planet. It is in a bad way. And a lot of people that are here are calling out, they want help very badly, and you can't help unless you are in the body here. It's very intense here. There's no way to get into the ... enough to help, without infringing on free will, unless you're in the body. There are no easy solutions here.
>
> AND THE OTHER REASON FOR COMING BACK?

> It was my own criticism of myself that I did not know how to give without receiving. I felt that I needed an experience that would express what I knew without expecting a return.
>
> **B**
>
> DO YOU HAVE SOMETHING ELSE TO LEARN, OR SOMETHING TO TEACH? SOMETHING TO BRING FORTH IN YOUR LIFE?
>
> Teaching is learning. That is one. They're both one.
>
> NOW ARE YOU FULFILLING YOUR ASSIGNMENT IN SOME WAY NOW?
>
> About to. All the pieces are ready. Not quite ready. Gathering together. They are gathering. This is a gathering time. The things that I must work with are not all gathered yet but are coming.
>
> NOW, WHAT IS THE NEXT DEVELOPMENT, WHEN WILL THIS PLAN BE PUT INTO EFFECT?
>
> A meeting. One piece, one piece—is a meeting, soon. Ah … only one piece. Other pieces, gradually, will come. Four years to do it.
>
> WHERE WILL THE MEETING TAKE PLACE?
>
> I don't know. That's only one piece of it … but that will bring … threads together, some of them.
>
> WHAT WILL BE THE RESULT OF THE MEETING, THE FINAL OUTCOME?
>
> More—more threads joining. To complete the—to complete … um, again, magnetism, electric, it has to do with the same threads, those threads, joining.

And so now is the time when the threads are beginning to come together, not only for this little band of "apples" but for so many others:

> … we have sought slowly to bring to you information relevant to the times in which you now find yourselves. We have sought through many of our channels, our peoples walking the surface of your planet, to present through all avenues open to us, whether these be that which you term fiction or fact, data or imagination, something of the change which is about to take place.[15]

It is indeed a strange story. Yet it will ring true to the many who read this who themselves have a feeling that they were put here on Earth to help …

somehow, some way, some day. The Confederation would say: meditate, and your purpose will unfold, from within.

Our subject, "A," far more than the other two, was focused during her regression sessions on the purpose of her coming here, and the precise reasons for which she had chosen this time in which to journey here. To close this chapter, I let a meditative Wanderer speak about her mission on Earth:

A

CAN YOU TELL ME ANYTHING MORE ABOUT "D," WHY HE CAME, OR ...

Yes, he comes before I do.

WHY? DO YOU KNOW WHY HE DOES THIS?

He will ... it will be necessary for him to be there at the so-called dawning of our appearance. This ... He will need the time also before any of us arrive to make his own advancements and to be ready for us. He will also know and convey information about the peoples on Earth. He will understand once again, as we all will, of the delicateness of free will, and the ways to help the people rather in a sneaky way.

It is a beautiful thing, if I may relate what I am thinking about here on the platform, it is a beautiful thing that all these peoples are coming to this one planet. And I sincerely pray, as I do each day, that the people will realize the fantastic thing that the infinite Creator is allowing. We feel very blessed in our hearts.

DO YOU KNOW WHY YOU GO TO EARTH AT THIS TIME? IS THIS A SPECIFIC TIME FOR EARTH?

All I can say ... it is a feeling that we all have. Feelings and vibrations from everything and everywhere. We receive also. It is a feeling like giving birth. It is time for Earth to be born. She has gone through many times of labor, many hard stages of development, but giving birth ... hopefully, the planet will live. But if it is the will of the infinite Creator, the Earth may not. We do because it is. No one guesses at the infinite Creator. But we develop; we have our task, and we do this because it is our task. We need to pass tests. We need to achieve oneness, dissolution in the infinite Creator, just as all peoples. We come to help give birth to the Earth. But we cannot give it life. That is the free will that is the communication between the Creator and all of the Earth. Not just in the voices of the people, it is in invisible and the unheard of, the tiny, tiny places inside of each person and each thing that communicates to the infinite Creator its will. And we can only help each of those tiny places realize its kingdom and its glory. And, if it hears, then so be it. It is a hard thing. It is a painful thing, for I feel its birth. I feel that the Earth is inside of me. And I worry because I have no real control over the life and death of this child. This is why I'm sad. I'm sad because we are all one, and it is hard to stand back and not know whether your child is going to live or die. And although its death will be its birth, I know what that illusion, death, can do when the mind is weak. I pray, as we all do, for the peoples on Earth to hear, even if it's with their inner ear, we pray for each soul to awaken, and we stand ready for that split second when someone might turn around and see. That is why we are here, nothing more and nothing less. We are here as Gods. But we are Gods that grovel, and know the blessing and the love that we give and receive from those who step on us. Because we were them also. It only takes time, that illusion, time, to stand up and be gods to someone else.

We pray for the Earth, that she will be born. Soon, there will be many things: confusion. At the time, there will be much busy-ness, as it is called. At that time there will be false witness and false rumors, and those who want to play mischief with this most important time. I see all of this standing on the platform. I see this with my mate. It is pouring through me, which is why I am able to talk of it. For soon this knowledge will be closed. For those of us who still know the reality there will be no miracles. Miracles are for the unfaithful. Miracles are tricks.

... tape ends, some material lost while another tape loaded in the recorder.

... and the ship just leaves.

AS IT LEAVES, I WISH YOU WOULD TAKE A LOOK BACK NOW AT THE PLANE THAT YOU HAVE JUST LEFT. CAN YOU LOOK AT THIS FOR ME IN THE SPIRITUAL OR IN THE PHYSICAL REALM AND GIVE ME ANY KIND OF DESCRIPTION? IS IT IN THE SAME DIMENSION AS EARTH?

It is ... (pause) It is hard. It is at least one vibrational level above Earth. Earth will, if it survives, it will go through a great change and will live through another birth. But that is where we are, because we are able to have such powers of mind that we can do these things with other planets in total harmony. This is something Earth will have to learn in its next phase.

It will be, as I remember from my past knowledge ... a beautiful time. But it is still one level behind my level, for soon we will go through a birth also. But it is not such a hard one.

THEN IN CHANGING FROM ONE VIBRATIONAL DIMENSION TO ANOTHER, IT IS SIMPLY A MATTER OF ATTUNEMENT, THEN?

Yes. The one that I kept looking back to from that? He is on a different vibrational level.

EVEN THOUGH YOU ARE IN THE SAME DIMENSION?

Yes. My teachers are at a higher vibrational level.

AND THIS IS WHY THEY HAVE A DIFFERENT GLOW ABOUT THEM?

Yes.

NOW, CAN YOU REACH THAT LEVEL?

Now?

EVER.

Yes.

DO YOU EXPECT TO ATTAIN THAT LEVEL AT SOME TIME ON THE EARTH PLANE?

I can obtain it if I stay on the Earth plane, according to my own development and on my awareness of who I am. If this is what is asked of me, then I will do this. But I may not stay here on the Earth. It is up to the infinite Creator. To my innermost soul. If my infinite Creator ... these things are not set, and no one knows the infinite Creator.

ON THE EARTH PLANE, THERE WILL BE AN ENTITY KNOWN AS JESUS CHRIST.

Yes.

IS HE FROM A SIMILAR VIBRATIONAL LEVEL AS THE PEOPLE YOU HAVE BEEN TALKING ABOUT?

Yes.

THEN EARTH BEINGS, WHEN THEY REACH THAT LEVEL, CAN ALSO ATTAIN THIS LEVEL OF VIBRATION?

Oh, yes. Oh, yes.

NOW, CAN THEY DO IT DIRECTLY FROM THE PHYSICAL PLANE, OR WOULD THEY HAVE TO LEAVE THE PHYSICAL PLANE AND THEN COME BACK?

It is most possible to do it while on this plane. But it takes what I have been talking about—the dissolution of time and space. It is a mental process that is beyond everything that is known here. If he can achieve that, if he can achieve being able to dissolve completely, he will be of much higher vibrational level, and whether his task is to stay here and be an illumined one or to go on any other of the infinite levels where people exist, that is up to the infinite Creator.

OK. DO YOU WANT TO POINT OUT ANYTHING ELSE, NOW, FROM THIS PARTICULAR POINT?

It is ... it is hard to explain, except that at this level, many planets ... it is like the make or break level. It is a most unstable situation because there is the equality and the battle between the illusion of bad and good. It is not ... it is erroneous to call it evil, that is why I say illusion. It is simply the remembrance in people of their earlier life, earlier vibrational plane, that is carried over, inherited, in the Earth itself. Which comes up on the other side of the higher vibrational that is most evident there also. It is a ... two, like magnets, in each particle, in each person, in each molecule, that keeps them from becoming steadied and ready and quiet for birth. There are old ... if I may call them that, old souls that only remember their more base vibrational level, and they add to the struggle. It is only after this level that things will be much easier.

Two postscripts to this chapter: first, it may have occurred to you to wonder why we didn't have all five of the subjects' regressions in this discussion. Unfortunately, neither "D" nor "J" have, up until this time, been hypnotizable.

Secondly, I would like to give credit to Mr. Lawrence Allison, an excellent hypnotist who has spent many patient hours with me working on these cases.

Chapter Nine

Death, Destruction, Chaos, And Other Bad Stuff

A comprehensive study of far-out ufology would not be complete without the inclusion of the doomsday prophecies. A substantial portion of alleged UFO messages deal with coming drastic Earth changes, along the lines of the Edgar Cayce predictions. Included in the list of disasters are polar shifts, earthquakes, instantaneous and mass kundalini experiences, divine revelation, total planetary transformation, and other items which should rival Saturday afternoon football for generating general interest.

What condenses out of all this prophesied mayhem is a story of cycles. A good man to start telling this story is one of the contactees of the fifties, George Van Tassel. He reported numerous contacts with extraterrestrials including a guided tour of a saucer of the type photographed by another early contactee, George Adamski.

Van Tassel claimed telepathic contact with the UFOnauts both at a distance and in person. By the latter I mean that he claimed that the very "normal" looking space man who accompanied him on the space ship would answer his questions before he could verbalize them. George published information he had received from the Great Pyramid at Giza to a time machine he was building as a result of instructions from the space people. This time machine, which he called an integratron, still sits in the Mojave Desert near Van Tassel's small airport at Giant Rock, California. He claims that the reason it won't work is that the space people have never come back and calibrated it for him.

Needless to say, Van Tassel was never taken seriously by the bulk of the scientific community. I spent a week at Giant Rock in 1964 getting to know George and doing a little more detective work. Although I have no way of vouching for the validity of his claims, I can say that he displayed the characteristics of the people who were involved in my telepathic experiments, and was able to display the same type of seemingly telepathic response with which I had become quite familiar in that connection.

At any rate he is one of the classic contactees and some of his material fits nicely into my theory of ufology.

> O mortals cast in density of form, I center the Light to guide your way. My Light is not seen by those who observe only the density of figure.

> Neither can I violate the Laws I have made in the Wisdom of My eternal ways. I cannot but stay at rest with you, hoping that the best will reach for Me, that I may bring your perception into the Light.
>
> Man closes doors, man hides himself. He binds himself to possessions of dust, not realizing all is lost to him and lost to Me. For only by the progression of thee do I progress. My parts are scattered throughout My boundless Being. I move in many ways to fashion My completeness. Each part shall find the resurrection in Me, though the time is recorded in the records lost in space. My eternity is only complete in the patience of Myself in thee.
>
> And so I wait within, with the knowing that My beginnings never end.
>
> O man, in the everchanging pattern of My thoughts I bring My creatures into being. In seeing motion all about, never doubt that I am there. For I am motion, change, and time, so that My rhyme of repetition may cycle all My parts.
>
> Your eyes reach out to see the stars, not realizing each has stars within. Though sin may barricade your way to Me, change will be your sword to rend the veil and I shall hail you in your victory over self.
>
> Though My time is naught to Me, time to you is meant to be a gauge to register progression in My ways.
>
> Motion is the Me in thee, O man, to manifest a change, so that in time you may escape the rhyme of rebirth repetitions and be timelessly the peaceful thought of Me—eternally.[1]

❧

> There are twelve densities in the system we occupy. Each of these is divided into twelve major cycles. Each major cycle is divided into twelve minor cycles. When a solar system moves out of one density into another, it is called a master cycle. The solar system that we are in is now in the arc between the Third and Fourth densities. For the planet Earth and this solar system, this is the time of times. The Earth is culminating a minor cycle, a major cycle, and a master cycle all at the same time. This will bring about a rebalancing of the planet on new poles. When this occurs, the great earthquake written of in Revelations will take place.[2]

George is saying that due to the rotation of our galaxy, or some more complex relative motion through space, our planetary system is making a cyclical transition which will result in changes in the basic atomic structure of our physical environment, including our physical bodies.

Another source says:

> ... our understanding of time relates to *magnetic cycles*. Perhaps we have imperfectly expressed ourselves on this score in that we cannot seem to convey to you the relationship between cyclic time—magnetic cycles—and your understanding of time.[3]

OAHSPE speaks of the termination of the previous cycle:

> So Jehovih said: Now will I prune the earth and her heaven. Behold the division of Wagga shall be hewn off and cast beneath the waters of the ocean. Her heaven shall be no longer tenable by the spirits of destruction, for I will rend the foundation thereof and scatter them in the winds of heaven.
>
> Go ye, therefore, down to the earth and provide nets and vanchas for receiving the spirits of darkness, and for receiving the spirits of mortals who shall perish in the waters. And provide ye a place in my exalted heavens suitable for them; and ye shall wall them about in heaven that they cannot escape, but that they may be weaned from evil.[4]
>
> My etherean ships of fire shall surround Wagga on every side. And I will cut loose the foundations of the earth, at the borders of the ocean and the mountains of Gan, nor shall any prop or corner-stone stay My hand. And I will send rains and winds and thundering; and the waters of the great deep shall come upon the lands, and the great cities shall go down and be swallowed in the sea.[5]

Here is the Hatonn source on the same subject; except that he is speaking of the end of the *present* cycle.

> There are many vibrations within this creation. It has been written in your Holy works that "in my Father's house, there are many mansions." This was a statement of these conditions. The mansion, or vibration, in which an entity finds himself is a result of his desire. If there is a separation, or choice, to be made, then it is up to each entity to select, according to his desire.
>
> For that reason, we visit your planet at this time, to attempt to help those who could wish to make their choice. There are many who have chosen already, even though they are not aware of it.

There will be an experience in this illusion, in the not-too-distant future, which will be alarming to some of the people of this planet. We are attempting to provide an understanding of the truth of this experience prior to its occurrence. Our service is to aid those who wish to choose a different mansion.

If an entity has chosen a particular mansion, then he will receive it. It is not a good or a bad place. It is simply a different place.[6]

There are several events that will occur. There will be events of a physical nature. These events will be, from the point of view of those who are living with the illusion, of a very destructive nature. However, there is no such thing as destruction. There is only change. This you must understand. If you understand this, then you will understand the truth of what is to occur.

There will be change, a physical change. This change will be very beneficial. However, the people of this planet who view these changes from their present state of ignorance will consider them to be quite destructive.

This is unfortunate. However, the people of this planet have had a sufficient length of time to become educated. They have, however, sought to educate themselves in the ways of their illusion, rather than the ways of the Creator. This illusion is so strong in their understanding that most of them have no awareness in a waking sense of reality. These people will be very difficult to communicate with. They will view the changes in their immediate creation as destructive and irreversible.

Q. Well, is it going to be an earthquake, or a depression, or what?

The changes will be of a physical nature. The depression of which you speak is of no consequence. It would be viewed as nothing compared to the physical changes that will occur. It will be necessary for members of groups such as this one who wish to serve to understand fully the reality of these changes, and to understand fully the accuracy of the statement made in your holy book which states that "Although you walk through the valley of the shadow of death, you will fear no evil." This must be kept uppermost in your consciousness. For you will walk through this valley. And you will demonstrate to those who seek your knowledge of truth and only your ability to demonstrate this knowledge will alert those who seek the knowledge that you are a true and knowing channel. For many false channels will at this time be lost. For they will not be able to demonstrate their knowledge of truth. For they will cling to the illusion that has surrounded them, and will display the fear that this illusion brings upon them.

This change is looked upon by those of us who understand it as an extremely beneficial change. It is also looked upon, by those members of groups such as this one who have realized the truth of this information, as extremely beneficial to all the peoples of this planet. It will be difficult for some of the members of groups such as this one to demonstrate an understanding of these truths, since they have been strongly affected by the illusion that has been created by the people of this planet.

However, this understanding is a necessity to be demonstrated.

Q. What's going to be happening, exactly?

Physical change, of all types.

There will be massive destruction wrought upon your surface. It will be of such a nature as to totally change the surface of your planet. This destruction is within your planet at this time. It has been put there by thought. It has been put there by the thought of the population of this planet through thousands of years of thinking this thought. This thought is of a vibratory nature. You are at this time passing through the last portion of what you know as the third density vibration. Shortly, your planet will be sufficiently within what you know as the fourth density vibration. At this time there will be a disharmony between the thought that creates the vibration that is your planet, and the thought that dwells within the density that is the fourth.

Much energy will be released of a physical nature. This energy will create physical changes within your planet. There will be changes within your land masses. Changes in your atmosphere.

Changes in all of the physical manifestations of your planet. This will be of a nature that will be considered to be cataclysmic. This is a very good thing. However, it will not be considered good by those that are within the illusion.

Labeling this change good or bad is something that is dependent upon the individual observing the change and his orientation. My friends, the reason for this change being of a cataclysmic nature is that the thought that has been generated upon and in your planet for the past several thousands of years is a thought that is out of harmony with the new vibration that your planet now goes into. The Creator never conceived of the condition that is shortly to manifest upon your planet. This condition is manifested as a result of the desire of all the individuals that dwell on this planet. They are not aware of this desire, but their desire has created this.

They have created a condition by their desire that is shortly to be severely out of harmony with where they will physically be. Due to this, there will be a large energy release, which will manifest itself upon your planet in the form of earthquakes, storms, volcanic eruptions, and in fact a shift of the poles of your planet with respect to their orientation in space.

This change that will shortly manifest itself upon your planet is, as I have said, a result of the mismatching of vibrations of your planet and its new position in space. This change will alert many of the people of your planet who are very lightly slumbering, and many of the ones who are slumbering relatively deep. Many of these people will at this time be what is known in many of your religions as "saved." It will save them, because they will get the violent awakening that is necessary to cause them to raise their vibrations that last amount that is necessary to get them off the fence, so to speak.

There will be those who are more deeply slumbering, so to speak, who will not make the transition. It is up to you to provide those who will be awakened with the information that they desire. We have stated that this transition is both good and bad. Ultimately, in its most broad sense, it is a good transition; however, it is an unnecessary transition. In a normal transition there would be no energy release, since in a normal transition, the vibration of the planet would match closely enough and be in harmony with the new and higher vibration. This would result in no energy release, and the planet would continue in a relatively normal sense from a lower vibration to the higher. Your planet is an aberration in the evolution of the spirit of the people of the planet and the planet. The change that will take place will be a beneficial change. However, the mechanics of the change will seem anything but beneficial.

Those of the people who dwell upon this surface at this time who are totally aware of the results of this change, and the reason for it, will not in any way be affected by this change. Those who are not aware of this, but who are aware of this in a spiritual sense, will be affected only emotionally, because they will not understand. There are the people we wish to communicate with.[7]

The UFOnauts emphatically feel that this catastrophic time is not absolutely necessary. We could avert it if we came into harmony with the new vibration. In fact, the precise timing of the Earth changes depends entirely upon us:

> We of course cannot interfere, but do ask that you who are on the Earth planet work metaphysically, mentally with love in your hearts to eliminate, as much as Spirit will allow to be eliminated, danger, fear, panic, and loss. Thank you. We are on the alert. We do not know when and how some of these will strike. But they are scheduled, from what we can gather of auric conditions and mass thinking in this section of the world, which is very serious at this time.[8]

❧

> But let me say to you this, that prophecies were given so that Man would have the opportunity to avoid these things. Prophecies do not necessarily need to be fulfilled, for Man's destiny lies entirely within his own hands. You see, prophecies are made by the realization of a pattern, but patterns can be changed, and you, my friends, the People of Earth, have it within our power to change and avoid these things.[9]

And from Case No. 3, Chapter 1:

> Then he gave us to understand that the little men might represent a threat for all of us in the future. But, as he was not sure whether the danger came from the particular type of individual who had abducted him or from other unknown types, he was at present prepared to have a further meeting with them in order to clarify the matter. In any case, he said, he was certain that the world was in great danger, without however knowing from where this danger would come. The danger had been revealed to him by the fair-skinned individual of friendly mien who had appeared mysteriously before him in the chamber, unperceived by the little men. The danger would involve the whole of mankind, and would possibly include intervention by unknown beings, in addition to other calamities. This danger might however be avoided if mankind changed their present behavior.[10]

The Confederation is hoping that we on Earth will become aware of what power our thoughts actually have, and its members are here to keep the message of love flowing to those on Earth who desire to hear it and learn from it.

> Your planet, along with its neighbors, is moving as your galaxy is, into a new area of space, a new vibration. In this creation, there is nothing but order. It is only necessary to look about you to see the order and perfection of this universe.
>
> You are about to experience a gift. This gift will be a new understanding of love. Some of you have already begun to experience this, and as the progression takes place, it will become more and more apparent to many of those of Earth.
>
> We are here to help with this experience. This is the reason that so many of your brothers from space, as you call it, are now here with planet Earth. We are here to serve and to help the Creator's plan bring to you the love that you desire.[11]

And from OAHSPE:

> So great was the wisdom of these Gods and Goddesses that to come within the earth's atmosphere was sufficient to enable them to read all the souls and prayers of mortals, and all the thoughts and desires of the spirits of the lower heaven belonging to the earth. To each and all of them the voice of Jehovih was ever present, and their power was like unto their wisdom.
>
> Jehovih hath said: To the corporean I have given power to hear one or two things as the same moment of time; but My Gods can hear intelligently tens of thousands of men speaking at the same time. Yea, they can find a way to answer them also.[12]

❧

> Fragapatti said: Autevat, my son, the All Light fell upon me, saying: My Son, go to the red star, the earth; her coat is red with mortal blood! Now, by her time she standeth more than two hundred years beyond the boundaries of Horub. For this, I called thee and thy attendants. How long will it take thee to go thither and survey the earth and her heavens, and return hither?
>
> Autevat, well trained in such matters, said: Of the earth's time, forty days. Fragapatti said: What number of attendants wilt thou require for so great a distance? And Autevat said: Twenty thousand.
>
> Fragapatti said: Provide thee, then, all thou requirest, and go at once. And if thou shalt find the inhabitants of the earth suitable for sacred records, commission thou the God or Lords to send second loo'is to raise up an heir for Jehovih's kingdom.

> Autevat said: Thy will and Jehovih's be done. And, duly saluting, he and his attendants withdrew, and, coming to Gatwawa, ordered an arrow-ship of twenty thousand gauge. In two days it was completed; and, during the time, Autevat had chosen his attendants. And so he departed, swiftly, like a ray of light, Autevat and his attendants, for the red star, the earth. To see what was the matter, that a God so far away as Fragapatti was, could feel and know the flow of human blood!
>
> For such is the all perfection of Jehovih's Sons and Daughters. Even mortals can sense things a little way off; but Jehovih's upraised Gods feel the breath of the stars, and know when they are disordered.[13]

> The planet Earth is now in a state of transition toward a greater unfoldment of man's progression; the world is not going to end![14]

> ... we are now diligently preparing the way for His footsteps to be heard throughout the world. The Kingdom is no longer at hand, the Kingdom is *here*, and He is shortly to manifest to all men. We have awaited this time with eagerness through the long centuries. Is it not then a time for great rejoicing even though some catastrophe shall come to the world? But through this catastrophic purification man shall inherit his godhood.[15]

> Full knowledge of our presence will soon be known to your people. There will be, at that time, great upheavals on your planet. We regret this cannot in any way be avoided. We knew this from the beginning. We, therefore, have warned man repeatedly to prepare for these events, both mentally and physically.[16]

And one last and extremely sensible insight into the contactee predictions of catastrophe, which we would do well to note as an accurate perception:

> "Orthon," a cosmic being, told a group of Danish contactees that a great cataclysm would occur on December 24, 1967. The press freely translated this as "the end of the world." Borge Jensen, spokesman for the contactees, told newsmen that Orthon and the Space Brothers had released the warning out of love for mankind. The world did not end, and one would have to debate the limits of "cataclysm," but on the date named by the space being, earthquakes rattled various parts of the globe (some registering as high as 7.25 on a Richter scale of 10), an inactive volcano in Samoa began vomiting new fire, and nearly the

whole of Europe was paralyzed by severe winter storms. Could it be that our Space Brothers merely exaggerate the scope of coming disasters in an attempt to get apathetic and skeptical Earthmen to act?[17]

Chapter Ten
Conclusion

In the previous chapters we've become familiar with the general foundations of the basic communication which I have extracted from the contactee and other UFO phenomena. The material we have examined is only a tiny percentage of the total contactee data available to the energetic researcher, but it does represent the general gist of most contactee data. I will not say that there are not some totally anomalistic contactee cases, but these seem to be in the minority. One of these cases is the strange and lengthy contact of the people from the planet UMMO, the original contactee reports coming from Spain. As a researcher said:

> Invited to address the gathering at the close of the Symposium, Secretary-General Fouere dwelt upon the unique nature of the UMMO reports. He said: "I have received dozens of messages from supposed extraterrestrials, transmitted by all types of contactees. They are always messages of a missionary or evangelical type, in which terrestrials are warned of the tremendous dangers resulting from their imprudent manipulation of atomic energy; or the others try to save us and redeem us. The UMMO messages, on the other hand, without attempting to convert us to any sort of cosmic religion.[1]

It is to be noted that although the UMMO material is not high-key in its zeal to save earth, the philosophical content of the messages are congruent with the basic Confederation philosophy. Noted researcher Brad Steiger, a man with quite a bit of experience in dealing with the contactee phenomena, gave this evaluation of the contacted message content in his excellent and perceptive book, THE AQUARIAN REVELATIONS:

> The philosophical and metaphysical content of the essential message allegedly entrusted to the contactee is nearly always the same. A distillation of the Outer Space Apocrypha would reveal such concepts as the following:
>
> - Man is not alone in the solar system. He has "space brothers" and they have come to earth to reach him and to teach him.
> - The Space Brothers have advanced information which they wish to impart to their weaker brethren. The Space Brothers want man to join an intergalactic spiritual federation.
> - The Space Brothers are here to teach, to help man rise to higher levels of vibration so that he may be ready to enter new dimensions. According to the Outer Space Apocrypha, such a

goal was precisely what Jesus, the prophets, Confucius and the leaders of the great religions have tried to teach man.

- Man stands now in the transitional period before the dawn of a New Age. With peace, love, brotherhood and understanding on man's part, he will see a great new era begin to dawn."
- If man should not raise his vibratory rate within a set period of time, severe earth changes and cataclysms will take place. Such disasters will not end the world, but shall serve as cataclysmic crucibles to burn off the dross of unreceptive humanity."[2]

You can see that I am not the only ufologist who has been putting the puzzle pieces patiently together over the years. These conclusions as to the content of the UFO message seem inescapable to the serious investigator. In fact, the missionary aspect of the UFO's contact is assumed to be present to the point where, in a recent case, the investigator was puzzled as to why the contactee hadn't responded properly to it:

> If Mrs. M's UFO experience was "designed" to inspire her with a missionary zeal, as has happened to other contactees, why has it not "worked" for her in this way, and for what deeper reasons other than to avoid notoriety has she avoided telling many people about her experience.[3]

To conclude this exploration, I will make a statement of the total UFO story as I have come to understand it, on the basic philosophical level. The UFO sources have a view of the universe and man within it upon which they build all their actions toward us. This is what we are getting from the bulk of these UFO contacts:

The stuff of which the universe is made is consciousness, a single, infinite consciousness. This by definition is the Creator. This consciousness created vibrations through infinite space. This basic vibration is identified in our physical science as the photon, the basic particle-wave called light. This light vibration is the raw material used to make everything that there is within the creation.

The vibrations which were fashioned from light exist over a large range of frequencies, only a small portion of which is apparent within our present physical reality. All atoms, whether within or outside of our physical reality are simply more complex rotations and vibrations of the basic photon.

We are then, a highly complex, vibrational, single, infinite, entity. Presently we are experiencing the illusion of individualization as separate entities, but still we have been created by the one consciousness, and our basic essence resides within the Creator's one consciousness. This original state has been allegorized by the Holy Bible's story of Adam and Eve. In that tale, the serpent coaxes the couple into eating the fruit of knowledge of duality (good and evil), and so they get ousted from the Garden. The UFOnauts say that the Creator created us with knowledge of our unity with all things, but also with free will and the ability to create as His sons and daughters. Through our free will, they say, man long ago decided to become individualized to the extent that we could no longer find our unity with one another. We were no longer one, we had entered into a man-made universe of duality, of separation from the original thought, which then resulted in the polarization of consciousness (good and evil). From this duality all of our present problems have been generated.

The original creative thought was a thought of the creation in which each part would act in service to the other parts, just as the parts of the body act as a unit, in mutual service to itself as a whole. However, in the man-created world the various parts have ceased being totally and mutually supported, and a far more complex world-reality has emerged. The question of why the world doesn't seem to work very well can be put in focus by imagining what would happen to the natural creation if trees got tired of turning Co_2 into oxygen and clouds decided not to rain any more. In some cases we humans are still capable of being biased towards service: we are shocked if a mother refuses to feed her new-born child. But we have strayed far enough into isolation to be unable to perceive the unity between us all, so that we tend to believe that there are some whom we should not serve, but oppose.

This Adam and Eve adventure of ours away from the original thought resulted in succeeding changes of vibration, as the structure of the individualizing consciousness proceeded to take form. Back when the individualized man was young he had the full Creator's ability to instantly create that which was imagined. Thus the Creation grew and grew. But as the consciousness of unity was lost, the Creation became progressively stratified so that it came to exist not as one vibration of love but as many vibrations, each a little less rapid than its predecessor. And so evolved the numerous densities of experience, all condensed from the same original vibration, each spanning part of the range from total unity to total separation. This makes for a vast creation of experience, considering that the original consciousness was infinite to begin with.

We are, today, encased in a consciousness many eons away from the condition of total unity. Most of us don't totally like where we've landed in the continuum of experience: worse, most of us don't even remember the journey we took to get here. According to the UFO contacts, we are at a point in the journey back toward the original thought where it is possible for at least some of us to realize our position and make a conscious choice about our own progress. We have been preparing to make this choice for almost a full cycle of experience at this level or density. The time to make the choice is now, for the cycle is ending.

> As fast as the ship passed the lights, the etherean musicians came aboard, being anxious to meet Hipacha and his hosts, especially the I'hins, and to congratulate them on being the first harvest from the lowest heaven at the end of a cycle. And strange to say there were just twice as many as Sethantes had prepared in the first dawn on earth. Fragapatti called the swift messengers belonging to the roads of Gon, in etherea, and he said unto them: Go ye to Sethantes, whose fields lie in the Roads of Gon, and say unto him: Greeting, in the name of Jehovah! The earth hath reached Obsod and Goomatchala, home of Fragapatti, who sendeth love and joy on behalf of sixty millions, first harvest of h'ak, grade sixty-five.[4]

Grade fifty is the minimum harvestable grade, according to OAHSPE, the grade indicating that the person is fifty percent for himself and fifty percent for service to others.

Now we are living within the third density of vibration, trying in our rather vague way to learn how to think, not in a complex and intellectual way but in the sense of coming into tune with the original vibration of unity.

I realize that some people are perfectly satisfied with life as it is. I am reminded of the circus janitor who cleans up after the elephants. Upon being interrupted at his malodorous work, shovel in hand, he looks up and smiles. "Say," we quip, "how come you keep on working here. What a job! Don't you want to leave and get a better job?" The janitor laughs in amazement, and replies: "What? And quit show business?" So, some people like this density, and, indeed, there are those who seek a level of experience even farther from unity than ours. If all upon our planet were striving for unity, then the UFOnauts wouldn't be nearly so elusive. But there are many who prefer their universe as it now is, and do not wish to be bothered with such nonsense.

In OAHSPE, we find Jehovih speaking "out of the light inherent" in the etherean gardens, stating the situation like this:

> Sixteen times have my etherean hosts redeemed the earth and her heavens from darkness into light, and yet ere the end of a cycle she

> falleth again, and her atmospheres with her. And now it hath come to pass that her heavens are filled with thousands of millions of spirits that know not Me and My emancipated worlds.[5]

Here is the "fallen mankind" described in another way:

> ... man so loved the earth and whatsoever ministered unto his ease and to his flesh desires, that he fell from his high estate. And great darkness came upon the earth. And man cast aside his clothes, and went naked, and became carnal in his desires. The Lord went abroad over the earth calling: Come to me, O man! Behold, thy Lord is returned! But man heard not the voice of the lord; for, by man's indulgence, the spirit of man was covered up in his own flesh.[6]

So, mankind, and all entities in the creation, dwell within various densities, in some degree sensitive or insensitive to the original vibration of unity or love which created the universe.

After all of these densities were formed in the Creation, the desire began to be generated to do the inevitable: make a full circle back to the original unity. Jacob's ladder, with every rung going higher, is a good analogy to this: man has inborn the inevitable desire to seek for the top of his ladder of experience. All over our infinite Creation, entities have progressed, at various rates, on this climb back to the original condition. As entities reach a certain point in their development, they begin to again grasp the nature of the Creator as service to all. At this point these entities reach their hands down the ladder, to help their brothers who are climbing below. *But the law of progression is sustained in perfect free will, so that only those who are reaching up for that help will receive it.* Men have an inalienable right to progress, or even regress, at their individual speeds; there is an infinite amount of time available.

The UFO source states that in the third density of vibration we have tools with which to make our experiences work for our progress: our physical or third-density body, and our higher self, which can detach itself from the physical and experience the finer vibrations of existence which interpenetrate our physical world. Most of the total humanity which has ever been in the physical is at present to be found in the finer planes of existence. The inhabitants of these astral and devachanic regions incarnate into a physical body primarily for the experiences which the physical world can offer. Some within the astral realms incarnate chiefly to experience the pleasures of the flesh. The more spiritually evolved souls of the devachanic regions often desire incarnation into the physical to mature themselves through the catalyst of physical experience, which is much more immediate and keenly felt than experience on higher planes. The astral's objective is easy to understand: he just wants to get back in the game and live it up. To get at the reason that the devachanic entity wants to incarnate, let me just give an example in story form. Mr. Good has, in his previous life on Earth, done a great many nice things, but like all of us, he was in some ways still selfish. After his death, back on the higher planes, he was able to view his life just passed as a whole, and in this perspective his mistakes were apparent. In the higher vibration to which he has come because his vibrations basically are a match with it, all of his companions have his desire for advancement, and thus it is possible to "see" with more discerning eyes what has occurred on the denser planes. The errors become obvious.

Now Mr. Good has an ambition: he wants to correct his mistakes in order to advance his level of consciousness. But this is not easy to do by pure force of will. It must be done in the dense level at which one acts and then seems to receive reactions from the outside. On the devachanic level it is obvious that all effects are the result of one's own actions.

> Even as to the square of the distance away from the earth, so are the grades of my resurrections.
>
> According to the exaltation of man's soul, so shall he inhabit the places I have made.
>
> According to his own soul's growth and development, so shall he ascend in my kingdoms, outward away from the earth, grade unto grade adapted I them.[7]

The great virtue of the physical world is the amount of pain which it can generate in consciousness. It is due to the stimulus of this catalyst, pain, that we gradually learn how to avoid pain, in an ever-ascending sense. Primitive man learns not to put his hand in the fire: spiritually-seeking man learns to combat his own pain by seeking to be of service to his fellow man. The pain of existence can be felt at the level of the physical body, within the mental or the emotional body, or solely within the spiritual body. Yet while we are within the physical this pain will have a far more urgent and pressing nature, and the decision to seek for its rightful surcease will have a far more pronounced effect upon our essential being.

So Mr. Good chooses another Earth life. Maybe this time he does a little better. He evaluates again. There is no limit to the number of tries a person can have. If necessary an entity could go through our earthbound experiences through eternity.

The analogy may be made to the apparatus for distillation of pure water. The denser vibrations are closer to the earth's surface, actually penetrating it, while the faster ones move at higher altitude. Entities continually make a circuit from a higher level back to the surface, then back again, upward, but hopefully to a higher vibration than before. This is a sort of percolating process producing finally a distillate of souls that are ready for a more refined distillery. This we have seen called the fourth density by UFO sources. OAHSPE describes the type of distillation desired upon this density of existence as follows:

> Jehovih had so made man and angels that, whosoever had learned to abnegate self and to labor for the good of others, was already above grade fifty, and his ascension should be perpetual thereafter; whilst they that were below grade fifty, who had not put away self, should gravitate downward, toward the earth.[8]

In our previous harvests, says OAHSPE, only a small percentage "made the grade":

> Loo'wan said: Great Spirit, I have heard, I have seen. We gather the earth's harvest for Thee, O Jehovih, but they are small. We gather the earth's harvests of dark spirits, O Jehovih, and they are ten times larger. Behold, there is no balance between them.[9]

> And as oft as they are raised up in light, so are they again cast down in darkness, because of the great desire of the spirits of the dead to return back to the earth. These druj return to mortals and fasten upon them as fetals or as familiars, and inspire them to evil. Go now to the earth, O my beloved, and find the division of the earth where most these druj congregate, for I will uproot their stronghold; I will break them from their haunts and they shall no longer carry My people down to destruction.[10]

In past harvest-times, it has happened that entire isolated populations of our world would reach a satisfactory vibration, with souls choosing to incarnate here to be with like-minded people, these populations being isolated from the rest of the world. In these circumstances, the UFOnauts have been able to make actual physical contact from the next vibration. The UFO sources feel that this open contact is highly detrimental to any culture not spiritually ready for it, for several reasons. First, it is demoralizing to realize that there are places one can't go. More importantly, the physical illusion is most effective when it appears totally real and of unquestioned importance. People who are more or less ready to graduate from this classroom of Earth do not need to have the illusion sustained for them; they are ready for a broader perspective. For those who are still learning, this perspective would be detrimental. It would instill, to some degree, doubt in the importance of the "training aids" of our daily experience. IS told Puharich and Geller that they had landed 3000 years ago. They apparently had found a culture sufficiently advanced in vibration to meet.

Right now, there doesn't seem to be a culture or nation sufficiently advanced as a whole to make possible a general or mass landing of fourth density entities. It may be possible that a very small, isolated group might be able to accept such a direct contact. But IS says, "And now we must land again." They are anxious to aid us, now, and to land, because of where we are in our system of cycles. We are at the end of a harvesting period, so that the Earth itself is making her transition to the fourth density. This transition is inexorable and involves not just our planet but the solar system as a whole.

I realize this is one of the harder parts of the UFO story to swallow. It is not easy to picture not just people, but every atom, molecule, particle and part of the solar system, in transition, so that the vibratory rate of all particles will increase one density level in vibrational rate. But the explanation of the cause of the natural catastrophes which a very large percentage of UFO contactees forecast rests on this basic premise of cyclical transition. For the planetary mayhem is said to be brought about due to the disharmony between the vibrations of our planet and the density into which it is transiting.

The planetary vibration is said to be the result of the total sum of man's individual vibrations through history. When the majority of the people advance in vibratory rate at the "normal" rate, the transition to the higher vibration, when time comes for it to be made, is smooth and without incident. But in our case, the majority of our people have not made the appropriate advances, and so there is conflict between our vibration as a planet and the vibration of the new volume of space into which we are passing. As the vibrations increase at the nuclear level and changes begin to occur, the resultant energy releases will result in thermal gradients sufficient to create great stresses in the Earth and therefore massive Earth changes. Through George Hunt Williamson, the source known as Brother Philip says,

> Concern yourselves with the sheep of the flock, those that have strayed or wandered away, for they must have the message of hope and faith in order to endure those tragic days ahead.[11]

Philip pictures the "sheep" to be those who have a sufficiently high vibration to make the transition into the next density, but have no intellectual knowledge of what is occurring. They see many "sheep" as sitting on the fence, poised between striving consciously to advance spiritually and striving instead for more physically-oriented goals to the exclusion of spiritual ones. It is their hope that the sheep may be alerted as these Earth changes begin, so that they may get off the fence, on the spiritual side. The disasters will frighten many, and the Confederation of Planets wishes to alleviate this fear, by putting the events into perspective with their spiritual significance.

Certainly, when we do experience a disaster such as a tornado, hurricane, or flood, we see much pride and glory washed or blown away. Physical structures are torn to shreds, people's belongings and treasures lost. Yet from these experiences people overwhelmingly report their renewed thankfulness to the Creator for sparing them what they see, now to be far more important: their loved ones. The experience seems to focus in people a feeling of being newborn, thankful for real blessings, and humble in the face of the omnipotence of the Creator.

The positively oriented group of UFOnauts are working to make available to people in just this frame of mind the information which gives the spiritual reason for the Earth changes. The Bible gives us, "Blessed are the meek, for they shall inherit the Earth." Taken in reference to the coming transition, the statement describes those of a sufficiently service-oriented attitude to be in harmony with Earth's new rate of vibration.

In the same message, Brother Philip says,

> … the spirit of Anti-Christ is ever more powerful, and it is drawn closer and closer towards the Earth, where it shall have its final death throes. But in those death throes it will take many down with it, and they will not find the Kingdom to be inherited, but must repeat again that great cycle of time that is now culminating in the scene upon your Earth world.[12]

This is spoken of in the Bible as the battle of Armageddon. The UFO sources see it as a battle of mind involving billions of entities both in the physical and in the finer densities of Earth's vibrations, with those billions knowing little or nothing of their part in the battle, or even that the battle is raging. Like most battles, only the "generals" know the overall objectives of the fight, and so in this battle the Masters on both sides—the sides being good and evil, or unity and separation—are doing their best to harvest the greatest crop of consciousness. Their objectives are completely within what we call the mental planes, but objectives won within these planes are inevitably manifested into the physical.

The increasing polarization of the good and evil forces within our planet's people is showing up now in, on the one hand, the great increase in people's desire to seek spiritually; on the other hand, the great increase in crime, war-mindedness, desire for individual power, corporate and personal greed and corruption, and the many other negative aspects of thought which are easily picked out of today's news. The significant fact of course is not that these things occur, but that they are increasing.

From Revelation: "And there shall be wars and rumors of wars and nation shall rise against nation." What kind of thinking causes this situation, which most assuredly now is occurring? The contactees say, very simply, thought of self rather than service. The problems of Earth, from small to vast, can be traced back to this one choice. The result of individuals choosing to serve self is, ultimately, hatred, war, and crime.

As we enter the cusp of this transition period, with the potential difference between the coming vibration of higher unity and the existing vibration of self-service or separation becoming greater and greater, the positive UFOnauts feel that the "sheep" have the greatest chance possible to use this Earth classroom effectively. People can make great progress in these "last days."

In addition to the positive UFOnauts in their craft who are here to aid us, there are many "apples" who are striving to aid Earth's vibration. They have to some degree remembered who they are and what their purpose here is, and they have entered many fields of endeavor to get the message of spiritual seeking spread. Some are in the various fields of communications through media, TV and motion picture production. Some are popular musicians, writing songs about things of the spirit that are on everyone's lips. Some write in modern parable of the eternal truths. Some find expression in their careers of all kinds, touching people through their very personalities and points of view, their simple examples of how to live in harmony. Quite often, the apples are not fully aware of why they have written these songs or words, lived this life, or done these deeds; he or she is simply following an inner direction which is trusted intuitively. I don't mean that one must be an apple to live or act in the described manner, but a great many who so live and act are apples. And all who are led to positive acts are benefiting not only themselves but the Earth vibration as a whole.

A footnote to the discussion about apples is the fascinating fact that the Beatle's recording company was called Apple Records. I have often wondered whether the Beatles were aware of George Hunt Williamson's book.

It is an unshakable tenet of the UFO sources that though they can aid their brothers of Earth in spiritual seeking, the first step, of choosing to seek, must be made under conditions of complete free will by the individual. Hence is formed the concept of providing an example of higher truth, which alerts the seeking consciousness without giving him any proof as such. To prove the "miracle" or "higher being" to be real is to force the choice of seeking on people. But this choice must remain to be accepted or rejected without prejudice: this is the mechanical structure of spiritual evolution. In 1963 a contactee in Warren, Pennsylvania, received:

> … there was a great being who descended into the Earth and parted the sea in testimony for the Israelites, but they did not understand. These miracles were not understood, and this shall not happen again.

The miracles we get now will continue to be of a controversial nature so that people who wish to refute them may do so. "Those who have the eyes to see, let them see."

IS was at first very hesitant about giving Puharich permission to have Geller's abilities scientifically tested:

> After you insisted that Uri be validated, counsel was taken higher and higher, and it was decided that Uri could be validated just this once. And he may never be allowed to do such work again under laboratory control.[13]

It would be in keeping with the contactee theory that they might feel that something on the order of scientific proof might be too strong a catalyst for us, so that they would be infringing on our free will. They were correct to allow Geller to be tested, for as they must have finally surmised, people who do not want to trust this proof, simply state that they don't believe that anything has been proven. The desired controversy over Geller has only been enhanced by these scientific tests!

I do not foresee a parting of the sea occurring in the near future; but I do predict that our UFOnaut visitors will continue to feed man on Earth tantalizing bits of evidence of the illusory nature of his world picture. Each of us will find the truth—in our own way.

"The Amazing" James Randi, a professional magician, is quite convinced that Uri Geller is no more than a conjurer, and that his supposed feats of psychic ability are actually well-done illusions. Randi's complaints about Geller include the point of Geller's inability or unwillingness to work when there are professional magicians around. Randi states that if he were trying to do illusions, he also would wish for no colleagues to be around, that is, if he wanted to fraudulently indicate to the public that his effects were not "tricks" but a demonstration of psychic ability.

He makes a good case on his own terms. The game has been rather expanded out from under him, of course, by the arrival on the scene, and the testing, of many children throughout the world who have the Geller-type abilities. But the book by Randi brings out one of the main strands of thought that weave into my theory. For this controversy between Geller and his many detractors points up one thing above all: this physical world is very real to us.

And it is for a purpose that this world is so real, so solid-appearing to us. All of us have incarnated into the physical to experience its catalytic effect upon our higher self. It is necessary for this illusion to be real, if we are to benefit from its manifestations. Our ultimate objective while we are in this physical illusion is to work our way out of it, mentally and emotionally. The clues which show the direction this effort should take are subtle, but numerous. It is necessary to set out to discover the true reality by an act of will: it is necessary to decide to seek the truth. The Biblical injunction, "Seek and ye shall find," is the heart of this concept. The truth is all about us, yet we are not forced to behold it. Only when we freely will to seek the truth, shall we find it.

So, the clues which help to start us seeking the truth can never be provable, blatant, and leaving no room for doubt. All the clues are open questions. The UFO phenomena as well as the Geller abilities will retain that quality of elusiveness, of unprovability, until such time as all of us already have begun seeking. When Randi said, "I cannot choose to believe something because I want to," he had an important truth by the tail, though I think he was holding it the wrong way. It is when we want to know the truth that the truth begins to come to us.

Some people see UFOs, and some don't. There is a reason for this discrimination. A person who is at the proper stage of mental evolution can tolerate the stimulus to seeking which is effected by the sighting. Likewise in other paranormal events, whether the event happens or not is highly dependent on the state of mind of the observers. When an attitude of seeking along the so-called spiritual path is manifested, the event is also manifested. One real skeptic in the group can nullify results. Randi says he is good at exposing Geller because he is a magician.

I say that I am good at verifying Geller's abilities because I understand the limitations of the phenomena. For the first time in recent history, we have increasing numbers of people performing what seem to be small miracles. This is happening now as a way of gradually breaking the illusion for those of Earth's people who are ready for a new understanding. People who are unwilling to take these clues, like Randi, will be perfectly able to ignore them. Total free will is part of the plan.

One more observation about "miracles." The bent metal and the UFO sighting seem like miracles to us. We are so jaded! A flower blooms, a baby is born, and we think that's no miracle! If we are going to understand the true nature of our environment, it will be necessary to turn off the intellect and become, as a little child, aware of the creation. It makes no difference whether Geller is really performing miracles. His function is to stimulate thinking, not to prove anything. There is no way of proving miracles, for the plan itself provides for rejection of any concept, and therefor for lack of provability. We are surrounded by not just a few miracles done by Geller and others, not just a history of miracles done by Masters such as Jesus, but by the infinite panoply of the "natural" magic of our world. How did this world of beauty and marvelous efficiency we know as nature come to be? Is it not also miraculous? Yet this beauty also can be accepted or rejected, depending on our philosophical attitude. The whole universe speaks to us. But we do not have to listen.

Endnote Listings

Chapter One
A Very Strange Phenomenon

1. Weldon, John, UFO'S: WHAT ON EARTH IS HAPPENING, Irvine, Ca., Harvest House, ©1975, p. viii.
2. Fuller, John, ed., ALIENS IN THE SKIES, New York, Putnam, 1969, p. 91.
3. Jacobs, David Michael, THE UFO CONTROVERSY IN AMERICA, Bloomington, Indiana University Press, 1975, p. 86.
4. *Ibid.*, p. 82.

Chapter Two
The Telepathic Contact

1. Puharich, Andrija, URI: A JOURNAL OF THE MYSTERY OF URI GELLER, Garden City, Doubleday, 1974,p.165.
2. *Ibid.*, pp. 174-5.
3. Norman, Eric, GODS AND DEVILS FROM OUTER SPACE, New York, Lancer, 1973, pp. 161-2.

Chapter Three
Reality, Etc.

1. Newbrough, John Ballou, OAHSPE, Amherst Press, Amherst, Wisconsin 54406, 1882, p. 596.
2. Whitrow, G. J., ed., EINSTEIN: THE MAN AND HIS ACHIEVEMENT, New York, Dover, ©1967, 1973, p. 71.
3. RECIPROCITY, Frank Meyer, ed., 146 Ross Hall, University of Wisconsin, Superior, Wisconsin 54880.
4. THE STRUCTURE OF THE PHYSICAL UNIVERSE, and several other of Larson's works, are available from the publisher, North Pacific Publishers, P. o. Box 13255, Portland, Oregon, 97213.
5. For further information about the Larsonian physical theory, contact NEW SCIENCE ADVOCATES, Ronald Satz, Secretary, 4010 North War Memorial No. 1008, Peoria, Ill. 61614.
6. Butler, W. E., THE MAGICIAN: HIS TRAINING AND HIS WORK, London, Aquarian, 1963, p. 48.
7. HOLY BIBLE, John 1:9-13.
8. Steiger, Brad, THE AQUARIAN REVELATIONS, New York, Dell, 1970, p. 11.
9. Bruening, J. H., Letter to J. A. Hynek, published in GRAY BARKER'S NEWSLETTER, No. 4, Feb., 1976, pp. 10-11.

Chapter Four
The Nature Of Man

1. Taylor, John, SUPERMINDS, New York, Viking, 1975, p. 11.
2. Muldoon, Sylvan, and Hereward Carrington, THE PHENOMENA OF ASTRAL PROJECTION, New York, Weiser, 1969.
3. Ostrander, Sheila, and Lynn Schroeder, PSYCHIC DISCOVERIES BEHIND THE IRON CURTAIN, Englewood Cliffs, Prentice-Hall, 1970, p. 197.
4. Watson, Lyall, THE ROMEO ERROR, Garden City, Anchor, 1974, p. 242.
5. Leadbeater, C. W., THE DEVACHANIC PLANE; THE ASTRAL PLANE, both published by Theosophical Publishing House.
6. Williamson, George Hunt, OTHER TONGUES, OTHER FLESH, London, Spearman, 1953,1965, p. 363.
7. Twitchell, Paul, ECKANKAR: THE KEY TO SECRET WORLDS, New York, Lancer, 1969, p. 10.
8. Newbrough, *op. cit.*, p. 782.
9. Sagan, Carl, THE COSMIC CONNECTION, New York, Dell, 1973, p. 17.
10. Randi, James, THE MAGIC OF URI GELLER, New York, Ballantine, 1975, p. 16.
11. Jung, Carl, FLYING SAUCERS: A MODERN MYTH OF THINGS SEEN IN THE SKY, New York, Signet, 1969,1959.

Chapter Five
A Solution To The Mystery Of The UFO

1. Emenegger, Robert, UFO'S PAST, PRESENT AND FUTURE, New York, Ballantine, 1974, pp. 59-61.
2. Rueckert, Carla, ed., VOICES OF THE GODS, unpublished manuscript, Louisville, 1974, pp. 6-7.
3. Nada-Yolanda, VISITORS FROM OTHER PLANETS, Miami, Mark-Age, ©1974, p. 28.
4. Steiger, Brad, REVELATION: THE DIVINE FIRE, Englewood Cliffs, Prentice-Hall, ©1973, p. 146.
5. Rueckert, *op. cit.*, p. 7.
6. Newbrough, *op. cit.*, pp. 85 and 191.
7. *Ibid.*, p. 477.
8. *Ibid.*, p. 196.
9. *Ibid.*, pp. 55-6.
10. Nada-Yolanda, *op. cit.*, p. 65.
11. Rueckert, *op. cit.*, p. 65.

12. Menger, Howard, FROM OUTER SPACE TO YOU, New York, Pyramid, 1959, 1967, p. 155.
13. Rueckert, *op. cit.*, p. 15.
14. *Ibid.*, pp. 15-16.
15. Nada-Yolanda, *op. cit.*, pp. 54-5.
16. *Ibid.*, p. 26.
17. Williamson, OTHER TONGUES, *op. cit.*, pp. 8-9.
18. *Ibid.*, p. 364.
19. Wallace, Baird, THE SPACE STORY AND THE INNER LIGHT, Detroit, unpublished material 1971, 1972, Article 2, p. 2.
20. Menger, *op. cit.*, p. 156.
21. Brother Philip, SECRETS OF THE ANDES, Clarksburg, Saucerian Pub., 1961, p. 149.
22. Brother Philip, tape recording, date unknown, place unknown, unpublished.
23. Wallace, *op. cit.*, Article 4, p. 2.
24. Nada-Yolanda, *op. cit.*, p. 61.
25. Williamson, George Hunt, THE SAUCERS SPEAK, London, Spearman, 1963, p. 9.
26. Rueckert, *op. cit.*, p. 19.
27. Brother Philip, SECRETS OF THE ANDES, *op. cit.*, p. 73.
28. Rueckert, *op. cit.*, p. 21.
29. *Tao Teh Ching.*
30. Puharich, *op. cit.*, p. 2A7.
31. Rueckert, *op. cit.*, p. 25.
32. *Ibid.*, pp. 27-9.
33. Rampa, Tuesday Lobsang, THE HERMIT, London, Corgi, 1975, p. 82.
34. *Ibid.*
35. Williamson, SAUCERS, *op. cit.*, pp. 146-7.
36. Brother Philip, SECRETS OF THE ANDES, *op. cit.*, p. 111.
37. Rueckert, *op. cit.*, p. 29.
38. *Ibid.*, pp. 29-30.
39. Steiger, THE AQUARIAN REVELATIONS, *op. cit.*, p. 26.
40. Williamson, OTHER TONGUES, *op. cit.*, p. 226.
41. Adamski, George, BEHIND THE FLYING SAUCER MYSTERY, New York, Warner, 1967, 1974, pp. 96-7.
42. Rueckert, *op. cit.*, pp. 141-148.
43. Nada-Yolanda, *op. cit.*, p. 153.
44. Steiger, THE AQUARIAN REVELATIONS, *op. cit.*, pp. 68-9.
45. Steiger, THE AQUARIAN REVELATIONS, *op. cit.*, p. 106.

46. Trepanier, Clyde, MAN, CONSCIOUSNESS AND UNDERSTANDING, VOLUME FOUR, Detroit, Understanding of Detroit, 1962, p. 1-24-62 (1).
47. Larson, Dewey B., QUASARS AND PULSARS, Portland, North Pacific Pub., ©1971, p. 15.
48. Rueckert, *op. cit.*, p. 160.
49. Trepanier, *op. cit.*, p. 1-24-62 (1-2).
50. Rueckert, *op. cit.*, pp. 174-8.
51. Trepanier, *op. cit.*, p. 6-6-62 (3).
52. Rueckert, *op. cit.*, pp. 180-3.
53. Menger, *op. cit.*, p. 171.
54. Wallace, *op. cit.*, Article 7, p. 2.
55. HOLY BIBLE, Luke 11:9-10.
56. Rueckert, *op. cit.*, pp. 186-7.
57. Nada-Yolanda, *op. cit.*, p. 86.
58. *Ibid.*, p. 94.
59. Newbrough, *op. cit.*, p. 58.
60. Wallace, *op. cit.*, Article 7, p. 10.
61. Van Tassel, George, THE COUNCIL OF SEVEN LIGHTS, Los Angeles, DeVorss, 1958, p. 41.
62. Rueckert, *op. cit.*, pp. 189-90.
63. Newbrough, *op. cit.*, p. 204.
64. Rogers, Walt, unpublished material, Wayne, Mich., undated, pp. 115-6.
65. Rueckert, *op. cit.*, p. 192.
66. Wallace, op cit., Article 9, p. 5.
67. Newbrough, *op. cit.*, p. 325.
68. Rueckert, *op. cit.*, pp. 197-9.
69. Rogers, *op. cit.*, p. 38.
70. Brother Philip, tape recording, *op. cit.*

Chapter Six
The Development Of Man

1. Steiger, THE AQUARIAN REVELATIONS, *op. cit.*, p. 33.
2. Rueckert, *op. cit.*, pp. 204-5.
3. Trepanier, *op. cit.*, p. 1-11-62 (1).
4. Wallace, *op. cit.*, Article 9, p. 2.
5. Van Tassel, *op. cit.*, p. 9.
6. Rueckert, *op. cit.*, pp. 206-9.
7. Trepanier, *op. cit.*, p. 2-15-62 (1).
8. Brother Philip, SECRETS OF THE ANDES, *op. cit.*, p. 29.

9. Rueckert, *op. cit.*, pp. 209-11.
10. Brother Philip, SECRETS OF THE ANDES, *op. cit.*, p. 69.
11. Rueckert, *op. cit.*, pp. 216-7.
12. Rogers, *op. cit.*, pp. 217-8.
13. Rueckert, *op. cit.*, pp. 217-8.
14. *Ibid.*, pp. 238-40.
15. Menger, *op. cit.*, p. 170.
16. Rueckert, *op. cit.*, pp. 240-2.
17. *Ibid.*, pp. 242-3.
18. Van Tassel, *op. cit.*, p. 28.
19. Brother Philip, SECRET OF THE ANDES, *op. cit.*, p. 69.
20. Menger, *op. cit.*, p. 170.
21. Williamson, THE SAUCERS SPEAK, *op. cit.*, p. 72.
22. Menger, *op. cit.*, p. 169.
23. Rueckert, *op. cit.*, pp. 252-257.
24. *Ibid.*, pp. 257-9.
25. *Ibid.*, p. 260.
26. Steiger, THE AQUARIAN REVELATIONS, *op. cit.*, p. 77.
27. Trepanier, *op. cit.*, p. 10-18-62 (2).
28. Rueckert, *op. cit.*, pp. 281-2.
29. Rogers, *op. cit.*, p. 37.
30. Van Tassel, *op. cit.*, p. 79.
31. Rueckert, *op. cit.*, pp. 283-4.
32. Nada-Yolanda, *op. cit.*, pp. 72-3.
33. Regardie, Israel, THE ART AND MEANING OF MAGIC, Cheltenham, Helios, 1971, p. 80.
34. Trepanier, *op. cit.*, p. 5-24-62 (1).
35. Rueckert, *op. cit.*, pp. 286-7.
36. Trepanier, *op. cit.*, 5-24-62 (3).
37. Rueckert, *op. cit.*, pp. 296-7.
38. Williamson, THE SAUCERS SPEAK, *op. cit.*, p. 52.
39. Rueckert, *op. cit.*, p. 314.
40. Nada-Yolanda, *op. cit.*, p. 52.
41. Van Tassel, *op. cit.*, p. 113.
42. Rueckert, *op. cit.*, p. 315.
43. Adamski, *op. cit.*, p. 99.
44. Rueckert, *op. cit.*, pp. 317-20.
45. Rogers, *op. cit.*, p. 52.
46. Wang Yang-ming.
47. Rueckert, *op. cit.*, p. 322.
48. Newbrough, *op. cit.*, p. ?
49. Williamson, OTHER TONGUES, *op. cit.*, p. 296.

50. Van Tassel, *op. cit.*, p. 27.
51. Menger, *op. cit.*, p. 168.
52. Eliot, T. S., "Four Quartets," in THE COMPLETE POEMS AND PLAYS, 1909-1950, New York, Harcourt, ©1952, p.145.

Chapter Seven
A Solution To The Mystery Of Uri Geller

1. Puharich, *op. cit.*, pp. 93-4.
2. Rueckert, *op. cit.*, p. 178.
3. Puharich, *op. cit.*, p. 160.
4. *Ibid.*, p. 165.
5. *Ibid.*, p. 166.
6. Menger, *op. cit.*, p. 154.
7. Williamson, THE SAUCERS SPEAK, *op. cit.*, p. 47.
8. Puharich, *op. cit.*, p. 174.
9. Brother Philip, tape recording, *op. cit.*
10. Williamson, OTHER TONGUES, *op. cit.*, pp. 431-2.
11. Puharich, *op. cit.*, pp. 174-5.
12. Nada-Yolanda, t)p. cit., pp. 46-6.
13. Puharich, *op. cit.*, p. 175.
14. *Ibid.*
15. *Ibid.*, p. 178.
16. Rampa, *op. cit.*, p. 110.
17. Puharich, *op. cit.*, pp. 178-9.
18. *Ibid.*, p. 182.
19. Williamson, OTHER TONGUES, *op. cit.*, p. 5.
20. Puharich, *op. cit.*, p. 183.
21. Nada-Yolanda, *op. cit.*, p. 26.
22. *Ibid.*, p. 25.
23. *Ibid.*
24. *Ibid.*, p. 58.
25. Williamson, OTHER TONGUES., *op. cit.*, p. 229.
26. Hatonn, contactee message, unpublished, 1976.
27. Puharich, *op. cit.*, p. 183.
28. *Ibid.*, p. 198.
29. *Ibid.*, p. 183.
30. *Ibid.*, p. 184.
31. *Ibid.*, p. 199.
32. *Ibid.*, p. 242.
33. *Ibid.*, p. 248.
34. *Ibid.*

35. *Ibid.*, p. 175.
36. Newbrough, *op. cit.*, p. 10.
37. *Ibid.*, p. 59.
38. Steiger, REVELATION: THE DIVINE FIRE, *op. cit.*, p. 144.
39. Puharich, *op. cit.*, p. 184.

CHAPTER EIGHT
THE WANDERERS

1. Williamson, OTHER TONGUES, pp. 207-8.
2. Nada-Yolanda, *op. cit.*, p. 48.
3. Williamson, OTHER TONGUES, *op. cit.*, p. 206.
4. Williamson, THE SAUCERS SPEAK, *op. cit.*, p. 78.
5. Nada-Yolanda, *op. cit.*, p. 122.
6. Steiger, REVELATION: THE DIVINE FIRE, *op. cit.*, p. 145.
7. Nada-Yolanda, *op. cit.*, pp. 7-8.
8. Newbrough, *op. cit.*, p. 92.
9. Newbrough, *Ibid.*, p. 24.
10. Nada-Yolanda, *op. cit.*, p. 33.
11. Williamson, OTHER TONGUES, *op. cit.*, pp. 206-7.
12. Steiger, THE AQUARIAN REVELATIONS, *op. cit.*, pp. 112-3.
13. Williamson, OTHER TONGUES, *op. cit.*, pp. 208-9.
14. Newbrough, *op. cit.*, pp. 781-2.
15. Steiger, THE AQUARIAN REVELATIONS, *op. cit.*, p. 103.

CHAPTER NINE
DEATH, DESTRUCTION, CHAOS, AND OTHER BAD STUFF

1. Van Tassel, *op. cit.*, pp. 143-4.
2. *Ibid.*, p. 30.
3. Steiger, THE AQUARIAN REVELATIONS, pp. 106-7.
4. Newbrough, *op. cit.*, p. 63.
5. *Ibid.*, p. 64.
6. Rueckert, *op. cit.*, pp. 130.
7. *Ibid.*, pp. 131-7.
8. Nada-Yolanda, *op. cit.*, pp. 56-7.
9. Trepanier, *op. cit.*, p. 10-19-62 (1).
10. Aleixo, Hulvio, "Bebedouro II: The Little Men Return For The Soldier," FLYING SAUCER REVIEW, 21:3-4, p. 33.
11. Rueckert, *op. cit.*, pp. 137-8.
12. Newbrough, *op. cit.*, p. 56.
13. *Ibid.*, p. 172.
14. Williamson, OTHER TONGUES, *op. cit.*, p. 313.

15. Brother Philip, SECRET OF THE ANDES, *op. cit.*, p. 26.
16. Steiger, REVELATION: THE DIVINE FIRE, *op. cit.*, p. 146.
17. Steiger, THE AQUARIAN REVELATIONS, *op. cit.*, p. 36.

Chapter Ten
Conclusion

1. Ribera, Antonio, "The Mysterious 'UMMO' Affair, Part 5," FLYING SAUCER REVIEW, 21:3-4, p. 44.
2. Steiger, THE AQUARIAN REVELATIONS, *op. cit.*, pp. 12-3.
3. Schwarz, Berthold Eric, "New Berlin UFO Landing and Repair by Crew," FLYING SAUCER REVIEW, 21:3-4, p. 27.
4. Newbrough, *op. cit.*, p. 247.
5. *Ibid.*, p. 62.
6. *Ibid.*, p. 58.
7. *Ibid.*, p. 786.
8. *Ibid.*, p. 418.
9. *Ibid.*, p. 62.
10. *Ibid.*, p. 63.
11. Brother Philip, tape recording, *op. cit.*
12. *Ibid.*
13. Puharich, *op. cit.*, pp. 222-3.

Bibliography

A. Recommended Reading On UFOs:

Fuller, John, ed., ALIENS IN THE SKIES, New York, Putnam's, 1969.

Fuller, John, INTERRUPTED JOURNEY, New York, Dial, 1966.

Hynek, J. Allen, and Jacques Vallee, THE EDGE OF REALITY: A PROGRESS REPORT ON UNIDENTIFIED FLYING OBJECTS, Chicago, Regnery, 1975.

Jacobs, David Michael, THE UFO CONTROVERSY IN AMERICA, Bloomington, Indiana Univ. Press, 1975.

Keel, John, THE MOTHMAN PROPHECIES, New York, Saturday Review Press, 1975.

Keel, John, UFO'S: OPERATION TROJAN HORSE, New York, Putnam's, 1970.

MUFON, MUFON 1975 UFO SYMPOSIUM PROCEEDINGS, July 5/6, 1975, MUFON, Seguin, Texas, 1975.[1]

Puharich, Andrija, URI: A JOURNAL OF THE MYSTERY OF URI GELLER, Garden City, Doubleday, 1974.

Reeve, Bryant and Helen Reeve, FLYING SAUCER PILGRIMAGE, Amherst, Wisconsin 54406, Amherst Press, 1957.

B. Recommended Reading On Related Subjects:

Butler, W. E., THE MAGICIAN: HIS TRAINING AND HIS WORK, London, Aquarian, 1963.

Holroyd, Stuart, PRELUDE TO THE LANDING ON PLANET EARTH, W.H. Allen Co., 44 Hill St., London W1X8LB, England.

Leadbeater, C. W., THE ASTRAL PLANE, Adyar, Madras, Theosophical Publishing House, 1970.

Leadbeater, C. W., THE DEVACHANIC PLANE OR THE HEAVEN WORLD, THE CHARACTERISTICS AND INHABITANTS, Adyar, Madras, Theosophical Publishing House, 1948.

---

[1] Note: Although most of these books can be obtained from their publishers, in the case of MUFON, the address to use in enquiring about their PROCEEDINGS is the same as for SKYLOOK magazine.

Manning, Matthew, THE LINK, New York, Holt, 1974.

Muldoon, Sylvan and Hereward Carrington, THE PHENOMENA OF ASTRAL PROJECTION, New York, Weiser, 1969.

Newbrough, John Ballou, OAHSPE, Amherst Press, Amherst, Wisconsin 54406, 1882.

Ostrander, Sheila, and Lynn Schroeder, PSYCHIC DISCOVERIES BEHIND THE IRON CURTAIN, Englewood Cliffs, Prentice-Hall, 1970.

Raudive, Konstantin, BREAKTHROUGH: AN AMAZING EXPERIMENT IN ELECTRONIC COMMUNICATION WITH THE DEAD, New York, Lancer, 1971.

Steiger, Brad, MYSTERIES OF TIME AND SPACE, New York, Dell/Confucian, 1974.

Steiger, Brad, REVELATION: THE DIVINE FIRE, Englewood Cliffs, Prentice-Hall, 1973.

Taylor, John, SUPERMINDS, New York, Viking, 1975.

Tompkins, Peter and Christopher Bird, THE SECRET LIFE OF PLANTS, New York, Avon, 1973.

Valentine, Tom, PSYCHIC SURGERY, Chicago, Regnery, 1973.

Watson, Lyall, THE ROMEO ERROR, Garden City, Anchor, 1974

Wilson, Robert, THE COSMIC TRIGGER, And-Or Press, P.O. Box 2246, Berkeley, CA 94702.

Watson, Lyall, SUPERNATURE, New York, Bantam, 1974.

C. Recommended Contactee Books:

Adamski, George, FLYING SAUCERS HAVE LANDED, Hackensack, Wehman, reprint.

Adamski, George, BEHIND THE FLYING SAUCER MYSTERY, New York, Warner Paperback Library, 1974.

Adkins, Diana, INTRODUCTION: CONFRONTATION, The Netherlands, Servire/Wassenaar, 1970. Order copies from the author, c/o Orb Institute, 3209-11 M Street N.W., Washington, D.C. 20007.

Angelucci, Orfeo M., THE SECRET OF THE SAUCERS, Amherst, Amherst Press, 1955. (Out of Print.)

Betherum, Truman, ABOARD A FLYING SAUCER, Los Angeles, DeVorss, 1954.

Fry, Daniel, THE WHITE SANDS INCIDENT, New York, Best Books, 1954

Layne, Mead, FLYING DISCS, San Diego, Borderland Sciences Research Associates, 1954.

Menger, Howard, FROM OUTER SPACE TO YOU, New York, Pyramid, 1959.

Nada-Yolanda, VISITORS FROM OTHER PLANETS, Miami, Mark-Age MetaCenter, 1974. Order Copies from Mark-Age MetaCenter, 327 NE 20 Terrace, Miami, Florida 33137, free catalogue also available.

Trepanier, Clyde, MAN, CONSCIOUSNESS AND UNDERSTANDING, Annual publication since 1959. Published by the author. Inquire for copies c/o the author, 14212 NE 75th St., Redmond Wa. 98052.

Van Tassel, George, THE COUNCIL OF SEVEN LIGHTS, Los Angeles, DeVorss, 1958.

Wallace, Baird, THE SPACE STORY AND THE INNER LIGHT, published by the author in 1972. Enquire for copies c/o the author, Box 158, Grosse Ile, Mich. 98138.

Williamson, George H., and Alfred C. Bailey, THE SAUCERS SPEAK, London, Spearman, 1963.

Williamson, George H., OTHER TONGUES, OTHER FLESH, Hackensack, Wehman, 1965.

These two sources below are not contactees as such, but their material is closely related to the contactee material and as such is interesting.

Phylos The Tibetan, A DWELLER ON TWO PLANETS, Hackensack, Wehman, 1952, 1970.

Phylos The Tibetan, EARTH DWELLER'S RETURN, Hackensack, Wehman, 1970.

Probert, Mark, THE MAGIC BAG, SAN DIEGO, published by the author, 1950.

D. Recommended UFO Periodicals:

Aerial Phenomena Research Organization (APRO) BULLETIN, 3910 E. Kleindale Rd., Tucson, Arizona 85712.

Center for UFO Studies (CUFOS), International UFO Reporter, 1609 Sherman Ave., Suite 207, Evanston, IL 60201.

Mutual UFO Network (MUFON), MUFON UFO Journal, 103 Oldtown Rd., Sequin, TX 78155.

Flying Saucer Review, FSR Publications Ltd., West Malling, Maidstone, Kent, England.

Made in the USA
Monee, IL
10 December 2024